KT-568-839

NLP at Work

WARWICKSHIRE
COLLEGE
LIBRARY

The Difference that Makes the Difference in Business
Second edition

WARWICKSHIRE COLLEGE
LIBRARY

Class No:
658.409

Acc No:
00525228

Sue Knight

NICHOLAS BREALEY
PUBLISHING
LONDON

WARWICKSHIRE COLLEGE
LIBRARY

Class No:
658.409

Acc No:
00525228

This second edition first published by
Nicholas Brealey Publishing in 2002
Reprinted with corrections in 2002, 2003

First published in 1995

3–5 Spafield Street
Clerkenwell,
EC1R 4QB, UK
Tel: +44 (0)20 7239 0360
Fax: +44 (0)20 7239 0370

PO Box 700
Yarmouth
Maine 04096, USA
Tel: (888) BREALEY
Fax: (207) 846 5181

http://nbrealey-books.com
www.sueknight.co.uk

© Sue Knight Books & Talks Ltd 1995, 2002
The right of Sue Knight to be identified as the author of this work has been asserted in
accordance with the Copyright, Designs and Patents Act 1988.

ISBN 1-85788-302-0

British Library Cataloguing in Publication Data
A catalogue record for this book is available from the British Library.

All rights reserved. No part of this publication may be reproduced, stored in a retrieval
system, or transmitted, in any form or by any means, electronic, mechanical, photocopying,
recording and/or otherwise without the prior written permission of the publishers. This
book may not be lent, resold, hired out or otherwise disposed of by way of trade in any
form, binding or cover other than that in which it is published, without the prior consent of
the publishers.

Printed in Finland by WS Bookwell.

Contents

Acknowledgments

I thank… first and foremost my husband, Spence, who feeds me the most wonderful meals while I write. And he feeds me with ideas, illustrations, examples, questions, challenges, feedback, and above all love and inspiration.

My family, who support me in everything and who are the reason for my work and my life.

My mum, who told me that I "would always fall on my feet." I couldn't wish for a more reassuring belief. And when I show her a new book says, "Where do you find it all to write about, Susan?" I do wonder.

Sarah Bacon, my PA. I feel very privileged to have such a sensitive and caring buffer between the rest of the world and me.

Nicholas Brealey, my publisher, whose patience and guidance know no bounds in reading the many, many versions of books that I explore with him.

Gene Early, my lifetime coach and guide.

John Grinder and Richard Bandler, the founders of NLP whose work inspires so many people in the world today.

Robert Dilts, for the caring and ecological work that he continues to do in his creative development of NLP.

Andy Wilkinson and Jo Twining, for taking the time to read chapters and offer feedback.

There are many more associates and friends who have made a difference for me. Thank you.

The NLP stories have now become a part of the folklore and it has become difficult to trace all the sources. Some of the stories are my own. I suspect that many came from David Gordon, an early pioneer of NLP. The stories that I heard when

I first studied NLP have stayed with me. I hope that the ones in this book do the same for you and that you learn through them in ways that perhaps you did not anticipate.

I dedicate this book to my sons James and Alex—my writing is my legacy. I wish for you the wealth that I have found in exploring this way of thinking about life. You are both with me in everything I do.

TRIBUTE TO SIMON

Last year I worked in Australia and I fell in love with the country and the people I met there. One of the people who assisted me on the training was a young man called Simon Blanda. He was the epitome of the welcome that I received in Sydney: He was fun, open, sensitive, and giving, and much much more. He filled the room with his charisma and his energy. We chose Simon as someone that we wanted the group to model because of his enormous capacity for building relationships. He was without doubt a model of excellence.

Just as I was completing this book I received news that Simon had been killed in a car crash. I am grateful that we had that precious time with him when we were able to learn a little of his very special magic. The modeling we did that day had a purpose that none of us involved will ever forget. I hope that this book helps us all to learn a little more how to give to life and to others in the way that Simon did, and to learn to model so that the qualities of the special people in our lives become the legacy for future generations.

Preface to the Revised Edition

When I wrote the first edition of NLP *at Work* over five years ago, NLP was virtually unheard of in the world of business. I wrote the book in order to make NLP much more accessible to people at work, especially those who recognized that everyone has a leader "within." I believed then as I do now that we can transform for the better the way we communicate with each other and the way we work. My experience as a consultant for over 30 years has shown me that humane communication is good business communication. My work is not just about making organizations good places to be, it is about making them successful places. I was aware of the quality and the enormity of the changes that could take place even though I could not predict them precisely. And I certainly could not have predicted the changes in my own circumstances.

I have transformed the way I work. More to the point, developments in technology have allowed me to work in a very different way to five years ago. I no longer administer a team of associates and instead collaborate with other entrepreneurial organizations via the web. I believe that we can create a culture of abundance in the way we work and consequently I have set up my own website with the goal of giving away as many of my thoughts and ideas as quickly as I can (www.sueknight.co.uk). Ideas grow into places where there is space for them. I now have five books published and NLP *at Work* has been translated into eight languages. As a result of the promotion of NLP through the books especially, I am very fortunate in that most business comes to me. We no longer do any mailshots or cold calls; my aim is to attract the people and the companies

1
What Is NLP?

"What we see and hear is what we think about. What we think about is what we feel. What we feel influences our reactions. Reactions become habits and it is our habits that determine our destiny."

Bob Gass

Neuro linguistic programming (NLP) is the study of what works in thinking, language, and behavior. It is a way of coding and reproducing excellence that enables you to consistently achieve the results that you want both for yourself, for your business, and for your life.

We live in a world of unprecedented change. We are immersed in unpredictability and complexity. The more we discover the more there is to discover. Every question reveals yet more questions.

Unprecedented change

We need skills and attitudes to help us learn how to make sense of chaos. We need to know how to find certainty within ourselves about what we want and what we believe when everything around us may seem to challenge who we are. We need to take care of ourselves and stand alone in our self-assurance and empathy for others, yet we need to be able to show others our weaknesses and ask for help. We need to know how to pick ourselves up when we are down, to learn from uncertainty and disappointment, to shape our direction and to be prepared to lose all.

We need the capacity to move more quickly than ever before and at the same time to stand still and drink in the richness of the moment. We need to know how to communicate with people of vastly different cultures and, more than anything, how to communicate with ourselves. We need to understand others' perceptions even if they are poles apart from ours and we need to listen to the wisdom of our own bodies.

We need to know how to laugh, to let go, to learn, to grow, to love, to mourn, and to move on. We need humility and graciousness and the strength to absorb our own and others' inconsistencies. We need the resilience to remain in situations that cause us pain and to be able to find the joy in everything and everyone. We need to know how to find the excellence that is within us all and to celebrate it with every part of our heart and soul. We need to forgive, forget, and allow ourselves and others to be who they truly are. We need to learn as we have never learned before.

How can we cope?

How, then, do we cope? In some ways the answer is a paradox. Far from embarking on courses of accelerated learning and speed reading to be able to learn faster, we need to look within ourselves and find our unique resources. In this way we can develop our own formulae for success. We need to be still to discern what is important for our specific vocation and what is not. We need to know how to learn from every situation, everyone and every intuition.

NEURO LINGUISTIC PROGRAMMING

Neuro linguistic programming (NLP) is a process of modeling the conscious and unconscious patterns that are unique to each of us in such a way that we are continuously moving toward a higher potential.

❏ **Neuro** By increasing our awareness of the patterns in our thinking, we can learn how these thought patterns influence the results we are getting in work and in life. The key to finding personal and business success comes primarily from within ourselves and learning about how we think enables us to tap into our inner resources.

❏ **Linguistic** Our language is our life. What we can say is what we can think and what we can do. Learning to understand and master the structure of our language is essential in a world where we trade increasingly through our ability to communicate.

❑ **Programming** We run our lives by strategies, in a similar way that a computer uses a program to achieve a specific result. By understanding the strategies by which we run our lives we give ourselves choice: choice to do more of the same or choice to enhance our potential and our individual excellence.

In essence, NLP is the study of our thinking, behavior, and language patterns so that we can build sets of strategies that work for us in making decisions, building relationships, starting up a business, coaching a team of people, inspiring and motivating others, creating balance in our lives, negotiating our way through the day, and, above all, learning how to learn.

We have strategies for everything we do. The good news is that we can learn how to refine existing strategies as well as learning new ones and even discarding those that are redundant. The bad news is that for the most part the critical pieces of these strategies are outside of our conscious awareness. We typically do not consciously know what we do and especially how we do it.

This is where NLP comes in. With NLP we can unpack not only the conscious elements but especially the unconscious ones so that we can learn how we do what we do. This allows us to do what we really want and achieve what we deserve.

"'The best thing for being sad,'replied Merlin ... 'is to learn something. That is the only thing that never fails. You may grow old and trembling in your anatomies, you may lie awake at night listening to the disorder of your veins, ... you may see the world around you devastated by evil lunatics, or know your honor trampled in the sewers of baser minds. There is only one thing for it then—to learn. Learn why the world wags and what wags it. That is the only thing which the mind can never exhaust, never alienate, never be tortured by, never fear or distrust, and never dream of regretting. Learning is the thing for you.'"

T.H. White, The Once and Future King

Thinking, behavior, and language patterns

THE RELEVANCE OF NLP

Combining "thinking about thinking" with technology

I am often asked "Is NLP still relevant?" and my answer is a resounding "Yes!" We need to learn how to use new technology in ways that are creative and different. If you do what you always did, you get what you always got. And it is the combination of "thinking about thinking" and technology that will set the new breed of leaders and entrepreneurs apart from the rest.

There is nothing else in the world of human development and learning as powerful as NLP. Emotional intelligence, spiritual intelligence, visualization, and various other new concepts in human resource development are mere derivatives of the NLP process.

"The only route to understanding would have to come through creating a practical working model in your mind that could be used to rise above the detail ... Every successful entrepreneur I've ever known has worked this way ... From this high level view of the world, they create simple, rule of thumb formulae that can be used as the basis for decision making."

Peter Small, The Entrepreneurial Web

There is so much to learn in both technology and personal development that it is impossible for anyone to learn everything. It is our ability to manage our thinking, our conflicts, and our experience that will ultimately make the difference between those of us who will lead the way into an increasingly new, exciting, creative, and cooperative future, and those who will rapidly fall by the wayside as they attempt to follow. This is what we can learn with NLP.

WHAT WILL YOU GAIN FROM THIS BOOK?

Success comes from within. Our success depends on our ability to be excellent in everything we think, say, and do. NLP provides us with a way to achieve this.

By mastering the concepts in this book and making them your own you will begin to excel more and more at what you do. You will achieve more of what you really want and become more of who you truly are.

Excellence is context specific. Many business models fail because they assume that what works in one environment will work in another, yet what makes a leading entrepreneur in one environment may be quite different to what constitutes success in another. NLP enables you to code excellence and enhance it so that you can establish what really works for you in your environment and with your skills.

Excellence is context specific

More specifically, NLP can support you in learning how to do the following:

❑ Accelerate your ability to learn so that you can not only manage change but initiate and embrace it, enabling you to lead the way in your particular specialism and field of work.
❑ Continually develop new ways of thinking that support you whatever the changes in the external world.
❑ Let go of the old, traditional patterns and habits that constrict your growth and release the hidden talents that are appropriate to today and the future.
❑ Embrace feedback in a way that enables you to develop new ideas and products with the involvement of all your customers, colleagues, and friends.
❑ Set compelling outcomes for yourself, ones that by their very nature take on a momentum of their own and maximize the chances that you will achieve what you want, both personally and for your business.
❑ Develop formulae for yourself to enable you to respond to, and more importantly take a lead in, the world of high technology so that you combine the best of high-tech thinking with awareness of yourself and others.
❑ Build high-quality relationships with significant people in all contexts of your life, whether that be face to face or via the latest technology.
❑ Heighten your awareness of yourself and others, so that you are sensitive to the subtle shifts in behavior and attitude that provide feedback on the effects of the way you communicate.
❑ Develop your flexibility so that you have more choices and consequently more influence over the situations in your life.

❏ Improve your ability to generate commitment, cooperation, and enthusiasm in the people around you.
❏ Manage your thoughts and feelings so that you are in control of your emotions and your destiny.
❏ Develop your ability to tap into your unconscious mind and draw on its superior power and potential.
❏ Accept and love whatever you have and in so doing to love yourself. Then you will be able to love others in a way that will transform your business and your life.

You will find your own applications and your own formulae for success—that is the real joy and power of NLP. In business especially, NLP is the difference that makes the difference in personal and business coherence, communication, strategic thinking, e-business, motivation, influence, negotiation, leadership, entrepreneurship, empowerment, self-development, visualization, reengineering … the list is endless. Overall, the purpose of learning NLP is to generate further learning. This is outside many people's understanding, especially those who want readymade answers.

HOW DOES NLP WORK?

NLP pays very little attention to what people *say* they do, as that usually bears very little or no resemblance to what they *actually* do. You might think that by asking top achievers how they succeed you would get precise answers. You would be wrong! The key to success is often unknown at the conscious level. The previously unknown pieces are sometimes referred to as the magic of NLP. However, it is not magic, merely an awareness of what really makes the difference that is so often missing in more traditional models and techniques. Using the tools of NLP you can elicit these unknown pieces so that you can "code" talent.

There will be things you do that you do not (yet) understand. Do you know, for example:

❏ What you do that is different in those relationships where you have exquisite rapport, where you know what the other person is going to say before they say it?

❑ How you control your feelings in some situations when in others you lose control?

❑ In those situations where you feel especially confident, how you generate that inner feeling of calm and certainty even when everything else is stacked against you?

❑ How it is that some of your remote communications achieve as much if not more than face-to-face conversations?

❑ What it is about the way you use technology at those times that influences people to want to do business with you?

❑ How it is that sometimes everything you do seems just right, you feel at one with yourself, and you achieve new personal bests?

❑ What happens at those times when you are able to shift gear to a more successful way of being so that you achieve more than you previously dreamt was possible?

When you know the answers to these questions and others like them, you begin to have more choice over the way you think, feel, and behave. You have more influence over the way in which you can respond to your unique calling in the world.

REFERENCES

Bob Gass (1999) *Word for Today,* UCB Broadcasters Ltd.
John Grinder & Judith DeLozier (1996) *Turtles All the Way Down: Prerequisites to Personal Genius,* Metamorphous Press.
T.H. White (2001) *The Once and Future King* (new edn), Voyager.

William James is usually considered the father of American psychology. He was once invited to deliver a series of lectures at Harvard on a topic of his choosing. These lectures were presented on the green and were special in that they were open to the public. After some deliberation, he chose boldly and the title for his first presentation was "Can One Prove The Existence of God," a topic sure to raise eyebrows in the early part of this century in New England.

Thus, it was with some trepidation that he watched the audience file into the lecture hall and, sure enough, at the very last moment, a little old lady rushed down the center aisle and deposited herself front row center.

Professor James presented his topic with his usual wit and charm. He noted as he worked his way through his lecture that the little old lady was very attentive and seemed to be enjoying herself—he did mark the fact that she seemed to laugh when no one else did. Nevertheless, all seemed quite in order.

At the end of the presentation, which was very well received, the inevitable queue formed. And, of course, at the end of the queue was the little old lady. When her turn came, she looked up brightly at James and said:

"Dr. James, I very much enjoyed your lecture. But I do still have one question."

"Please, Madam, ask your question!" returned William James courteously.

"Well, Dr. James," she replied with a glint in her eye. "If there's no God, what keeps the earth from falling down?"

James quickly reviewed his options … he considered such explanatory notions as centripetal force, gravitational systems … but wisely chose to respond in a way as to learn something from this woman. Turning his attention back to her, he said, "Madam, I would be happy to answer your question, but tell me what it is that you believe that keeps the earth from falling down?"

"Why that's very simple, Dr. James, the earth is resting on the back of a gigantic turtle!"

James mused to himself over her extraordinary response for a moment and then with a hint of triumph in his voice asked the obvious question. "Then pray tell me, Madam, what keeps this gigantic turtle from falling down?"

"No, no, no Dr. James!" replied the little old lady. "You can't get me there … it's turtles all the way down!"

Taken with permission from the preface to Turtles All the Way Down by John Grinder and Judith DeLozier.

Part I

The Elements of NLP

A journey of discovery

NLP brings together many techniques that have been around for years and combines them with discoveries that are new. It is both a study of masters of change, some of whom are no longer alive, and a recognition of the talents that exist within each person today. NLP is a journey of discovery.

When I decided to write the first edition of this book my publisher and I discussed in detail what would be an appropriate structure. NLP didn't evolve in a neat chronological sequence, it exploded into the world of therapy and then did the same in the world of business. More recently, the enlightened few have realized its significance in the world of technology. So how could I structure the subject in a way that enables you quickly to grasp the elements and begin to appreciate and experience the power of the whole? I experimented with many approaches before we decided to use the name Neuro Linguistic Programming as the basis for the structure. Easier said than done!

The elements of NLP don't fit perfectly into the categories of Neuro, Linguistic, and Programming. Nevertheless, these headings act as useful umbrellas under which to introduce the subject. I ask for the tolerance of the purists among you who could argue about the exact categorization of each of the elements. The feedback I have received since the first edition is that readers have found this structure helpful and so I have continued with it and expanded the content of each section.

Equally, I would emphasize that the book is by no means

complete in its coverage of NLP. I have chosen those pieces of the subject that I believe serve as a useful introduction and are most relevant to work and our rapidly evolving world. However, this book now goes a long way toward being a useful source document for those who want a comprehensive introduction to NLP and for those who are taking their learning further and studying to NLP Practitioner level and beyond.

NEURO

The first "technique umbrella" is **Neuro**. Neuro is to do with the way we use our minds, our bodies, and our senses to think and make sense of our experience. The more awareness we have of our thinking patterns, the more flexibility and therefore the more influence we have over our destiny.

Thinking patterns

I start this section with Chapter 2, Thinking patterns. The discovery of the unique ways we think opened the doors to many of the models for change covered in the subsequent parts of the book. Many books encourage you to "think positively," to "stay calm," to "keep control." NLP is much more than this, offering the "how" to achieve these results.

NLP is "thinking about thinking," and this chapter in particular will help you expand your thinking power. NLP does this not by prescribing fixed techniques that work for some, but by enabling you to explore what it is that you do when you "think positively," "stay calm," and "keep control." You have your own unique ways of accessing and using these kinds of resources, no matter how infrequently or how briefly you may have used them in the past. Once you understand the elements of your personal "program" you can run that program when you choose. This chapter will raise your awareness of how you do what you do, a stepping stone to what Peter Senge, in his book *The Fifth Discipline*, calls personal mastery.

Increasingly, you will find that leadership models and models for change talk about mental maps. With NLP you can discover the nature of your own mental map and how it influences everything you do.

Immediately following Chapter 2 is a questionnaire, "Identify your preferred thinking pattern." I have included this here so that you can begin to recognize some of the patterns in your thinking, especially in the way you use your senses to think and therefore to communicate. This questionnaire is an expanded version of the one in the original edition of the book.

Also in the Neuro section is Chapter 3, Filters on your world. The filters through which we experience the world govern our perception of situations and people. By recognizing these filters we can understand more about our ability to relate to the unique styles of others. For example, have you ever noticed how in meetings some people talk about what is different about ideas and proposals, whereas others search for what they like and how these ideas compare to other similar ones? And have you ever experienced people who are inspired by a vision of the future trying to get through to others who want to dwell on the problems? We need to learn how to accept all the differences and similarities that exist between us if we are to function as one.

Unique styles

At the end of this chapter I have included another expanded version of a questionnaire introduced in the original book, "Identify your filters." Working through this questionnaire will help you to apply the previous chapters to yourself and increase your ability to learn how to detect the patterns that influence the way we live and work.

A new chapter in this part of the book is Chapter 4, Thinking with your body. This is such a central part of NLP that in a way I am amazed that I did not have it as a separate chapter before. So many people have come across the more traditional theories of body language where, as an example, scratching your nose means that you are lying and folding your arms means that you are defensive. NLP offers a very different kind of understanding, one that is unique to the individual and respectful of the person. It does not put gestures into predetermined boxes but enables us to develop the subtlety of attuning to our own body language and that of each person we meet, no matter what the context of the communication.

In this chapter you will learn how to recognize different patterns in behavior and consequently different patterns in thinking. In this way you can improve how you communicate with anyone in any situation.

Under the **Linguistic** heading are Enriched communication, Precision questions, Metaphor, and two new chapters in this revised edition, Hypnotic language and Metamessages.

LINGUISTIC

The ways of using language to facilitate change formed a large part of the early work of John Grinder and Richard Bandler, the founders of NLP. In business, language is one of the most readily available forms of influence. The chapter on language patterns explores how you can use each of your senses to enrich your language and bring it alive.

With precision questions you can learn how to generate quality information, the lifeblood of business. Precision questions are also undoubtedly one of the most powerful tools for challenging the constraints that people create for themselves.

Whereas precision questions work largely at the conscious level, metaphor is a way of utilizing the unconscious mind in the process of change. Learn how to recognize and use metaphors to engage your listeners' minds and elegantly bypass conscious resistance.

The first of the new chapters is Chapter 7, Hypnotic language. In my quest to promote NLP in the world of business I initially played down the role of hypnotic language. I wanted to concentrate on how we could make the unconscious conscious, rather than promoting the use of working with trance. I have since moved on. Business has also moved on and I think that there is now a much greater understanding that hypnotism is more than a stage performance. My aim in including this chapter is to help you realize just how much we are influenced by the hypnotic language that is around us every day, and through this awareness how we can learn to use this language to good effect. Many of the techniques that are essential to business and our personal development rely on our willingness to draw on our unconscious minds and hypnotic language is a way to work with that.

Chapter 9, Metamessages, reflects the aspects of NLP that I have found to be especially important in business and that are often overlooked or misunderstood. Unconsciously we are always an example of something; the key questions are whether we are aware of the example we are giving to the world and whether that example is what we would choose. Understanding this bigger message and how we can be the example we want is the subject of this chapter.

NLP is a process of modeling exceptional talent in ourselves and in others. I have expanded the **Programming** section of the book to reflect the increasing importance and interest in this, the essence of NLP. In modeling you learn not only how to bring together all the skills of NLP to elicit and code exceptional talent, but also how to access the hidden resources within yourself so that you can begin to realize your true potential. In this section I have included a new perspective on modeling, one that builds on the introduction I offered originally.

In this section there is a new chapter, Strategies for successful living, and a new theme, the TOTE. This is not to do with gambling, but is the structure of the way we achieve results in our lives. In this chapter you will learn how to unpack and code the elements of the programs that govern results so that you can reproduce the parts you want for yourself and for others.

All of these elements can be used in different ways. As independent techniques they will enable you to improve the quality of your relationships and gain greater control and choice over the way you live your life and the results you achieve. Additionally, even though many of these elements were discovered through the process of coding excellence, they are now also used to enhance the quality of the coding process itself. For example, your awareness and understanding of the finer distinctions in language and behavior will enable you to discover the difference that makes the difference in the models of excellence you choose to study.

You may come across people with different views and thinking as to what constitute the elements of NLP. That is fine. I believe it is important that we each take NLP for what it is, a process of discovery. The elements I have included here are an introduction to NLP. Not only are more elements already known and taught, but undoubtedly more are being discovered as I write. I offer you these core skills as a way of developing your awareness and sensitivity both to yourself and to others. If you achieve that, you will already have begun the process of change—one that can support you in leading a life that is significant and fulfilling.

PROGRAMMING

Neuro

"The spiritual life is a life beyond moods. It is a life in which we choose joy and do not allow ourselves to become victims of passing feelings of happiness or depression."

Henri J.M. Nouwen, The Road to Daybreak

Many traditional models of change and influence have sought to bring about change through manipulation of other people and the environment. The reality is that we cannot change other people, we can only change ourselves. Our environment is tempered by the mental models we hold. There are some people, for example, who only see good in others. They have no representation for bad. In their world bad doesn't exist.

Our thoughts leak out in everything we do, often in ways that are outside our conscious awareness. These thoughts send out signals to the world about what we want, what we believe, and who we are. And the world responds to those signals. Consequently the key to influencing the responses is to change the inner signals. NLP offers us the opportunity to manage these inner representations and signals. In doing so we begin to tap into the potential of the world's most powerful computers—our minds. By learning how to manage our thoughts we can:

❏ Change our experience of situations and people.
❏ Influence the reactions we get.
❏ Hold memories in a way that supports the person we want to be.
❏ Create the future we want.
❏ Build the relationships we would really like.

That list is only for starters. We can learn to manage our minds in ways that work for us to lead the lives we are meant to lead.

2
Thinking Patterns

"All too often content and style are overlooked by designers caught up in whizz-bang technology."

@demon (demon newsletter)

*I*f you want to know how to get your message across in a way that is readily understood, then learning how to recognize and choose appropriate thinking patterns is key to your success. Each step forward in this skill will lead to increased mastery of your experience. Combined with other NLP skills and techniques, it gives you the ability to reproduce with consistency not only other people's talents, but also your own. By learning how you do what you do, you turn luck into planned achievement.

Learning about thinking patterns is part of the skill package we require to deal with the many different cultures with which we come into contact. Most of the teams I consult with are now multicultural. Even if the team members originate from the same country, each person still has their own style, their personal culture. We need to learn how to recognize, understand, accept, and relate to these different styles if we wish to navigate our way in business professionally and successfully.

Unique thought patterns

By exploring the structure of how we think we can begin to understand the subtleties of different cultures. And we can do this as we encounter them—we do not need to research for months in advance of a possible encounter or journey. The value of learning NLP is that we can use it in real time.

The connections you make and the way you represent memories, ideas, and information are unique to you. Everyone has their own way of thinking. When you understand the nature of these representations, you begin to influence your thinking, your emotions, and consequently your experience. What you think is what you are.

You take in information through all the senses of sight, hearing, touch, taste, and smell. You represent this information in your mind as a combination of sensory systems and inner feelings. These thinking patterns are a part of how you "code" your experience. By learning to manage your thoughts you learn how to create the life and career you want for yourself. Life is literally what you make it.

PREFERENCES IN THINKING PATTERNS

Let's explore some differences in thinking patterns. Think of "coffee." What comes to mind?

A picture? Maybe you imagined coffee cups and a coffee maker.

Or maybe you heard the hiss of the coffee machine. Or the noise of the coffee being poured into the cup.

Then again, maybe it was more of a feeling. The feel of the coffee cup perhaps. Or the taste or aroma of the coffee.

Possibly it was a combination of some or all of these different ways of thinking.

These different ways of thinking are:

Pictures, sounds, and feelings

- ❏ **Visual** You think in pictures. You represent ideas, memory, and imagination as mental images, e.g. a picture of a cup of coffee.
- ❏ **Auditory** You think in sounds. These sounds could be voices or noises, e.g. the sound of a coffee machine.
- ❏ **Feelings** You represent thoughts as feelings, either internal emotions or the thought of a physical touch. We will include taste and smell in this category of feelings, the taste of the coffee for example, or the aroma.

You will find that you probably have a preference for some systems over others, both in the way you think and in the way you communicate.

When we are relating to the world at large it is vital that we appeal to all senses. In this way we "catch" all the preferences that our readers, our listeners, our viewers, and our potential clients might have. At the time of writing there is a backlash against some e-business propositions; at the same time there is a boom in interest in "clicks and mortar" businesses. These are established high street businesses (the mortar) that have developed ways of attracting people to their premises through the web (mouse clicks). Given what we know about our need to appeal to all senses this is not surprising. The combination of the technology with a physical outlet appeals to both our intellectual and physical needs. So people are currently more likely to search for what they want on the web but follow through with a visit to a store where they can see, hold, touch, and talk through the items they want to buy.

Is it any surprise that communication is one of the most widely recognized problems in business? Consider the level of frustration so many people express with the meetings they attend. Even when an objective is agreed, it is likely that each person at the meeting will represent a successful conclusion in a different way. For example, outcomes could include:

Imagined outcomes of a business meeting

❏ **Visual** An image of all the agreed actions written up on a whiteboard with names against each one.
❏ **Auditory** People talking to each other at the close of the meeting, making comments such as: "That's been really useful. I know exactly what my department has to do next."
❏ **Feelings** Thoughts about shaking hands with other people at the meeting and a satisfied, warm feeling.

We don't know what we don't know

You may already recognize preferences in your thinking, and they may of course vary from one scenario to another. To check out any preferences use the questionnaire on page 30, "Identify your preferred thinking pattern."

This year my husband got a new company car with a satellite navigation system. We have used this on many occasions and we can choose the style in which the directions are represented. If my husband selects the settings he chooses the smallest-scale map that can be displayed and will often choose the symbolic indicators for which way to turn in preference to a pictorial map. If I am using it I choose the pictorial map with the largest scale possible. When traveling through France I like to see where we are in the context of the whole country, whereas my husband likes to see the details and names of the immediate vicinity. So we tend to switch from one form of display to another when we are together to keep us both satisfied.

What is significant is that the makers had the wisdom to offer this choice. The ability to offer choice has become a key differentiator in business. To do so we need to understand the way our customers think, even if they themselves do not consciously know (and they probably don't). It is this awareness of unconscious need that is so much more important than standard customer surveys. We don't know what we don't know! We need to be able to offer choices that our customers only realize are important to them when they experience the difference.

A clue to the way we think is in how we move our eyes. For example, is there someone near you now who considers themselves a good speller? Ask them to spell "phenomenon." Watch their eyes as they do so. If they are really skilled, ask them to spell "phenomenon" backwards. Good spellers will typically look up, eyes right or eyes left, to see the word in their mind's eye. (Some may look straight ahead but in a defocused way.) Because they can see it written out they have no difficulty in spelling it backwards. It is as if it is there on the page in front of them.

Did your schoolteacher ever say to you: "You won't find the answer on the ceiling"? The truth is that you probably would! Your eyes are an indication of how you are thinking. I have come across managers who when interviewing candidates for a job have been suspicious of people who break eye contact. The implication for them is that they may very likely have recruited people who do not think!

The details of all the eye movements and their meaning are in Chapter 4, Thinking with your body.

Eye movements

FINER DISTINCTIONS IN THINKING

Within each of the main thinking patterns of visual, auditory, and feelings there are finer distinctions. For example, the color and clarity of an image, the tone and volume of a sound, the strength and location of a feeling. People who have control over their emotions and their experience have the ability to manipulate these fine distinctions in their thinking. Learning to exercise and extend your range of thinking patterns leads to mental agility, just as physical exercise leads to bodily flexibility.

You return home and walk into the kitchen area. The working surfaces are clean and white. On one surface is a blue ceramic bowl filled with fruit, vivid green apples, purple grapes, and several bright yellow lemons. You pick up one of the lemons and feel the textured surface with your fingertips. You raise it to your nose and smell the sharp aroma. Also on the surface is a sharp kitchen knife and a wooden chopping board. You place the lemon on the board and slice through the middle of it. A fine mist of lemon juice sprays into the air. You pick up one half of the lemon and see the defined segments and pips, some of them cut through. You raise this half to your mouth; the sharp aroma is even stronger now. You sink your teeth into the skin.

Body and mind are one

At this point the saliva flow in your mouth will probably have increased. This is the power of thought. The way you think affects your internal state, which in turn triggers a physical reaction, in this case the saliva flow. Your mind cannot distinguish between what is imagined and what is real.

For example:

Jim often had to give presentations as part of his work. Although he felt comfortable in one-to-one meetings, whenever he had to present to target groups of half a dozen or more he felt uncomfortable and nervous. It was worse if he knew about the presentation several days in advance because he would start to imagine what could go wrong. In particular he would imagine a dark room, and although there were people in his image of the room their faces would be a blur. He would typically start telling himself in a harsh, critical internal voice the problems he might have. For example, he wouldn't be able to explain his points clearly, he would lose his place in his notes, people would get bored. If he heard himself speaking it would be in almost a whisper. He could see people straining forward to hear, or sitting back and looking away. He would feel a heavy, sick feeling in his stomach, his heart began to beat faster, and his mouth felt dry. Beads of perspiration would break out on his forehead and hands.

And all this even before he gives the presentation!

We "dry run" our lives in our minds to such an extent that we influence the eventual result. Our lives are self-fulfilling prophecies. We are what we think.

MANAGING YOUR THINKING PROCESS

Think about something you did last week. Now think of something you could have done last week but didn't. The question is, how do you know you did one and not the other? After all, these are only memories, one remembered, one created. How often have you had the experience of not knowing for sure whether you did something or not? "Did I lock the front door?" "Did I turn off the light?"

Think of something you did yesterday that you will do in an identical way tomorrow. It might be getting out of bed, brushing your teeth, or setting the alarm. How do you distinguish between the one you did yesterday and the one you will do tomorrow? In fact, *can* you distinguish between what you did yesterday and what you will do tomorrow?

Past, present, or future

Many people distinguish between the past and the future according to where they position the images in their mind. For example, the past might be behind you or to your left. The future for some people is in front of them or to their right. Where is your past? Where is your future? And where is the present?

Identify two people, one you like and admire and one you dislike. Now take the one you like and admire. In your thinking about this person:

❑ Do you see him or her and, if so, what is the quality of the image? For example is it bright or hazy, color or black and white, moving or still?

❑ Are there any sounds associated with the thinking?

❑ What are the qualities of the sounds? Are they loud or faint, harsh or soft?

❑ What is the location of the sound?

❑ And what about the feelings? What exactly do you experience and where?

Now think of the person you dislike and consider the same questions. What is similar in the quality of your thinking about the two and what is different? The content is irrelevant. It is the *nature* of your thinking that makes the difference.

This ability to distinguish between the various aspects of your own and other people's experience is a way of determining the difference that makes the difference between those who do achieve what is important to them and those who don't.

VISUAL DISTINCTIONS

Let's consider these distinctions in thinking patterns in more detail.

Brightness	Bright or dim? Dull or sparkly?
Clarity	Dim and hazy or sharp and in focus?
Size	Larger than life, life size, or smaller than life?
Color/black and white	Full color, shades of grey, partial color, black and white?
Location	In front of you, to one side, behind you?
Distance	Close to or distant?
Motion	Still snapshots or movies?
Speed	Fast/slow?
Framed/panoramic	Enclosed in a frame or panoramic?
Sequence	In order/random/simultaneous images?

Associated/dissociated   Are you seeing as if out of
your own eyes (associated) or
can you see yourself in the
picture (dissociated)?

Now take a few simple images and experiment with them.

Think, for example, about your journey to work. You can
change your experience of this journey to make it better or worse
by experimenting with your thinking about it. Start by changing
some of the visual distinctions. For example, if it is dim turn up
the brightness. Then put it back as it was. If it is still make it into
a movie. Each time you experiment with a distinction return it to
its original form before you experiment with another. This way
you will be able to establish how a change in a specific distinction
affects your experience of the situation, in this case the journey.
You may find that your thinking about the journey becomes more
relaxed, more stressful, more interesting, or maybe more
exciting.

You may find initially that you are not aware of any pictures
in your thinking. This is not unusual. If this is the case, do the
exercise with your eyes closed and allow yourself to become
aware of what you do notice.

Volume	How loud/quiet?	
Speed	Fast or slow?	
Location	Where is the source of the sound? Is it in front of you, to one side, behind you?	
Distance	Is the sound close or far away?	
Voice/sound	Is it a voice or can you hear other sounds? If it is a voice, whose voice and what tone is it in?	
Pitch	High/low/mid range?	
Continuous	Is the sound continuous or intermittent?	

**AUDITORY
DISTINCTIONS**

Take another memory, for example your last disagreement at
work. Experiment again, this time with the auditory distinctions.
For example, if you can recall voices make them soft and
whispery. Now give them a different accent. Make them loud
and boomy, remembering to return the memory to its original
state before experimenting with the next distinction.

Note how this experiment affects the quality of the memory.

What starts as an unpleasant memory can become an amusing one merely by changing the nature of the voices. Give someone the voice of a cartoon character, e.g. Bugs Bunny. What effect does that have?

FEELINGS DISTINCTIONS

Pressure	What sort of pressure can you feel? Is there a sense of being pushed, a general or specific pressure?
Location	Where in your body do you experience any sensations?
Motion	Is there movement to the feeling? Is it fluttery, steady, intermittent, tingling?
Temperature	Hot/cold/damp?
Intensity	Strong/weak?
Pace	Is it a fast feeling, a slow one?

Now think of a time when you felt joy. What does joy feel like to you and where exactly in your body do you experience it? Experiment again. This time experiment with the intensity of the feeling. Can you turn it up and down? Return the feeling to its original state. Change the pace of the feeling. Continue to experiment with each element of the feeling, returning it to its original state before you experiment with the next one.

You will find that in each case there will be one or two key distinctions for you. By changing these distinctions you can change the quality of your experience.

Jim experimented with his thinking about presentations, first thinking about one-to-one meetings in which he felt confident and relaxed. He discovered that the key distinctions for him were brightness, focus, and the tone of voice with which he spoke to himself. By bringing the quality of his thinking about presentations into line with his thinking about one-to-one meetings, by making the image bright and in focus, and by softening his internal voice tone, he noticed that he felt a steady rippling feeling in his chest. This was the same feeling he experienced in one-to-one meetings. This, for him, was the feeling that he associated with confidence.

There are some general trends in the distinctions associated with feelings of confidence, happiness, and certainty. Not surprisingly, there are expressions in everyday language that reflect this. For example:

❑ "The future is looking brighter" as opposed to "The future looks black."
❑ "That's becoming clearer" as opposed to "That's unclear."

The richness of your internal thinking leaks through into your communication and into the way you influence yourself and others. Enrich your thinking—enrich your life.

SUMMARY

Once you have experienced something it becomes a memory. When you react to a memory you are reacting to the way you store that memory in your mind. Managing the distinctions in your thinking gives you the ability to influence and change the nature of your memories, so that you can store them in a way that results in your feeling the way you want to feel.

Many people become skilled at storing memories in a way that leads to depression, anger, or other negative feelings. Why choose these when you could choose pleasure or peace? The same is true for the future. Why make yourself worried or frustrated about an event that hasn't occurred when you could be making yourself confident and comfortable? You might choose to keep some of the worry in the form of concern. The point is that you choose the state you want rather than its choosing you. Our ability to manage our state is more and more important as the world around us defies control and becomes increasingly unpredictable.

You can be sure that you already use distinctions in your thinking patterns in this way. Whenever you change your experience of something you are almost certain to have reprogrammed the way you think about it, even though you may not have realized that this was what you were doing.

SHORTCUT TO MANAGING YOUR THINKING

THE SWISH

The SWISH is a technique for utilizing these distinctions in thinking to replace a problem state with a desirable state. It is fast and powerful, as well as being great for dealing with unwanted behavioral habits. Note that the SWISH will not necessarily be ideal for deeper, more significant issues. There are other techniques later in the book that can help with these.

1   First, identify the response in yourself that you want to change. What exactly is the reaction you would like to replace? For example, you might want to change a state such as anxiety or apprehension.
2   Identify precisely what it is that triggers this response. There will be something specific that immediately precedes your reaction. Identifying this trigger is a key part of the process. If, for example, it is a response to the way in which someone speaks to you, identify what it is they say or what it is about the way they say it that triggers your reaction. Re-create this in your thinking in exactly the way it happens. If it is the way in which someone speaks to you, then hear them saying the words in exactly the way they do. If it is the sight of an audience in front of you, imagine yourself in that situation looking out at the audience in the way you do. See exactly what you see as if you were there.
3   Now determine which facets of the way you think about this trigger have the greatest effect. There will be some elements that intensify your reaction. The SWISH lends itself most readily to visual triggers and most often the size and brightness of the image have the greatest impact. For example, if it is the sight of a certain person who works for you that triggers a response, experiment with each distinction in turn, putting the image back the way it was before you experiment with the next one. The aim is to find the one or two that intensify the response. Although these elements are currently triggering the response that you don't want, the aim of the SWISH is to hook these elements to the response that you do want. In so doing, you are making your own resources work for you rather than against you.

4 Think about something completely different to "break your state." For example, what color was the front door of the house in which you lived last?

5 Now imagine the person you would like to be, irrespective of what you have been in the past and irrespective of any specific behavior. This is an opportunity to imagine how you would like to be, the sort of qualities you would really like to have, the style that fits with who you truly are. Imagine this as if you are looking at yourself as an observer, dissociated. Develop this until you have an image that is compelling and desirable. Check that this "you" really fits in with the significant people in your life—it needs to be a real benefit to them too for you to be this new way. Explore how this fits with whatever sense of purpose you have, with your beliefs and values, with every aspect that is important to you. Check that this new you meets any needs that you may have been satisfying in less healthy ways in the past. If, for example, you have been getting attention for being stressed, check that you are going to get the level and quality of attention you need from this new way of being in the world.

6 Think of something completely different to break state again—for example, your telephone number backwards.

7 Make an image of the trigger, the stimulus that prompts the response that you want to change. Use the key factors that enhance the trigger. For example, if the distinctions of size and brightness intensify the trigger, make this image bright and big.

8 Take the image of the "new you" and make it small and dark. Place this small, dark image in the corner of the bigger image.

9 Very quickly make the large image small and dark and *at the same time* make the small image large and bright. Do this as fast as you can: The speed is important. You can make a sound to accompany this movement, a SWISH sound, hence the name of this process. (You can choose another sound if you wish.) The sound can become the association for the feelings of becoming the new you.

10 Break state again. Clear the images so that you start afresh. Create a new image so you break the image before you start again, otherwise you may set up a loop in your thinking.

11 Repeat the process five times and check to see if it works.

You will know this when you either experience or imagine the trigger for the original state and your response to it has changed to what you want it to be and you SWISH into the new you immediately. If this is not happening, go back and experiment with different parts of the process until it does.

THOUGHT PROVOKERS

1 What sort of jobs do you think would best suit people whose thinking preference is (a) visual? (b) auditory? (c) feelings?
2 Think of a successful outcome of a regular meeting that you hold/attend. How do you think about this? Is it a picture? Do you hear sounds or conversation? Do you experience certain feelings?
3 Look at a website that appeals to you. Which senses does it employ to capture your attention?
4 Think of a part of your work that you really enjoy. Now think of a part that you enjoy less well. How do the distinctions in your thinking vary?
5 Think of someone with whom you have a really good relationship. Now think of someone you find it difficult to deal with. Compare the differences in your thinking about each person. What are the main distinctions?
6 Take out a letter or email that you received recently. Which senses are you using as you read it?

REFERENCE

Steve Andreas & Connirae Andreas (1987) *Change Your Mind: And Keep the Change*, Real People Press.

One day a traveler was walking along a road on his journey from one village to another. As he walked he noticed a monk tilling the ground in the fields beside the road. The monk said "Good day" to the traveler and the traveler nodded to the monk.

The traveler then turned to the monk and said, "Excuse me, do you mind if I ask you a question?"

"Not at all," replied the monk.

"I am traveling from the village in the mountains to the village in the valley and I was wondering if you knew what it is like in the village in the valley?"

"Tell me," said the monk. "What was your experience of the village in the mountains?"

"Dreadful," replied the traveler. "To be honest I am glad to be away from there. I found the people most unwelcoming. When I first arrived I was greeted coldly. I was never made to feel a part of the village no matter how hard I tried. The villagers keep very much to themselves; they don't take kindly to strangers. So tell me, what can I expect in the village in the valley?"

"I'm sorry to tell you," said the monk, "but I think your experience will be much the same there." The traveler hung his head despondently and walked on.

A few months later another traveler was journeying down the same road and he also came upon the monk.

"Good day," said the traveler.

"Good day," said the monk.

"How are you?" asked the traveler.

"I'm well," replied the monk. "Where are you going?"

"I'm going to the village in the valley," replied the traveler. "Do you know what it is like?"

"I do," replied the monk. "But first, tell me, where have you come from?"

"I've come from the village in the mountains."

"And how was that?"

"It was a wonderful experience. I would have stayed if I could but I am committed to traveling on. I felt as though I were a member of the family in the village. The elders gave me much advice, the children laughed and joked with me, and the people generally were kind and generous. I am sad to have left there. It will always hold special memories for me. And what of the village in the valley?" he asked again.

"I think you will find it much the same," replied the monk. "Good day to you."

"Good day and thank you," replied the traveler, smiled, and journeyed on.

QUESTIONNAIRE: IDENTIFY YOUR PREFERRED THINKING PATTERN

The aim of this questionnaire is to help you identify any preferences you have in your thinking patterns. This is in no way a definitive analysis but is merely to intended to raise your awareness of how you think. Your thinking patterns can vary from one circumstance to another or you might be very balanced in your profile. Through awareness you can consider the choices you are making and whether they are influencing you and others in the way you would choose. The real advantage of learning the different thinking patterns is to be able to use them in real time.

For each of the following questions, think about the item, the person, or place described and tick the sense(s) that come to mind. The examples given are just that, examples. Be aware of what you are thinking before you look at the examples with each option. Check your answers on the analysis sheet provided at the end of the chapter.

You may tick as many senses as are true for you for any question. You may, for example, have one sense ticked for one question and five for another question. Work through each question and be aware of what comes to mind the moment you see it. Then tick the relevant sense(s). Go through each question in turn and answer them all immediately.

1   Petrol
    a   An image of some sort, e.g., a car, a petrol station?
    b   A sound, e.g., the sound of petrol pouring into a tank, the sound of an explosion?
    c   A touch, e.g., the feel of the pump handle?
    d   A smell, e.g., the smell of the petrol?
    e   A taste, e.g., the taste of petrol (assuming you know!)?

2   Your best friend
    a   A sound e.g., the sound of their voice?
    b   An emotion, e.g., your feelings toward them?
    c   A smell, e.g., the smell of their perfume?
    d   A taste, e.g., the taste of a meal you ate with them?
    e   An image, e.g., what they look like or a place you have been to with them?

3   The way you would most like to spend your time
    a   The sounds associated with doing this, e.g., the sound of people's voices or the sounds of the environment?
    b   A taste, e.g., the taste of a favorite meal?
    c   A smell, e.g., the aroma of your environment?
    d   An image, e.g., where you would be or who you would be with?
    e   A touch or an emotion, e.g., how you feel when you think of spending your time this way, the sensation of your muscles working in your body?

4   What you did yesterday
     a   A taste of some sort, e.g., what you ate?
     b   An image or picture, e.g., the scene of where you were?
     c   A sound, e.g., of a conversation?
     d   A touch, sensation, or emotion?
     e   A smell, e.g., of your environment?

5   A time you didn't enjoy very much
     a   A smell, e.g., of something distasteful?
     b   A sound, e.g., what you heard or what you were saying to yourself?
     c   A taste, e.g., of a bad meal?
     d   An image, e.g., the feel of something, or an emotion, how you felt at that time?
     e   What you were feeling?

6   Your favorite restaurant
     a   A touch or emotion, e.g., how you feel being there?
     b   What you see, e.g., the people you are with, your surroundings.
     c   What you hear, e.g., the conversation, the music?
     d   A taste, e.g., of the food?
     e   A smell, e.g., the aroma from the kitchen?

7   Something from your childhood
     a   A smell, an aroma, a perfume?
     b   A touch or an emotion?
     c   An image?
     d   Sounds or voices?
     e   A taste?

8   Your work
     a   A sound, e.g., of equipment or voices?
     b   An image, e.g., the picture of what you do?
     c   A smell, e.g., of your surroundings?
     d   A touch or an emotion, e.g., the texture of what you can feel or how you feel about your work?
     e   A taste?

9   Where you might be tomorrow
     a   An image or picture?
     b   An emotion or touch?
     c   A taste?

d   A smell or aroma?
e   A sound?

10   Something you find difficult to do
a   An image or picture?
b   A taste?
c   A sound or an inner conversation?
d   An associated emotion or a touch?
e   A smell?

11   Something you find rewarding
a   An emotion, e.g., a feeling of satisfaction, or a touch, such as the physical sensation of a sport?
b   A taste?
c   A smell?
d   A sound, e.g., what you say to yourself or the sound of voices or your environment?
e   An image, e.g., of what it looks like?

12   Something you find amusing
a   A sound, e.g., what someone says or what you hear?
b   An image, e.g., something or someone you see?
c   An emotion, e.g., the sensation of amusement, or a physical touch, such as the feel of something?
d   A taste?
e   A smell?

13   A goal that you have for the future
a   What you are seeing?
b   What you are hearing?
c   What you are feeling?
d   What you can taste?
e   What you can smell?

14   Your expectations for the rest of this week
a   Your image of what you see happening?
b   Your emotions about what you expect?
c   An aroma?
d   A taste?
e   How you are feeling?

15   What you are doing this moment
    a   What you can smell?
    b   What you can see?
    c   What you are hearing?
    d   What you can taste?
    e   What you are feeling?

Thinking patterns analysis

Circle the letters you ticked for each answer and total the number of ticks in each column:

	Visual	Auditory	Feelings	Taste	Smell
1	a	b	c	e	d
2	e	a	b	d	c
3	d	a	e	b	c
4	b	c	d	a	e
5	d	b	e	c	a
6	b	c	a	d	e
7	c	d	b	e	a
8	b	a	d	e	c
9	a	e	b	c	d
10	a	c	d	b	e
11	e	d	a	b	c
12	b	a	c	d	e
13	a	b	c	d	e
14	a	e	b	d	c
15	b	c	e	d	a

The higher the score, the higher the preference. It is usual for visual to be a preferred sense and for taste and smell to be lower preferences. However, there are no rights and wrongs in this—it is merely important to know what you do currently prefer. You may want now to check this out with your actual experience in situations and see what preferences are influencing your responses to situations. If you do not score anything for a sense it does not mean that you do not have this sense; it just means that you are not aware of it.

Ultimately, if your outcome is to develop your flexibility and influence, then you would want to practice being aware of using all senses so that you have the flexibility to adapt to differing circumstances.

Personal development: Increasing your awareness

As a result of doing this questionnaire you may want to develop your awareness of some of your senses. One of the simplest ways to do this is as follows:

1   Choose the sense for which you would like to raise your awareness.

2   Choose a time of day (it need not be more than 30 minutes) when your role is less significant and you can direct some of your attention to how you are doing what you are doing.

3   Program yourself with the question "What am I seeing/hearing/feeling/tasting/smelling?" (Choose whichever one you want to concentrate on.) If it helps, write the question down so that you have it in front of you for that time. If you are working at a computer you could put it as the screensaver.

4   Do this as many times as you want to until you recognize that you are unconsciously being aware of this sense. You could do the questionnaire again after three or four weeks to see if your scores have changed for this particular sense.

5   Now repeat the process for another sense.

3

Filters on Your World

"The appliances and machines around us will soon remember us individually and anticipate our needs."
Don Peppers and Martha Rogers, Enterprise One to One

Technology is smart and is becoming ever more intelligent at knowing and responding to, even influencing, our individual needs. In a culture so infused with technology, we had better get pretty smart at knowing our clients' needs. If we want to build lifelong relationships, either in our personal lives or, as is becoming the expectation, in our business lives, we need to learn how to read other people's styles and needs with ever-increasing sophistication.

Getting smart at detecting needs

The better able we are to detect needs, the better able we are to present ourselves, our products, and our services in a way that keeps our customers satisfied. Companies talk today about doing much more than keeping customers satisfied—they talk of customer delight. To delight our customers we need to be able to "model" their thinking and behavior to ensure that we appeal to what really matters to them. We not only need to "read" these styles, we need to have the flexibility to respond to them.

I recently decided that I would learn some Danish so that I could open my next program in Denmark in the native language. I felt that this would be respectful of the time that my delegates there give to listening to me speak in English. I asked a Danish delegate on a program I was running in England if he would translate a passage I had prepared so that I could practice what

I wanted to say. I asked if he would send the translation to me via email. He made a decision that it would be more helpful for me if he were to record the translation so that I could hear the words instead. In his heart he was being helpful, but auditory is not my preferred choice for learning a passage like this. I wanted to see the written word, having already learned some of the pronunciation.

It can be tempting to make choices about presenting material in ways that fit our own preferred ways of thinking rather than in ways that suit the preferences of our customers. We often think that we know best in terms of what our customers "should" have. And we make unconscious as well as conscious choices about the people with whom we choose to do business, depending on how well they skilfully match our needs. In the instance I quote what happened led to learning for us both, but in business making the wrong choice might cost you the work.

In the choices we make about how to present ourselves to our customers, the margin for error has become significantly smaller. The way we use the internet is a good example of this. If you haven't grabbed your potential clients' interest by relating to the way they think within six seconds of their logging on to your web pages, research shows that they will not wait to make sense of what you are saying—they will move on.

In this chapter I illustrate some fundamental needs. There are hundreds, even thousands of needs and it is your skill in detecting not only those I have explained here but the unique ones you can discover for yourself that will determine your success in working with, dealing with, communicating with, and living with other people. If you do not yet know how to do this, you need to do your homework fast. If other business people do not overtake you, technology most certainly will!

So let's consider some of these patterns in thinking and communicating that affect how we present ourselves so that others can relate to what we are doing and saying, and so that we can relate to them in a language and style they understand.

LEARNING TO RELATE SUCCESSFULLY

Have you ever bought a car and suddenly become aware of all the other cars of the same type on the road? Or have you ever had an experience, maybe an insight about yourself, only to discover that many of your friends have had the same or a similar experience, even though you weren't aware of that before? Do you see the wineglass as half full as opposed to half empty by looking for what is there as opposed to what is not? These are examples of ways you filter what happens to you to let some information in and keep other information out. This is what constitutes perception.

Here is a conversation that highlights the need to be able to understand and relate to different filters.

When Janet and Bill had a conversation, each found the other frustrating. Janet liked to discuss the details of what was needed, whereas Bill preferred to discuss the broader strategic concepts. For example, Janet would say, "I'd like Peter to go to the next meeting," and Bill would reply, "We haven't decided on the main areas of the plan that didn't work." Janet's conversation centered on future actions, whereas Bill concentrated more on the past. Janet would pay attention to the similarities between one situation and another: "This is like another idea I have about what we might do to improve the office layout." Bill would concentrate on the exception by saying things like "No, this is different" or "We didn't include an overall plan." It was as though Janet and Bill were talking different languages. They had different filters on their experience. They didn't find meetings with one another easy!

Different filters

When two people in conversation are using the same filters there is usually a high level of rapport. If the filters you use are different to those used by your partner then, as with Janet and Bill, you may experience discord and frustration. By using similar language patterns to your partner you are increasing the level of mutual trust and influence.

Learning to recognize the filters that you and others use is a first step. Developing your flexibility in the way you use the filters gives you a greater chance of finding a way of

Flexibility

communicating with each person you meet. There are hundreds of filters that we use every day to translate experience into perception. What follows is a "starter set."

In our example, for Bill to build rapport and thereby his understanding with Janet, he could have replied in the following way:

Janet	"I'd like Peter to go to the next meeting."
Bill	"Yes, Peter would make some useful contributions. Let's note that, so when we have decided what areas of the plan didn't work we can also decide who else we might want to include."
Janet	"This is like another idea I have about what we might do to improve the office layout."
Bill	"You come up with lots of ideas, Janet. Can we discuss those when we have gone through my idea about the overall plan?"

We don't always know what will work in advance, but by having an awareness of what is and what isn't working we give ourselves choice. Choice is the key to success.

Let's explore some of the filters.

ASSOCIATED/DISSOCIATED

Think of a conversation you had recently with one of your colleagues. As you think of this conversation, pay attention to how you are thinking about it. For example, are you seeing, hearing, and feeling the situation as if you are in your own body, i.e., seeing it out of your own eyes, hearing it with your own ears, and experiencing the feelings of being there? Or are you experiencing the situation as if you are outside of your own body, i.e., seeing yourself in the situation, hearing yourself as if you were an observer? The experience of being in your own body is referred to as *associated* and the experience of being outside of your own body is known as *dissociated*.

Pay attention for a moment to your surroundings. You may begin to notice what you see around you, the quality of the light, the colors and shapes, the shadows, and the clarity of the scene. As you notice the scene you may begin to hear sounds close to you and farther away. As you become aware of even more sounds, turn your conscious mind toward them. Be aware of the location of the sounds, their loudness or softness, their tone and speed. You can become aware of what you feel, of the textures and pressures on your body. Sense those parts of you that are touching the ground or a chair. Allow yourself to notice any smells or tastes that you experience. As you do this, pay attention to the feelings within you, to any tensions or internal emotions, their precise location and intensity.

This awareness of yourself through all of your senses is an associated state.

Now step back or stand behind the chair in which you were sitting and see yourself sitting or standing, as you were a moment ago. Look at yourself so that you can see the whole of you. Notice how the "you" there interacts with the environment. Be aware of how the "you" there in front of you looks and sounds.

In this dissociated state you will be detached from the feelings.

The ability to associate and dissociate is a foundation skill of NLP. To experience the emotions and feelings of a situation fully you need to be associated. To distance yourself from the emotions of an unpleasant or traumatic situation, you need to dissociate.

One of the people responsible for the counseling and support of the crew in the London Fire Brigade discovered that the members of the crew who experienced the highest levels of stress were those who relived their memories in an associated way. As they recalled what had happened, they re-experienced the emotions they had felt at the time. So as well as experiencing the trauma of each situation they were experiencing it over and over again and subsequently intensifying the stress they felt. The counselor also established that those who had the lowest levels of stress were those who were able to dissociate from what they experienced.

Dealing with stress

Games software designers have discovered that by developing software that "associates" us into the role of one of the players so that we are playing the game as if we are seeing it through our own eyes and hearing it through our own ears, we feel the game as if it were real. Considering that feelings that are the source of motivation to buy, giving us this emotional experience is a very powerful way of selling not only this game but future ones. We need to be aware of how these tactics are used *on* us and how they can potentially work *for* us.

Giving and receiving feedback

We can no longer plan years in advance: Life and business have become increasingly unpredictable and chaotic. What we have to learn to do is present our ideas and products partly formed and develop them through the involvement of and feedback from our customers. We can only do this if we have developed all the skills of giving and receiving feedback. One of these elements is our ability to dissociate from feedback that we might otherwise take personally and reject, and then associate once we have the resources we need in order to let the feedback in and act on it. Chapter 19, Giving and receiving feedback, outlines the steps for doing this.

The skill lies in choosing either an associated or a dissociated state for a purpose. The appropriate choice depends on your desired outcome. You might choose to dissociate to protect yourself from painful emotions, or you might choose to associate in order fully to experience all the feelings of a situation. Did you know that for most people decision making takes place through a feeling? If your preferred style is to keep yourself and others dissociated, don't be surprised if you and they struggle to make decisions! If your business depends on supporting others in making decisions, you need to know how to associate and how to help others do the same.

One of the directors of a marketing company found that she was struggling to get potential clients to make a decision about the work her company was proposing. She ran through what she had presented and how she had done that. What we noticed was that she came across very objectively and factually. Everything she said was logical, but she did not give space for feelings. Her voice communicated a consistently auditory way of thinking; the tone was even and slightly hard. There were few pauses in her presentation.

Given the feedback about her style and the likelihood of her client's needing to make decisions through a feeling, she associated into the presentation and changed her tone of voice to make it softer and lower toned (communicating and inviting feelings). She spoke with greater certainty, whereas before she had raised her voice at the end of most sentences. The next time she presented to this customer they stopped her part way through the presentation and told her that she need not continue—they liked what she was saying and she had got the business. This presentation and subsequent ones broke the record for time needed for the client to make a decision.

TOWARDS/AWAY FROM

Think of a goal you have for yourself right now. It can be a personal goal or a work goal. It can be short or long term. Be aware of how you are thinking about this goal. Are you imagining what it would be like to achieve the goal, i.e., what you are seeing, hearing, and feeling? Or are you aware of what stops you and what you don't want? For example, if you are thinking of slimming, do you imagine yourself slim and fit or do you think of the food you want to avoid and the weight you want to lose? What is in your mind? Your ability to think about what you really want is known as *towards* thinking. Your ability to think about what you don't want is known as *away from* thinking.

I have just received a request for some training with the senior management team of one of my clients. Their request is framed as follows:

"How to avoid letting strength of personal view get in the way of management."

This is a classic "away from" statement. Before I commit to the work I will want to know what it is that they really want. And I have drawn some conclusions already!

The concept of towards/away from is explained further in Chapter 15. In the context of goal setting, people who think

Don't worry!

"towards" are more likely to achieve what they do want. Those who think of what they don't want are likely to achieve just that. For example, if you tell yourself not to worry you are effectively programming yourself to worry. If you think about being confident, that is what you start to feel.

MATCH/MISMATCH

Look at the shapes below and describe their relationship to each other.

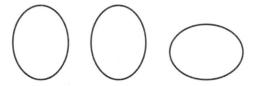

What do you notice? Do you notice in what ways they are similar, i.e., they are all oval, or do you notice that two are upright and one is on its side? In effect, do you look for what is the same—*match*—or do you look for what is different—*mismatch*?

When meeting a person for the first time, someone who sorts for a match might think of similar people, similar situations, or how the other is like them. Someone who sorts for a mismatch will identify what is different about this person and this situation compared with others they know and themselves.

Job profiles

Certain professions train people to think in a particular way. For example, I have come across more mismatching patterns of thinking in professions associated with information technology and finance than I have in many other fields of business. There is no right or wrong. Certain jobs depend on a person's ability to match, just as some depend on an ability to mismatch. A software engineer trained to uncover system "bugs" may be skilled at mismatching, looking for what doesn't fit, as indeed will someone in accounting whose job it is to find the imbalance. What matters is how appropriately these skills are used. If used appropriately they are fine, if not they can cause problems.

The "yes, but" pattern in conversation is an example of mismatching.

"I'm really pleased with the way this project has gone."

"Yes, but there's a danger we're going to get overconfident."

"You're right. Let's review objectively what we've achieved so that we build some of the good practices into future projects."

"That's all very well, but we don't have the time right now."

"Well, how about putting a date in the diary in a few weeks' time?"

"That's easy to say but not so easy in practice. Things change so rapidly around here."

As someone once said to me, everything before the "but" is bull****!

Dealing with this in conversation can be hard work unless you are another mismatcher who enjoys a good argument.

BIG CHUNK/SMALL CHUNK

Look around you at the room you are in. How would you describe it to someone who has not seen it before? Do you pay attention to things such as spaciousness, feel, and style? Or do you pay attention to number of windows, color of furnishings, the details? Is it a mix of both? The spaciousness, feel, and style are examples of *big chunk* thinking, whereas the details are *small chunk*.

This pattern of thinking can apply to anything. For example, if you have set a specific goal for yourself you could *chunk up* to more global goals or *chunk down* to milestones, which you could set along the way. In most work situations the application of big chunk/small chunk thinking is equally relevant.

Let's suppose you are in a cookery class. You need an orange for the dish you are preparing. Another member of the class also needs an orange, but there is only one. Without flexibility in thinking the usual solution would be to accept the facts as they appear and cut the orange in two, taking half each. If, however, you chunk up in relation to your needs in the situation by asking "What do you need the orange for?" you will discover broader needs. For example, you might want the orange for a cake and your colleague may want it for a soufflé. If you chunk down on the request for the orange by asking

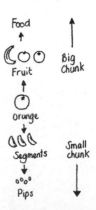

Food
↑
Fruit
Big Chunk

Orange

Segments
Small chunk

Pips

"What specifically do you need for your soufflé?" you might discover that the other person needs just the pulp. You know that you only need the skin, the zest, for your cake. It is possible for you both to have exactly what you want.

Chunking up and chunking down is the essence of skilled negotiation. It opens the doors to the likelihood of achieving a win/win position, in which both parties achieve all they want.

PAST/PRESENT/FUTURE

Where in time do you put your attention? Some people live their lives in the past, thinking about what has gone before. Some people live for the moment, and their attention is on the present. Some are continually planning and thinking about the future. You may have experienced these kinds of questions that look to the future:

❑ What's for dinner?
❑ How long until we get home?
❑ Where are we going on holiday?
❑ What's next on the agenda?
❑ What I want to achieve by the end of the project is…

Or you may know someone who concentrates on the past:

❑ What did you say earlier?
❑ Did you see what that person was wearing?
❑ Do you remember when we were on holiday?
❑ The last meeting we had was important.

There is no right or wrong, no good or bad, but this does have implications for how people communicate with each other. A friend called to invite me to a school reunion to talk over old times. As someone whose attention is more on the present and the future, the thought of reminiscing about the past didn't strike me as an attractive proposition!

ACTIVITY/PERSON/OBJECT/PLACE/TIME

Think of the best meal you ever had.

The filter you use will determine your memory of this. For example, if you sort by:

Activity	You recall what you and others did at this meal. Maybe you had a memorable conversation or the waiter dropped the plates.
Person	You remember the meal in relation to who was there.
Object	Your memories are associated with the food, a present you were given, the pictures in the restaurant, the type of furniture.
Place	Your memories are of the location: the restaurant, the town, the country, or possibly the location of the table at which you sat.
Time	You remember the time and date, an anniversary or another special occasion. You might remember that it was the first day of your new job or a farewell dinner at the end of term.

INTERNAL/EXTERNAL

How do you know when you've done a good job? Which of the following responses would be most likely to be true for you?

I know I've done a good job when:

❑ I see people using the results of what I have produced.
❑ I feel good inside.
❑ I know I've met the standards I set myself: We get more orders.
❑ I can say to myself, "That was a job well done."

Externally referenced people rely on external sources for their evidence of fulfilment. For example, they rely on what other people say and do. They may also rely on external factors such as "more orders," or "people use the results of what has been produced." *Internally* referenced people use their own internal

Dependence and independence

feelings, images, and voices as their evidence of fulfilment.

Your preference here will make a big difference to the way you work. If you are externally referenced you may be more likely to depend on having others around you. If, however, you are internally referenced, then you are independent of external people and events.

People who are independent in style are usually internally referenced. This is a characteristic pattern of senior managers. They can be concerned about what happens outside themselves; they need to be! However, they do not depend on external circumstances to feel satisfied. Can you imagine a managing director who depended on having his staff tell him that he was doing OK? Some of the leading figures of our time have succeeded because of their ability to persevere despite the external feedback they have received.

CONVINCER PATTERN

I was explaining to a client how he might restructure his management team. He seemed unsure, although he accepted the principle of what I was saying. We discussed the plans in a number of different ways. I eventually reflected his uncertainty back to him. He replied, "I just don't see it, Sue." I explained again and he replied, "I just don't get the picture." At that point I drew it on the whiteboard. "Now I see what you are saying," he said.

Everyone has a specific means by which they become convinced. In this client's case the principal factor was that he needed to see the ideas visually before he was convinced they would work. So part of what makes someone convinced is the channel through which they receive the information.

Other people might equally well have been convinced by:

❏ Hearing what I had to say.
❏ Trying it to find out if it worked in practice.
❏ Reading the plan in more detail.

There are differences in the way people need to receive information within these broader categories. Some people need to be told a number of times or have a number of examples before they are convinced. Others need to be convinced over a period of time; time is the deciding factor for them. Some people make decisions on the bare outlines of the facts—they don't need the detail in order to be convinced—yet others need to have something proved to them over and over again. They will be convinced, but only for one situation and one context at a time.

If your job involves you in having to convince others to achieve the result you want, you need to know the pattern by which they operate. You can then match this pattern in the way you present your information.

"Bring in someone who can take the pulse of your customers online."

David Siegel, Futurize Your Enterprise

With NLP, and especially by learning to recognize the ways in which your customers take in information through filters, you can provide a level of sophistication in your support that few have yet achieved. Most people know what they need to know, but as yet few know how to gain that knowledge. Learn to recognize the filters in yourself and others and you will master the "how."

To find out more about the filters you use, refer to the questionnaire on page 50, "Identify your filters."

Making decisions

SUMMARY

The filters on your experience determine how you make sense of reality. Nature has shown us that it is the animals and plants that have learned to cooperate with each other and their environment that survive. By learning to recognize filters in yourself and others, you begin to build bridges of communication. There are no rights and wrongs about the filters and there are many more than the ones I have covered here. Your filters can vary over time and context, and they are part of what makes you unique.

THOUGHT PROVOKERS

1 Read the following passages and determine which filters each author is using.

   a I'm someone who enjoys life to the full. I play squash, I write, I work full time as a salesperson, and I have a young family who keep me busy in any spare time I have! I get a lot of satisfaction from what I do. I set myself goals and I know by my own standards when I have achieved them. I enjoy travel, particularly to Europe, and I love eating out.

   b I can be a difficult person, or so others tell me. I can usually see the alternative point of view. I enjoy a good discussion, some would say argument. I like perfection. If something isn't quite right it irritates me. I spend a lot of time working and I am meticulous in the way I go about that. I am a programmer and the work I do requires attention to detail and the ability to see immediately if something is wrong.

   c I am a good listener. People come to me with their problems. I have always had this sort of role, not only in my work life but also with my friends. I have spent most of my life in the same part of England. I have always liked the people here. I can recall some very special occasions that I have spent with friends in the past. I have always been a bit indecisive about what I might do next. I have always let others push me into new situations or jobs, and have tended only to change if I have been dissatisfied with what I was doing at the time.

2 Take a letter or email that you have received recently. What filters do you detect in the language the writer has used?

3 Take a letter or email that you have written recently. What filters do you detect in the language you have used?

4 Compare the filters you are using in response to a communication from someone else. To what extent have you matched/mismatched the filters the other person is using?

5 Select one of your key customers. Take examples of their behavior and writing and identify some of their key filters.

6 Take a context in which you want to appeal to a wide audience, one in which people will have a wide range of filters. Identify how many filters you are using in the way you are presenting yourself, your products, and your services.

REFERENCES

Fiona Beddoes-Jones (1999) *Thinking Styles: Relationship Strategies that Work!*, BJA Associates.

Shelle Rose Charvet (1997) *Words that Change Minds: Mastering the Language of Influence*, Kendall Hunt.

Don Peppers & Martha Rogers (1998) *Enterprise One-to-One*, Piatkus.

David Siegel (1999) *Futurize Your Enterprise: Business Strategy in the Age of the E-Customer*, John Wiley.

One of our course delegates was recounting an incident with his three-year-old daughter.

"How many times do I have to tell you to put your toys away?" he asked her.

"Four times," she replied categorically.

QUESTIONNAIRE: IDENTIFY YOUR FILTERS

The aim of this questionnaire is for you to identify any characteristic patterns in the filters in the way you think. It is also a way for you to begin to identify which filters you might want to develop in order to increase your overall flexibility and influence.

There are no rights and wrongs to the questionnaire. You may find that you already have a very flexible style in your thinking or that there are some areas it would be useful to strengthen.

The questions vary in style, so follow the instructions. Do each question in turn and answer with whatever comes to mind as you read it. Your immediate, "off the top of the head" answer is the most appropriate. There is a key to analyzing your answers at the end of the questionnaire.

Answer the following questions for each area that is relevant to you.

1 Think of yourself exercising. Be aware of what you are thinking before you answer the following questions. Tick the thoughts that either match or are most like those that came to mind. Tick as many of the answers as are relevant (it might be one or all six).
   a   Getting fit/feeling good about the physical aspects of yourself.
   b   Avoiding injury/what might be a problem and how you want to avoid that.
   c   Having a sense of personal achievement.
   d   Losing weight.
   e   Enjoying the environment/the company of other people/the experience.
   f   Taking your mind off the pressure of work/getting away from problems.

2 When you think of changing your job, which of the following are you most likely to think about?
   a   The kind of work you would most like to do.
   b   The situations and people you don't like and want to avoid.
   c   The satisfaction you will get from doing what you want.
   d   The frustrations you experience currently and leaving those behind.
   e   The things that your current job doesn't give you.
   f   The kind of work that satisfies your needs and how a new job might provide that.

3 When you make a decision to go on holiday, which of the following do you do?
   a   Think of the problems of organizing a holiday or what might be difficult to arrange.
   b   Begin to imagine yourself on holiday; transport yourself there in your mind ahead of time.
   c   Think of what your holiday will be like.
   d   Remind yourself of all the benefits of taking a holiday.
   e   Think of some of the problems you have experienced on previous holidays.
   f   Think of everything you have to do first.

4 Think about the rest of this month. What are you thinking of?
   a What you really want to achieve by the end of the month and you are feeling good about.
   b How much you have got to do.
   c Something you have kept putting off and should finally get finished.
   d What you are looking forward to and what it will be like to achieve the goal you have in mind.
   e The positive emotions around what you believe you will have achieved by then.
   f The problems you face.

5 Write one sentence that explains the relationship of the following shapes to each other:
   a

   b

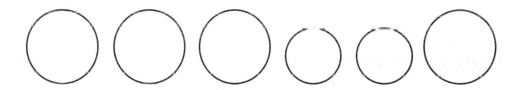

   c

6   Think of something you are in the process of buying: a car, a house, a book, an item of clothing (it could be anything). Which of the following are you doing?

a   Looking for aspects of this purchase that are the same as similar purchases you have made before.

b   Thinking the purchase through to discover in what ways it doesn't meet your needs.

c   Comparing the purchase with a mental or actual list of characteristics you want to have.

d   Searching for something that is different to what you have had before.

e   Seeking to find out how this product matches up to similar products.

f   Wanting something that is unique.

7   In conversation, which of the following applies to you?

a   You like a good argument.

b   You look for a common agenda.

c   You push for agreement.

d   You test out someone else's views to find out where they are wrong.

e   You find yourself using the expression "Yes, but…"

f   You find that you are usually in the company of people who share your ideas.

8   Think of yourself in relation to the other people with whom you have contact at work.

a   Do you consider yourself to be quite different to the rest?

b   Would you say you are very like the other people?

c   Do you think you stand out from the rest in any of the following ways: what you do, what you wear, how you approach situations and work, how you behave, the skills you have?

d   Do find you have a lot in common with them?

e   Do you feel somewhat of an odd one out in any respect?

f   Do you find that you generally work harmoniously with them?

9   Write down three or four sentences describing your home to someone who has never been there before.

10 Tick any of the following that are characteristic of you:
  a   Thinking about holidays you have had.
  b   Savoring the things you see, hear, and feel around you now.
  c   Reviewing how successful your work has been.
  d   Planning what you will do in the future.
  e   Paying attention to what is happening around you.
  f   Mulling over conversations you have had.
  g   Deciding how you will spend your day.
  h   Enjoying every moment.
  i   Dreaming of where you would like to be.
  j   Being aware of how you feel.
  k   Anticipating what is going to happen.
  l   Reminiscing.
  m   Attending reunions to go over past times.
  n   Living for now.
  o   Imagining what you want to happen in the future.
  p   Typically absent (daydreaming)/thinking about future times when in the company of others.
  q   Typically absent/reviewing things that have happened before when in the company of others.
  r   Totally connected and giving full and undivided attention to the people you are with.

11 Think of the best meal you have ever had. What are you thinking about?
  a   Who you were with.
  b   Objects associated with the meal, e.g., the food, a present you were given.
  c   The place: the restaurant, the town, the country, the location.
  d   The date, time, or occasion.
  e   What you were doing.

12 Think of how you most like to spend your time. Which of the following do you think about?
  a   Being with particular people.
  b   What you are doing.
  c   What you are involved with, e.g., golf clubs, a book, the garden.
  d   Where you are.
  e   A particular time, e.g., a Sunday afternoon, Christmas, the summer.

13 Think of something important that is going to happen in the future. Which of the following were part of your thinking?
  a   The date, time, or occasion.
  b   What will be happening.
  c   The people involved.

d   The things associated with the future.
e   The place.

14 Suppose you were going out this evening. What would be important to you?
a   Who you could go with.
b   Where you would go.
c   What you might do.
d   The timing of what you would do.
e   How you would be doing what you are doing.

15 How do you know when you've done a good job? Tick the ones that are true for you.
a   Someone praises me.
b   People tell me.
c   I feel good inside.
d   I know I've met the standard I set myself.
e   I get results from the success.
f   I just know.

16 How do you know when you are enjoying yourself?
a   People around me are happy.
b   I feel happy with myself.
c   I have space and time for myself.
d   Other people are pleased with what is happening.
e   I appreciate the effect I am having on events around me.
f   I have a good feeling.

17 How do you know when you have made a right decision?
a   I just know.
b   It is confirmed by others.
c   I get reassurance and agreement from others.
d   It is a gut feeling.
e   I feel good about it.
f   It pleases others.

18 What would have to be true for you to be convinced of a new idea or approach? Tick the ones that are true for you.
a   I'd need to be able to picture it in some way.
b   Someone would have to explain it to me.
c   I'd need to try it out to know that it worked.

d   I'd need to see the idea mapped out in some way.

e   I'd want to discuss it thoroughly.

f   I'd need time to think it through.

g   I'd need to have the idea explained or presented to me a number of different times.

h   I'd like the details.

19 What has to be true for you to buy something significant? Tick the ones that are true for you.

a   I need to see it.

b   I need to talk it through with someone.

c   I need to try it out/try it on/use it/experiment with it.

d   I need to go over it a number of times before I decide.

e   I have to research the details of what is involved about the purchase.

f   I want to think about it over time.

g   I want to know what it looks like.

h   I want to hear what others have to say about it.

20 Think of an important decision that you have made in the last few months. What was true for you?

a   I talked it through with others before deciding.

b   I made sure that I saw the outcome before deciding.

c   I tried it out first.

d   I thought about it over time.

e   Some aspect of the decision was shown to me.

f   I asked for/got others' opinions.

g   I went over it a number of times.

h   I researched it/got as much information as I could beforehand.

Questionnaire analysis

In this analysis the question numbers are grouped under the particular filters to which they most relate. This is not a definitive analysis—it is a pointer to some of the patterns in your thinking. The aim of the questionnaire is to raise your awareness of what you and others actually do.

Away from/towards thinking
Questions 1, 2, 3 and 4 relate to the "away from" or "towards" ways of thinking. Circle the letters of all the answers you ticked:

	Away from	Towards
Question 1	b	a
	d	c
	f	e
Question 2	b	a
	d	c
	e	f
Question 3	a	b
	e	c
	f	d
Question 4	b	a
	c	d
	f	e
	_____	_____
	_____	_____

Add up the number of letters circled in each column and write the total at the bottom. The column with the greatest number of ticks indicates your likely preference. If the scores are equal then it is likely that you use both ways of thinking. If there is a significantly higher score in one column than the other then this indicates a strong preference.

Match/mismatch thinking
Match/mismatch is analyzed in questions 5, 6, 7 and 8.

In question 5 your preference for match or mismatch is indicated by whether you identified what was similar in each of the shapes, for example:

a They are all rectangles, they all have four corners, they all have straight sides.
b They are all circles.
c They are all arrows, they all point roughly upwards.

The above are all examples of sorting for a match.

If you tend toward the mismatch, then you will have answers similar to the following:

a   Two are upright, one is on its side.
b   Two circles are smaller then the other four.
c   Two arrows are pointing up and right, one is pointing up and left.

Mismatch is indicated by any description in which you have sorted for what is different.

Put a tick in the column that most resembled your choice for each part of question 5 below. For questions 6, 7 and 8, circle the letters you ticked:

		Match	Mismatch
Question 5	a		
	b		
	c		
Question 6		a	b
		c	d
		e	f
Question 7		b	a
		c	d
		f	e
Question 8		b	a
		d	c
		f	e

Add up the number of letters circled in each column and add in the ticks for question 5. Write in the total for each column. The column with the greatest number of ticks indicates your likely preference. It is possible to have both ways of thinking, so you may find that your score for each is the same or similar.

Big chunk/small chunk thinking

In question 9, your preference will be indicated by the number of words of each type that you have used in your description.

Go through your sentences and count up how many descriptive words you used in the following categories:

a Abstract, global descriptions, e.g., spacious, airy, dark, traditional. These are words that are nonspecific. More examples of this kind of description would be: roomy, large, small, comfortable, convenient, well situated.

Number of abstract words in your example =   (write in your total here)

b Detailed, precise descriptions, e.g., *n* x *n* meters, temperature, number of doors, windows, etc., color of surroundings. More examples of this kind of description would be: brick building, three bedrooms, 10 x 4 garden, end terrace, combined kitchen/dining room, in SW16 district of London.

Number of precise words in your example =   (write in your total here)

If you have a larger total for (a) your preference is big chunk thinking. A larger total for (b) would indicate a preference for small chunk thinking. It is possible that you have used both and that the scores are equal.

Past/present/future

For question 10, circle the ones you ticked in the following columns:

Past	Present	Future
a	b	d
c	e	g
f	h	i
l	j	k
m	n	o
q	r	p
_____	_____	_____
_____		

Write in the total of letters circled in each column. The highest score represents your more preferred style, the lowest score your least preferred style.

Activity/person/object/place/time

Circle ones you ticked in the columns below:

	Activity	Person	Object	Place	Time
Question 11	e	a	b	c	d
Question 12	b	a	c	d	e
Question 13	b	c	d	e	a
Question 14	c	a	c	b	d
	_____				
	_____				

Your relative preferences are indicated by the number of ticks in each column, i.e., the more ticks the greater the preference. It is possible to have a similar number of ticks in all of the columns, indicating a balanced preference.

Internal/external reference
Circle the letters you ticked in questions 15, 16, and 17.

	Internal	External
Question 15	c	a
	d	b
	f	e
Question 16	b	a
	c	d
	f	e
Question 17	a	b
	d	c
	e	f
	_____	_____

Add up the numbers of letters circled in each column. The number of ticks in each column indicates your relative preference, i.e., the more ticks the greater the preference

Convincer pattern
The answers you ticked in questions 18, 19, and 20 indicate the importance of the following elements in your strategy for being convinced about something:

Visual demonstration (Vis dem)
Auditory explanation (Aud expl)
Active experimentation (Act expm)
Visual presentation (Vis pres)
Auditory discussion (Aud disc)
Time
A number of explanations/presentations/practicals (No)
Details (Det)

Circle the letters that you ticked for each of the questions.

	Vis dem	Aud expl	Act expm	Vis pres	Aud disc	Time	No	Det
18	a	b	c	d	e	f	g	h
19	a	b	c	g	h	f	d	e
20	e	f	c	b	a	d	g	h

Add up the letters circled in each column. The ones for which you have scores are elements that you want to be present in your convincer strategy.

PERSONAL DEVELOPMENT: INCREASING YOUR FLEXIBILITY

The analysis of the questionnaire indicates preferences in your thinking style. Overall, the more choices you have available to you, the greater the influence you can bring to situations. Having identified some of your preferences through the questionnaire you can now check them out for yourself in everyday situations. If you recognize any that are not a preferred choice for you, then you can strengthen them in the following ways.

1 Choose the filter that you want to strengthen, e.g., towards thinking or matching.
2 Choose a time each day when you will commit to paying attention to this filter. Make it a time when your contribution does not require 100 percent attention or a context that is not critical to your work. You might choose a social context, for example.
3 Decide that you will pay attention to how you and others use this filter (or not) in this time. You might want to write down the name of the filter so that you keep it in mind, or you might want to have it displayed somewhere you can see it easily.
4 Review the examples that you collected of how this filter was used (or not) and with what effect.
5 Do this until you feel that you have the choice of this filter easily available to you.
6 Repeat the process with another filter.

4

Thinking with Your Body

"It is impossible to not communicate."

Paul Watzlawick

Given that NLP is a process of identifying the difference between outstanding performance and everything else, we need ways to elicit this difference if we want to reproduce the performance. And this difference is very often the elusive part of what we do.

Suppose that I am skilled in the way I can build rapport in business meetings with potential new clients and you want to know how exactly I do that. I could tell you that when I prepare for a meeting with a new client, I think about the outcomes for the meeting. I can also tell you that I review what I know about the company and pay attention to how I build rapport throughout the process, but especially in the first few moments of our meeting. That is all very sound, but the question is: Does what I have told you contain the piece that really makes the difference?

If you were skilled in modeling you might notice that between talking about the outcomes for the meeting and reviewing what I know about the business already, I look fleetingly up and to my right. What I am doing for this moment is imagining visually what this company would be like if it were to do the kind of developments I have imagined will make a difference for it. I do this each time I approach a new client, but I take this thought so much for granted and it is so unconscious that I don't include it in my description of what I do (until recently when I modeled the process). However, this eye movement of looking up and to the right is a very strong clue that what I am doing at that moment is creating a visual image I have never seen before. By being sensitive to the eye movements you know that I am creating something visually, even though you may not know the content of what I am doing. This clue can give you the prompt to ask me something like: "What do you think about just after you have considered the outcomes?" You could be more specific and say: "At that moment what are you picturing?" That could be the prompt for me to realize that I am creating this visual image. This is one small clue that opens the door to one of the most significant pieces of my thinking when I meet a new client.

By learning to be sensitive to body language you can begin to detect the pieces of the strategies that really make the difference. And these are the pieces that otherwise lie undetected. It is the ability to detect body language patterns in this way that is unique to NLP and makes the process of modeling so special and important in the way we learn.

THE EYES HAVE IT

Our eyes give powerful clues to the way we are thinking. Ask someone close to you now to spell Mississippi. If there is a choice, ask someone who claims to be good speller. What are their eye movements? Watch carefully, because some of the movements are fleeting. Most good spellers visualize the word they are spelling by picturing the word as if it were on a screen in front and slightly above them. They typically look up and to their left, but some may look up and to their right or straight ahead with a defocused stare. Each of these eye movements indicates visual thinking, a key part of a successful spelling strategy.

The way we use our eyes indicates the kind of thinking that is going on. For example:

Eyes up and left (your left)—Visual remembered
This is where we look when we are remembering images we have seen before, e.g., the face of our partner, the last place we went on holiday, our workplace, what we did yesterday.

Eyes up and right (your right)—Visual constructed
This is where we look when we are constructing images we have not seen before, e.g., ourselves in a location we have always dreamt of but never been to, a colleague with an expression on their face we have never seen, our home redesigned, the vision for our business.

Eyes straight ahead defocused—Visual
The clue as to whether this is remembered or constructed can be determined by how the weight is distributed in the rest of the body: to the left and it is remembered, to the right and it is constructed.

Eyes to the side and left (your left)—Auditory remembered
This is where we look when we are remembering sounds that we have heard before, e.g., a favorite piece of music, the sound of a friend's voice.

Eyes to the side and right (your right)—Auditory constructed
This is where we look when we are creating a sound that we have never heard before, e.g., someone we know speaking in a completely different tone of voice.

Eyes down and left (your left)—Auditory digital, inner dialog
This is where we look when we are having a conversation with ourselves or asking questions in our heads.

Eyes down and right (your right)—External feelings and emotions
When we experience feelings this is where we look.

The direction may vary in that left and right may be reversed, but visual is always up or straight ahead defocused, and auditory is always looking toward the ears, which can be a good way of remembering it. There is a theory that left-handed children of left-handed parents are more likely to have the sides reversed.

HOW ELSE DO WE THINK WITH OUR BODY?

It is virtually impossible to lie with body language, which is one of the reasons it is important to be aware of what thoughts are being communicated through this medium. Body language is everything in our behavior with which we communicate other than words. However, the way we say those words, e.g., the tone, the volume, the pitch of our voice, is our body language.

So in detecting whether we are thinking in a visual, auditory, or feelings way, not only can we use eye movements as clues, we can also detect clues in body language.

For example, someone thinking in a *visual* way will typically:

❑ Speak quickly in a high voice (they are trying to use words to get across the images they can see, so need to speak quickly to do this).
❑ Breathe high in the chest—rapid, shallow breathing.
❑ Gesture high in the air, often trying to depict the images they can see internally.
❑ Often show tension in their body.

Someone thinking in an *auditory* way will typically:

❑ Speak in a rhythmic way, almost tunefully.
❑ Talk mid tone.
❑ Breathe mid chest.
❑ Gesture lower than someone who is thinking in a visual way.
❑ Often have their head tilted to one side as if to accentuate the amount they take in through their ears.
❑ Frequently touch their ears and mouth and often have their hand against their face as if on the telephone.

And someone thinking in a *feelings* way will typically:

❑ Speak in a resonant way, slowly with frequent silences.
❑ Breathe low in the chest—deep, slow breaths, as if sighing.
❑ Gesture down and to their right (you have heard the expression downright angry—down and right is usually where people go when accessing feelings).
❑ Have "laid back" body posture, relaxed and free moving.

Remember that these are only clues. The key with NLP is to calibrate to what is true for each person you meet. In this way you respect everyone's unique culture.

So body language is:

Intonation	Stresses	Voice
Tone	Speed	
Accent	Hesitations	
Rhythm	Emphasis	
Pauses	Frequency of response to others	
Facial expressions	Head movements	Head and face
Eye movements	Facial lines	
Muscle movements	Eye contact	
Muscle tension	Head position	
Skin color	Mouth expressions	
Body movement	Proximity to others	Body
Posture	Timing of movements	
Arm and hand gestures	Breathing rate	
Frequency and nature of touch, both self and others	Breathing position: high, mid, or low in chest	
Body rhythm—the kind of movement or stillness that is characteristic	Position and direction of legs and feet	

All of these elements and more are communicating our innermost thoughts every moment of every day. It is not that people don't recognize these signals—they do. The staff in one company I worked in knew very well that when the managing director's lip became taut and whitened slightly, it was time to stop asking questions! We do all read one another's body language, but many of us have become used to ignoring signals we detect unconsciously. We have learned to delete or distort what we pick up intuitively. By developing our conscious awareness of what these signals might be telling us, we start to draw on an immense untapped potential in our communication.

THE IMPORTANCE OF READING BODY LANGUAGE

Learning to be aware of body language and the differences between one person and the next and one culture and the next creates a marked improvement in how well we understand and influence other people and they us. Some people seem to have a natural ability to influence, creating a climate of instant rapport in which all parties feel at ease with each other. Others may find these people eminently approachable, easy to talk to on any issue with an obvious advantage in any negotiating, communicating, or influencing situation.

Among the first to publish material dealing with these issues was Albert Mehrabian in 1972. In a series of controlled experiments, he was able to demonstrate that non-verbal signals were significantly more influential than other stimuli.

Mehrabian concentrated on the face as the source of the nonverbal information. Other researchers have since demonstrated similar results with the other elements of nonverbal behavior. The outstanding conclusion that has been reached by many of these researchers is that typically more

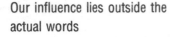

Our influence lies outside the actual words

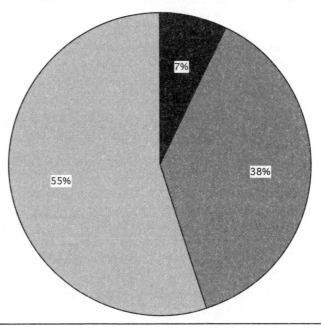

■ Content—the words only

▨ Vocal influence—intonation, tone, accent, rhythm, pauses, stresses

▦ Nonverbal influences—facial expression, eye movements, muscle movements, skin color

than 90 percent of our ability to influence lies outside of the actual words we use.

If we don't understand and respect difference, we are liable to judge what we don't know as negative. For example, in the UK there is a very much higher expectation of feedback to what we say (even if it is just a grunt) than is the norm in many other cultures. Consequently, we can find lower levels of response to what we say (especially when we are talking over the phone) very disconcerting. We might, for example, be tempted to misread it as disinterest.

We do not only limit ourselves by what we can say, but the choices we make about how we use words make communication even more risky. When we don't understand what we hear, in a meeting for example, most of us are unlikely to say so. If we don't entirely agree with what someone is saying, most of us are likely to say that they do agree or say nothing. However, whatever choices we make with the words that we do and do not use, our nonverbal behavior does signal what we truly feel.

By learning to pay attention to body language signals we can:

❏ Know when to end a conversation.
❏ Tell to what extent the person to whom we are speaking has understood what we are saying.
❏ Determine the level of agreement we have achieved.
❏ Recognize the degree to which we have touched the core motivation of the person to whom we are talking.
❏ Establish how we represent time and the impact of that on the way we use our time.
❏ Tell when we have created a connection and the beginnings of a relationship.
❏ Determine when we have established a deep level of rapport.
❏ Recognize what kind of emphasis in a presentation will work best in getting our message across.
❏ Tell if we have read and respected the culture of the person with whom we are dealing.

In the NLP process of modeling particularly, it is by watching and listening to body language that we can:

❏ Find out how someone structures their thinking to achieve what they do.

❏ Elicit the unconscious (and therefore taken for granted) ways of thinking that make the difference in the results we achieve.

❏ Do an inner benchmarking of excellence rather than relying only on external behavior.

❏ Deduce the values and beliefs behind someone's behavior.

❏ Recognize other people's different emotional states.

Nonverbal patterns

By developing our sensitivity to body language signals we can tell when someone has changed the way they are thinking. We can begin to determine what strategies they are using when they are achieving what they want and when they are not.

I was talking with someone about their goals for their work and their life. This person talked about two goals. The first was a goal they had been given in their work. As she talked about this her face was pale, her lips were taut, and she sat forward with her shoulders hunched. Then she talked about a goal that she had to travel and work in Canada. The moment she began to think about this her face flushed slightly, her shoulders dropped, the muscles of her face relaxed, and she began to move her arms in a fluid, easy way as she gestured while she spoke.

What we established (with not too much difficulty) was that when she was thinking about her work goals she was very much into problem thinking, concentrating on what she had to do and what she ought to do. She was also dissociated in her thinking as she did this. When she thought about her goals for working in Canada, she immediately imagined herself there doing the kind of work she really wanted. She was thinking about this in an associated way; she could see it as if she were looking through her own eyes and hearing it through her own ears. Most important of all, she was feeling what it was like to be there. The body signals she was evidencing for the second goal were characteristic of what was, for her, compelling motivation.

Most people have two key characteristic states: one when they are aligned and in touch with their unique skills and attitudes, and one when they are out of touch with who they are and their true capabilities. Each state has its own characteristic thinking patterns and beliefs and characteristic body language. By learning to recognize the characteristics of each and the distinctions between the two, we can learn how to choose the most effective one for the outcomes we want to achieve.

TRADITIONAL WAYS OF READING BODY LANGUAGE

You may have read books on body language saying that, for example, if someone is crossing their arms it means that they are defensive. Or maybe you have heard that if someone touches their nose with the back of their finger this means they are lying. In my experience it is foolish and disrespectful to make such judgments.

The way body language is used in NLP is very different. In NLP we respect that each person has their own unique patterns of body language. The challenge is to be sensitive to that and not make assumptions—positive or negative—about what those signals mean. We might find, for example, that crossed arms for one person mean something completely different to what they mean for someone else. One of the aims of NLP is to heighten our awareness of patterns in body language for everyone we meet so that we can learn how to flex our behavior to connect with them if we so choose and in a way that is respectful of who they are.

MIND AND BODY ARE ONE

What we think is how we are. Through our body language we show our skills, our values, our beliefs, what kind of person we are, our cultural preferences, and even our purpose in life. By a handshake you are revealing everything that anyone can ever know about you if they have the sensitivity to be attuned to this. And we show what we are feeling at any particular moment. If we are expecting disagreement in a meeting we are about to attend, we will show that in our body language.

When Peter was expecting disagreement in a meeting he typically engaged in a negative inner dialog imagining the worst

What we think is how we are

that each person might say to each other. Consequently his eyes went down and to his left. At the same time the muscles in his face tautened and he lowered his head. You wouldn't have to have too many meetings with Peter in this state to begin to know what was going to happen next!

If we are remembering a happy memory we also show it in our body language.

When Julia thought about the success she had achieved in her involvement with the board of directors she looked up and to her left initially (remembering what one of the most successful meetings looked like). She then started to smile slightly and looked down and to her right (as she associated into her feelings when the board had achieved a major agreement about the way forward in the business and had done so in a very creative way). She looked sideways and to her right as she imagined some of the conversations she expected to have in the next meeting. All the time she was rhythmically swinging her foot from side to side.

Body language reveals the truth of inner thoughts and feelings

Our body language reveals the truth of our inner thoughts and feelings and there is little we can do about the subtlest of signals that we communicate to the world at large.

SPOTTING THE FILTERS

In Chapter 3 I explained some of the different filters we use to think and communicate. We can often detect these filters through our language. And we can deduce the kind of thinking that someone is doing by the patterns in their body language. Remember that the patterns are only clues, not absolute proof. It is our awareness of patterns in body language, verbal language, and our knowledge of a person over time that enable us to get closer to what is really going on in their thinking. Nevertheless, the more we read the signals, the more we are likely to choose the way of communicating with each person we encounter that will enable us to relate to them effectively. Let's explore some of these body language patterns in more depth.

In Chapter 3 I described how we might be associated, engaged in what we are saying and thinking by experiencing situations standing our own shoes. In this state we are connected with our feelings. Or we can be dissociated, observing and listening to events as if we are a fly on the wall. In this latter state we are disconnected from our emotions.

Our body language changes dramatically according to which of these states we are in. In meetings it is easy to detect those people who are in an associated state. They usually lean forward and gesture animatedly to show their feelings. They often interrupt as their emotions rule their actions. When talking about their feelings, they hold their hands to their chest close to their heart. In contrast, someone who is dissociated is usually sitting or leaning back. By putting some distance between themselves and the situation they keep themselves objective. They do this mentally as they do it physically. When dissociated they often talk about themselves and point to themselves as if to an imaginary self in the air in front of them (which in their thinking is often how it is). Try selling to someone who stays in a dissociated state and you will probably find that it is hard if not impossible. For most people the decision to buy is associated with a feeling. The skill in this kind of influencing situation lies in knowing how to achieve that and recognizing when you have it.

BODY POSTURE AND MOVEMENT

Try selling to someone in a dissociated state!

BODY TENSION AND RELAXATION

The ease or tension we hold in our body is an expression of the way we are thinking. Think for a moment about something you must or should do today. Notice what happens in your body as you do this. Now think about something you would really like to do. Imagine yourself doing this. Notice what has happened to your body. How are your shoulders, your neck, and your back? Can you tell what expression you have on your face?

When we think in terms of problems or what we don't want in our lives we concentrate on what we want to move away from. This kind of motivation is often based on moving away from pain or discomfort. Consequently, the body language we demonstrate when thinking this way is one of tension. In this problem state we are likely to frown, hold our shoulders tense and hunched, and show tension in other parts of our body. Not surprisingly, one of the most common reasons for absence from work is back problems. What do you think that says about how a large proportion of the population feels about the work they do?

On the other hand, when we imagine what we do want we have corresponding body language. This is how people who think this way influence the achievement of their goals: They are acting as if they already have achieved them and the world responds accordingly. Their behavior is likely to "hang loose," they are relaxed, have loose facial muscles, easy moving limbs, flowing movements. If we watch and listen to the way we are using our bodies, we can get clues about what we are doing that is either helping or hindering us to achieve what we really want.

Acting as if we have already achieved our goals

Our posture, our gestures, and our facial expressions and lines communicate the habits we have developed in our lives. Take a look in the mirror: What is your face telling you?

What is your face telling you?

OUR RELATIONSHIPS WITH OTHERS

Some of us like to be liked and to please other people and some of us would rather have confrontation and argument. Sometimes we prefer one approach in one context and another in a different context. Whichever approach we like better shows in the way we behave. Someone who searches for similarity (matching) will seek to be like the person or people they are with in every way they can. They will move like them, dress like them, look like them.

You may have noticed how couples who are close to each other seem to grow to look alike. This is not surprising when you think that people who are fond of each other or in love will match each other's behavior and expressions. Over time the lines that form on their faces will be similar. Even if their basic face structure is different, the habits they form together will show in the way their bodies develop over time. Take a look at your partner: Do you like what you see? You may be looking at a mirror image of yourself!

So someone who creates a climate of rapport naturally— someone who is very approachable and is easy company—is usually someone who matches others around them. This doesn't mean that they agree with everything other people say. However, they will be searching for the opportunity to support other people in some way, building them up rather than knocking them down. Their behavior, including their movements, their posture, their facial expressions, their gestures, even the rate at which they blink and breathe, will be similar if not the same as the person to whom they are relating at that moment. In fact, this is the most appropriate and acceptable behavior for someone if they disagree with the content of what is being said. They can communicate at a nonverbal level that although they do not agree, they do support the person. You may have noticed how some people with critical feedback to give will simultaneously touch the other person on the arm or on the shoulder. In effect, what this is saying is that I am still connected to you even though I am giving critical feedback.

Notice what happens when someone whose preferred style is to match in this way is faced with someone who mismatches. As the other person changes to be different the matcher will look confused, and will often be shocked into silence. Mismatching behavior is alien to them. Alternatively, they will skillfully follow the other person, not allowing them to be out of synchronization.

Similarly, someone who searches for difference, preferring to mismatch, will show that in the way they behave. They will use body language that is contrary to the person they are with. If their partner in conversation is leaning forward in an associated manner, the mismatcher will lean back, dissociated. It is a pattern for them to be different and they will show it in the way they dress, behave, and speak.

You can easily notice someone who prefers to mismatch—they stand out from a group as the one whose behavior is different to the rest. Mismatching externally with others often stems from conflict going on inside the person and they may indicate this conflict by talking about or experiencing parts of themselves at odds with each other. They show this by spatially indicating the parts as being in separate hands, hence the expression "on the one hand… on the other hand…" Trying to match someone whose preference is to mismatch can feel somewhat like nailing jelly to the ceiling! This kind of behavior is characteristic of someone who may have difficulty in relationships, who may not be easy to converse with, and who seems to put obstacles in the path of any connectedness to anyone else.

Nailing jelly to the ceiling

Consider your office or your home for a moment. Do you know where everything is? Do key items have their place in your environment? If you have an office and use a computer you

SPATIAL FILING CABINETS

very likely file different sorts of information in their allocated places. Even if you are not orderly about this, it is likely that there is some method in your world. My son tells me that he knows exactly where everything is in his bedroom!

We do the same with the space around us. You will have a place in that space where you represent the past, the present, and the future. Think about it now. Where are your past memories: behind you, to one side, above you? Ask someone close to you—you might be surprised to find that they have their time zones allocated to very different parts of their personal space.

It is as if we have a spatial filing cabinet that goes with us wherever we go. We typically have a place for parts of ourselves that we like and identify with and quite another space for the parts of ourselves that we would prefer to dissociate from.

Often when I am coaching I note where these parts are stored. I can gradually make the person I am coaching aware of this storage system so they can make more choices in how they use it. It is often the case that we keep the parts of ourselves that we like close to our chest and the parts that we don't like at arm's reach in front or to one side of us. Watch people's hands and where they gesture as they speak to you and you will learn where they store their memories, parts of themselves, visions for the future, and much more.

We give clues about how we make decisions by where we gesture. Think for a moment about how you make decisions. How, for example, did you decide to read this book? Did you have a choice of books or was its purchase part of a planned approach and this was one step in a sequence? Whichever it was indicates your preference for choices or procedures. And if I had asked you to explain that choice to me, I wonder how you would have indicated your preference in your body language. Someone who prefers choice tends to wave their hands in an arc in front of them indicating the array of choice that lies before them. Someone whose preference is procedural is much more likely to make a chopping action, moving their hand away from them indicating the steps stretching before them in sequence. British Prime Minister Tony Blair frequently makes this chopping action during his talks, indicating his sequential procedural thinking.

Have you ever noticed a person who, when making a suggestion in a meeting, glances in the direction of someone from whom they are seeking approval? It may not be the person to whom they are making the suggestion, but it is the person whose feedback and acknowledgment they rely on for feedback on how they are doing. This is characteristic of someone who is externally referenced, in that they *need* feedback from an external source to know how they are doing.

Someone who is internally referenced has an internal yardstick that they use to know how they are doing. Someone with this preference is much more likely to look straight at the person to whom they are making a suggestion, or even not to look at anyone but perhaps to be looking at the next item on the agenda. Someone who is externally referenced is much more likely to seek feedback than someone who is internally referenced.

LOOKING FOR
APPROVAL

USING BODY LANGUAGE TO INFLUENCE OUR STATE

It works the other way round: How we behave influences how we think and feel. If we hunch our shoulders and tense our necks, we are likely to think about the problems in our lives. If at the same time we look down and (usually) right, we will also feel the emotions attached to those problems. Saying "keep your chin up" to someone who is feeling down is very sound advice. By lifting our heads up we disconnect from our feelings, which are experienced in a head down position for most people. And when we say "distance yourself from it" we are inviting our listener to imagine themselves outside of themselves in their thinking and to dissociate from their feelings. By changing one or two factors in the way we are thinking about a situation, we can significantly change how we feel about it.

"Keep your chin up!"

1 Work with a partner to do this.
2 Ask your partner to think of a time when they didn't feel at ease with themselves, when they felt out of balance, possibly stressed in some way. Ask them (but only briefly) to step back into this time so that they are seeing, hearing, and feeling it again.

SHORTCUT TO USING
BODY LANGUAGE TO
ACHIEVE AN ALIGNED
STATE

3   Note their body language. See how many characteristic
    elements of this state you can detect.
4   Ask your partner to break state (think about something
    completely different).
5   Ask your partner to think of a time when they felt
    completely at one with themselves. Ask them to associate
    into this time by seeing it, hearing and feeling it from their
    own shoes.
6   Note their body language. How many characteristic
    elements of this state do you detect?
7   Feedback to your partner what you noticed to be the
    differences between the body language of each state.
8   Ask them to do the same for you.

SUMMARY

Our bodies can know much more than our minds alone. If we
limit our learning to what we can know intellectually, we
significantly compromise what we can learn. We live in an age
when learning is key. We not only need to learn how to learn,
we need to use every resource to do so. Whole body learning
comes from using our bodies to tell us what our minds don't
consciously know. And the quickest and most effective way to
learn how to respond to the different cultures we come into
contact with each day is to listen and look at the body
language.

Making people aware of their body language can often have
the effect of lifting them out of the issue so that they take a
more dissociated view of what is happening. This can be
valuable if they are so emotionally caught up in an issue that
they cannot break out of it. Awareness of body language
creates a meta state from which we can watch and listen to the
patterns of what is happening and how it is happening.

THOUGHT PROVOKERS

1 Watch someone talking in regular conversation on a TV program. Notice where they put their hands. Notice also where they look when they speak. You don't need to know what their gestures mean, just be aware of them.

2 Ask someone you know to compare the holiday they had last year with the one they plan to have this year or next year. Notice where they look or indicate with their hands when they are talking about the past compared to when they are talking about the future.

3 Listen carefully to someone on the phone. Determine when they are associated and when they are dissociated, by the emotion (or absence of it) in their voice.

4 Pay attention to one person in the next meeting you attend. (Choose a meeting where you do not have a key role so that you can give time to observing someone else.) Determine how much of the time they are in the present with the other people in the meeting and how much time they spend elsewhere. Do this by noticing their eye movements.

5 When you are next with someone from a different culture (and that might still be from the same country as yourself), adopt as much of their nonverbal behaviour as you can. What do you learn about their underlying values (what has to be true for them to behave in this way) when you do this?

According to my mother's elder sister, our favourite aunt (who could count up to ten in Bushman and utter his formal greeting for our delight although invariably she went dangerously purple in the process), it was fatal to remark on the Bushman's smallness in his presence. More, it was often perilous to show in one's bearing that one was aware of dealing with a person smaller than oneself.

Our old 'Suto hands strongly supported my aunt with their own colourful illustrations. They said they had always been warned never to show any surprise if they unexpectedly came upon a Bushman in the veld in case he took it to imply they could have seen him sooner had he not been so small. When, unexpectedly, one ran into a Bushman the only wise thing to do was promptly to blame oneself for the surprise and say, "Please do not look so offended. Do you really imagine a big person like you could hide without being seen? Why, we saw you from a long way off and came straight here!" Immediately the fire in those shining eyes would die down, the golden chest expand enormously and gracefully he would make one welcome. In fact the oldest of the old Basutos once told me one could not do better than use the Bushman's own greeting, raising one's open right hand high above the head, and calling out in a loud voice: "Tshjamm! Good day! I saw you looming up afar and I am dying of hunger."

Laurens Van Der Post, The Lost World of the Kalahari

Linguistic

"Language and word choice form a manager's primary tool. Used wisely, sound guidance can grow from the seeds of aligned words. Used poorly and all you get are weeds."
    Michael Lissack and Johan Roos, The Next Common Sense

I n the beginning was the word. Your words are your life. Your language is an embroidery of patterns of words that tell your story. Your language is either your gateway to learning and choice, or your jailer.

In business especially language is a powerful tool. It is the currency of business transactions. By learning to develop mastery of your language you can:

The power of language

❏ Improve the quality of the information you exchange with others in whatever medium you choose.
❏ Increase the level of understanding you create with your communication.
❏ Influence the outcomes of situations.
❏ Empower yourself and others by challenging the constraints that show themselves in language.
❏ Bypass conscious resistance by engaging the unconscious mind.
❏ Communicate in a way that is captivating and compelling.
❏ Enrich your language and consequently your life.
❏ Learn what messages you are communicating to others' unconscious minds and discover if they are those you want to be communicating.

❏ Learn how to recognize the signals that you and others are sending through your body language.

The opportunity to practice your skill with language is available to you not only when you interact with others, but especially when you interact with yourself.

5

Enriched Communication

"Words as I speak or write them, make a path on which I walk."
Diane Glancy

Personal success relies largely on our ability to communicate. What we say matters little compared to how we say it, no matter what medium we use to convey the words. To communicate with influence it is important that we are able to use language that engages the hearts and minds of our listeners. We can choose language that leaves people cold and disinterested or we can choose language that engages their hearts and their minds and that they find compelling.

The quality of language is one of the significant factors that makes the difference between outstanding leaders and influencers and those who would aspire to achieve their standing but who do not ignite the hearts and minds of their listeners in the same way. The richer our language, the richer our internal experience and the richer the experience of those with whom we engage.

One of the early discoveries in NLP was that skilled communicators use language in a way that creates a climate of trust and understanding. The difference that makes the difference lies in the speaker's instinctive ability to adapt their language to match the language of the person to whom they are speaking. This way of building rapport through language is explained in Chapter 16.

A study of powerful communicators also revealed that they naturally use language that is rich in its use of all the senses. For example:

"A lover's eyes will gaze an eagle blind;
A lover's ears will hear the lowest sound,
When the suspicious head of theft is stopp'd:
Love's feeling is more soft and sensible
Than are the tender Horns of cockled snails:
Love's tongue proves dainty Bacchus gross in taste."

William Shakespeare, Love's Labours Lost

It is reassuring to know that you don't have to be Shakespeare to write and speak with compelling, enriched language. I first came across NLP when I attended a course on creative writing more than 12 years ago. I wanted to be able to write with interest and style. The course I attended was run by two people, one an author, the other a consultant who had "coded" the writing skills of this author in order that we might reproduce some of his writing style for ourselves. I became curious about this process of coding talent, which is how I came to be interested in NLP.

Since then I have modeled many writers. I had the privilege of listening to Brian Keenan, author of *An Evil Cradling*, talking about the process he went through to write this book about his harrowing experiences as a hostage in Beirut for four and half years. His discussion of the writing was as compelling as the writing itself. Both his spoken and his written communication are rich in the use of all senses. When he spoke to our course you could have heard a pin drop, such was the quality of his communication.

Business language

You can code the writing or speaking style of any great communicator. It sometimes seems that the qualities of compelling communication have been stripped away to leave the cold, neutral language that fills so many hours of business presentations and pages of reports. By studying the difference between the people to whom you are more likely to give your attention and those whose reports you shove to the bottom of the pile, you will uncover the secret of enriched communication.

SENSORY-SPECIFIC LANGUAGE

Studying the Shakespearean passage you will find that it contains language appealing to the eyes, the ears, and the feelings: "gaze an eagle blind," "hear the lowest sound," "soft," "tender,'"gross in taste." Needless to say this is very skillful writing. Typically the majority of people have visual as a first preference and this is the choice with which Shakespeare starts. Feelings language is what encourages the reader to associate and connect with what is being said and this is at the heart of this passage. And finally he leads to us a less usual form of language—leaving a sweet taste in our mouths?

Of course, you may not want to communicate exactly like Shakespeare in one of your project review meetings, but you probably do want to capture and hold your audience's attention. And you want to speak or write in a way that increases the likelihood of your listener or your reader understanding what you say.

To do this it is important to be able to have the choice of using all the senses in the way you speak or write. You will discover that your listeners and your readers have preferences, as in the following example.

All senses

Pete and Joe rarely agreed. They each complained that they found the other frustrating. As senior managers in a rapidly growing organization, it was vital that they understood each other's point of view. Whenever they got together to make decisions Pete wanted to get a grasp of the situation and make decisions based on his gut feeling. He'd had a lot of success working this way. Joe, on the other hand, liked to talk his ideas through in full. Typically he would have a list of points that he wanted to discuss. Pete quickly got frustrated with this and usually cut the meeting short. Their inability to reach a satisfactory conclusion had resulted in Pete moving Joe to a new position where they had less direct contact.

It seemed as though Pete and Joe were speaking a different language; in a way they were. Pete thought and talked mainly in terms of feelings. He made decisions based on "gut feel." Joe had a very auditory way of communicating, he would "talk his ideas through" and have "points to discuss." They were using different senses to communicate, or rather try to communicate.

If your means of communicating is the same as the person to whom you are speaking, then you are literally talking the same language. If like Pete and Joe you use different systems to communicate, then you will have difficulty understanding and accepting what the other has to say.

Your speech is an expression of the way you think. For example, if you think visually you are more likely to say:

❏ I get the picture.
❏ It's clear now.
❏ I see what you mean.

If, however, you think in an auditory way you are more likely to say:

❏ That sounds good.
❏ It rings bells for me.
❏ I hear what you are saying.

If your experience is more feelings based then you are likely to say:

❏ That feels right.
❏ It made an impact on me.
❏ I was moved by what you said.

The language of taste and smell also comes into this category of feelings:

❏ It left a bad taste in my mouth.
❏ I smelt something fishy about that suggestion.

Some of the key words for each of the three systems are:

Visual	Auditory	Feelings
see	sound	impact
focus	hear	taste
clear	tell	feel
bright	say	touch
picture	click	smell
hazy	bang	tense
color	talk	rough

view	volume	bitter
dim	loud	relaxed
look	snap	whiff

Some of the key expressions for each of the three systems are:

Visual

Things are a bit hazy
I take a dim view of that
The future looks bright
The outlook is bleak
Seeing things through rose-tinted glasses
He is in a black mood today
We're in the pink
I look forward to seeing you
Things are looking up
We've a clear way forward
A colorful expression

Auditory

I tell myself to take care
I'm glad to hear it
Tell me how it is
My teeth are chattering
Things clicked into place
Let me explain
We're in harmony
Listen to yourself
We're in tune with each other
It was music to my ears
I'm pleased you said that

Feelings

Racked with pain
The sweet smell of success
Get in touch with reality
A taste of fear
I've got a grasp of what you mean
Warm regards
I've got a handle on it
I was moved
It was a blow to my pride
Let's firm up on this
I savored the moment
Hold on

Excellent communicators naturally use the system preferred by the person to whom they are speaking, at least initially. This ensures that they are talking the same language and are more easily understood than if they were to use a representational system that was disliked by their listener.

CAPTIVATING LANGUAGE

Ships that pass in the night, and speak each other in passing;
Only a signal shown and a distant voice in the darkness;
So on the ocean of life we pass and speak one another,
Only a look and a voice, then darkness again and a silence.
"The Theologian's Tale: Elizabeth," Henry Wadsworth Longfellow

You'd scarce expect one of my age
To speak in public on the stage;
And if I chance to fall below
Demosthenes or Cicero,
Don't view me with a critic's eye
But pass my imperfections by.
Large streams from little fountains flow.
Tall oaks from little acorns grow.
*   "Lines Written for a School Declamation," David Everett*

These, I believe, are examples of compelling, inspiring language. By developing your ability to use all sensory systems in your language, you will be developing your ability to communicate in a way that is interesting and compelling. Contrast the following:

As you walk down the corridor to the main office you will see a pink notice on the wall to the side of the EXIT door. Read this—it will remind you of the emergency procedures we have demonstrated this morning.

This has a very different effect to saying:

Be sure to take account of the emergency procedures on the way out.

The first example is more likely to engage the listeners' attention. It uses sensory-specific language, and it encourages association into the experience of reading the procedures. It is therefore likely to be more memorable than the dissociated, neutral language.

Or compare the following two passages:

Things have been difficult for some time now. As a result of this our objective for the next period is to introduce a quality program. It will be crucial to the future success of the company. By giving attention to quality we will be understanding and meeting the requirements of our customers, both internal and external. I cannot stress the importance of this enough.

Neutral

For the last year our sales and it seems our spirit in this team have fallen. Because of what I feel to be the problem and because you tell me that our focus of attention now needs to be different, I have written out my thoughts on our outcomes for the year to come. I would like to explain these to you; I'd like you to listen and ask yourself, "How can I make this work for me?" I want to hear the answers to this question. My vision of the future is one where each of the people staff and clients alike—with whom we come into contact will see a new image emerging, one that communicates attention and care and concern that we really meet their needs. I believe we can do this by ensuring that we see each and every one of them to ask them all, "What do you really need from us in order for you to feel that you are being served well?" and "What would have to be true for you to want to continue to keep us as your main supplier for the next three years?" We will know when we have achieved our goal when our customers invite us to meet with them to discuss their needs and when they say, "You understand us and demonstrate that you will act to ensure our needs are met."

Enriched

Each style of communication has its place. Unfortunately, neutral, abstract language is often used in business through habit rather than choice. If you want to increase understanding, motivate, and inspire, then enriched communication is the way to do it.

SHORTCUT TO USING ENRICHED LANGUAGE

1   Choose something that you want to communicate to someone. It could be via an email, a letter, a report, or a presentation.
2   Think of the person to whom you are going to communicate. What would you say is their preferred sense for communicating (they may of course be fairly balanced, but most people have a preference)? If you are not sure, take a look at any communication that you have had from them. If you are communicating to a group of people, you can use all senses and it is appropriate to do so.
3   Imagine yourself associated into the situation that you want to communicate so that you can see, hear, and feel it. (This could be a past, present, or future situation.)
4   Choosing the preferred sense of your reader or your listener, write down what you are seeing/hearing/feeling (depending on what you think is their preferred sense). Now do the same with each of the other senses. Aim to convey with language what it is that you see, hear, and feel. If you are not sure of some of the vocabulary, check back to the lists on page 85.
5   After you have communicated what it is that you wanted to say, check out to what extent you achieved your outcome.
6   What have you learned about how to use enriched communication in the process of doing this?

SUMMARY

Enriched communication is the essence of motivation and commitment. Appeal to the eyes, ears, and feelings of your listeners and you will have their understanding and their attention. Inspirational leaders throughout history have instinctively had the ability to capture the hearts and minds of their audience. By understanding the components of enriched language, you too can inspire and delight your listeners. Bring your business meetings and presentations alive with your skilled use of language.

THOUGHT PROVOKERS

1 For someone you haven't met before, how could you prepare to present your ideas so that you take account of each of the visual/auditory/feelings systems?

2 Rewrite these sentences using enriched language:
   a It is important to me that I progress within this organization.
   b I want to know what we aim to achieve with this meeting.

3 Select someone you work with. Listen to the language they use. Identify any preferences for visual/auditory/feelings systems.

4 How can you ensure that you address each of the senses when giving a presentation?
   a Visual.
   b. Auditory.
   c. Feelings.

5 Pick one of your favorite books. Read through the first page and note examples of each of the sensory systems that you detect being used.

6 Watch the adverts on television. For each one, note which senses it appeals to predominantly.

7 Log on to the internet and select a website. Which senses does the home page appeal to? How attracted are you to continue to explore this site?

REFERENCE

Brian Keenan (1993) *An Evil Cradling*, Vintage.

Gregory Bateson was one of the influences on John Grinder and Richard Bandler, the founders of NLP. Much of his thinking about change and learning has been incorporated and developed in the concepts of NLP. Some of his discoveries about learning came from the time he spent studying porpoises, which involved watching porpoises in performances for the general public.

In particular, audiences were shown how a porpoise learned to do a trick. As the porpoise circled in the pool the trainer would wait and watch for the porpoise to do something different: flipping its tail or spinning around. As soon as it did this different behavior—it didn't really matter what it was as long as it was different—the trainer would blow a whistle and give the porpoise a fish. As soon as the porpoise repeated the behavior, the trainer would once again blow a whistle and give the porpoise another fish. In this way the porpoise learned what it had to do to get its reward and would demonstrate the new behavior in order to obtain the fish.

There were usually several shows each day so at the next show naturally the porpoise would swim out into the pool and begin to demonstrate the new behavior that had previously earned the fish. Of course, this time the trainer wanted to demonstrate to the audience how the porpoise learned new tricks and consequently didn't give it the fish. The porpoise would become increasingly frustrated and toward the end of the show would do something else: jump out of the water, for example. As soon as it demonstrated this new behavior the trainer would blow the whistle and give it a fish. The porpoise quickly realized that this was what it needed to do and would continue to jump out of the water, and each time it did so the trainer blew the whistle and gave it a fish.

At each subsequent show the same pattern was repeated, the porpoise getting increasingly frustrated each time until in desperation it performed a new behavior by chance, at which point the trainer immediately blew the whistle and gave it a fish. The frustration in the porpoise increased to such a point that occasionally the trainer would break the procedure and give the porpoise a fish without its demonstrating a new behavior.

Eventually after many shows the porpoise seemed to change dramatically and became very excited as it was waiting to be let into the show pool. When it was released into the pool the porpoise put on an amazing performance that included eight completely new behaviors, some of which had never been witnessed before.

When asked about the unearned fish the trainer replied, "Those fish were to maintain my relationship with the porpoise. Only by maintaining our relationship can we communicate in this way and achieve the kind of results you have just seen."

6

Precision Questions

"Language is the only homeland."

Czeslaw Milosz

L eadership is no longer a choice in organizations—it is a
necessity. To choose to follow others is to put your
business at risk. Only those businesses that cut a new
groove and present a unique product in a unique way, but a
way that is true to who they are, stand any chance of capturing
a share of the market.

Our ability to lead depends on our willingness to tolerate
ambiguity, take risks, and assume responsibility for our own
destiny. And it requires the capacity to inspire others to do
the same. When we think of leadership we often think of the
process of leading others, yet true leadership starts with the
ability to lead oneself. NLP, specifically the questioning skills
developed by John Grinder and Richard Bandler, provides a
way to lead both yourself and others.

Leadership is a necessity

*One day on holiday in Dorset we were joined by another little
boy. He and my son Alex decided to build a sandcastle. When
they were doing this I overheard them talking about school.
Alex asked him what he liked doing best at school. "I don't
know," he replied. "I'm not very clever." He was six years old
and his words reflected a choice he had made or had learned
already that would affect his potential for the future.*

Linguist Noam Chomsky distinguished two levels of language:

Two levels of language

❏ *Surface structure*—everything we say, either to ourselves or to other people.
❏ *Deep structure*—the underlying meaning of what we say, containing information neither expressed nor known consciously.

A number of things can happen between the deep structure and the surface structure of the language. The intention of the communication may be lost or changed in the process of converting one to the other. The more aligned we are between what we say and what we truly mean, the more coherent our message and the more likely we are to fulfill the role of leader, no matter what the context.

The only person who can look after you is you

The only person ultimately who can look after you is you. The responsible organizations are the ones who encourage their people to take this kind of ownership for themselves.

In the Cork, Ireland, branch of Pfizer every employee has total responsibility for their personal development, their personal learning, and their personal career. There are no managers— everyone is part of one team and everyone shares in the responsibility for business strategy.

Our language is rich in clues about our willingness and skill to take on this kind of responsibility. We need to learn habits to support this way of working. And more significantly, we need to learn to recognize the habits we have that hinder this way of working. Language is a good place to start to begin to make that kind of a difference.

LAZY LANGUAGE

Look at the expressions below. Read them quickly. What do they say?

Now read the following passage. How many *f*s are there?

FEATURE FILMS ARE THE RESULT OF YEARS OF SCIENTIFIC STUDY COMBINED WITH THE EXPERIENCE OF YEARS

The expressions actually read "Once in *a a* lifetime," "Paris in *the the* spring," "A bird in *the the* hand." We often distort what we read and hear and see to fit in with our expectations. In the passage there are six fs. How many did you count?

These simple exercises illustrate the sort of processes that occur in our thinking every day. We delete, distort, and generalize information so that it becomes disconnected from its deeper meaning. We typically use an imprecise form of language in speech, lazy language. This is at the heart of many business problems often paraphrased as communication issues.

Do you have a "they" in your company? I have worked with many different companies and have discovered that there is one cause of all the problems: "they."

DELETIONS, GENERALIZATIONS AND DISTORTIONS

Do you have a "they" in your company?

- ❏ *They don't communicate effectively.*
- ❏ *They introduce changes without consultation.*
- ❏ *They don't listen.*
- ❏ *They expect you to know what's going on.*
- ❏ *They keep you in the dark.*

They are very elusive. They are never in the same room as the people who are talking about them. They are very often one or two levels higher in the management structure, even when the people referring to them in one case were the board of directors themselves! Alternatively, they are an unknown quantity outside of the organization, a group of people who represent existing and future clients, suppliers, members of a holding company, and so on.

The "they" syndrome illustrates our tendency to put the source of problems (and therefore the possibility of change) outside of ourselves. They are elusive and impossible to pin down, which leads to our giving over responsibility and the possibility of influence to circumstances and people outside of ourselves.

Questions that challenge and influence constraints

John Grinder and Richard Bandler made a study of these language patterns. They developed and refined a set of questions designed to challenge and influence the constraints that people put on themselves. These reconnect the speaker with their experience and are influential in triggering change. By learning to challenge our lazy language we create greater coherence in who we are and we increase the constructive influence that we have on ourselves and subsequently on others.

A word of warning: The questions can be experienced as intimidating and aggressive if they are used without regard for the person you are questioning. Before using these questions on anyone other than yourself, I encourage you to read the section on building and maintaining rapport, Chapter 16, so that you maintain the trust and respect of the person you are questioning. We don't always have permission to use these techniques on other people, so the place to practice and make a difference is on ourselves.

It is by developing ourselves that we influence others

I really want to emphasize this point. Far from building rapport, NLP techniques used enthusiastically but without permission will do more harm than good. It is by developing ourselves that we influence others. A goal to aim for is to be such an attractive example to others that they want some of what you have got. Then and only then do you begin to have permission.

DELETIONS

Deletions are examples of language where parts of the meaning have been omitted. A client just commented to me as he finished a phone call, "He is saying that there is a big reorganization at work." The client did not say who "he" was.

VAGUE SUBJECTS

This is where "they" come into their own. It is a way of avoiding responsibility and ownership. This kind of language pattern implies that the speaker has no influence over what is happening around them. Other examples of vague subjects are:

People don't let you make decisions.	*Which people exactly?*
Customers make life very difficult.	*Which customers are you referring to?*
He said.	*Who said?*

This kind of question reconnects the speaker with their thinking about the source of their problems. It also gives you specific information, rather than leaving you to guess or mind-read who is implied by the statement.

VAGUE ACTIONS

If someone says "She ignored me," you could guess what is meant and you would probably be wrong. The question to ask is, "How exactly did she ignore you?" Your aim in asking this question is to find out exactly what behavior the speaker experienced to lead them to conclude that "she ignored them." The speaker is evaluating the behavior in a way that may not be true. In this case, "Ignored" is a vague action.

The question "How did she ignore you?" or "How specifically did he/she/they do that?" challenges the way you and others interpret and evaluate actions. Appraisal action plans seem to spawn vague actions.

❏ Fred needs to improve his time management skills.
❏ Jane will build on her experience as a sales executive.
❏ We are going to develop Harry's ability to delegate.

Such statements are often "copouts," a way of avoiding thinking about how exactly the manager and the jobholder will bring these changes about. Not surprisingly, many of the suggested changes don't happen. When challenged, the next most popular copout statement is "We are going to send him/her on a course!"

Vague verbs are often "copouts"

COMPARISONS

Comparative words include more, less, better, worse, fewer, well, badly—anything that suggests an evaluation against some yardstick. The difficulty in understanding what is meant by these occurs when the yardstick is omitted:

COMPARISONS

That was a brilliant report.	*Compared with what?*
My presentation was a disaster.	*Compared with what?*
The company is doing well.	*Compared with what?*
We are going to build a better world.	*Better than what exactly?*
We want to be the best company.	*Compared to whom?*

Performance objectives and measures of job success often seem to contain this kind of comparison:

Fewer customer complaints.	*Fewer than what?*
More sales leads.	*More than what or than whom?*
Better management communication.	*Better than what, precisely?*

ABSTRACTIONS

Abstractions take the action out of life. As a language pattern, an abstraction immobilizes the owner of the words. Abstractions are a way of taking a verb, an action word, and turning it into a noun, an abstract thing. This is called "nominalization." In doing so you take away the action. You are probably very familiar with examples of this such as communication, discussion, relationships, action, empowerment—and even abstraction itself.

To test for an abstraction, if you can put "ongoing" in front of the word—ongoing communication, ongoing relationship—it is probably an abstraction.

The way to challenge an abstraction is to question to find out who is doing what and how. For example, if someone says "It was a difficult conversation," your question could be, "Who was talking to whom and how was it difficult?" If someone says, "We have problems with our communication," "How do you want to be able to communicate differently?" would be a way of introducing the possibility of the speaker's beginning to move forward to a way of developing new skills.

OPINIONS AS FACTS

An "opinion as fact" statement occurs when the speaker expresses an opinion as if it were a truth by deleting the fact that it is an opinion:

❏ This is the right way to do the job.
❏ It's bad to be inconsistent.

"According to whom?" is the key question.

This sort of statement can be received as aggressive. An alternative way to express the same thing would be to say:

Opinions expressed as facts can be aggressive

❏ I believe this is the right way to do the job.
❏ Joe thinks it's bad to be inconsistent.

Opinions as facts are value judgments, characteristic of people who believe that their map of the world is the right one. The owners of such statements have closed the door to the possibility that there are other opinions, other ways to do things. Asking the question "According to whom?" reconnects them with their personal ownership of these views. They may discover that the owner is someone from their past, their parents or teachers. "It's wrong to leave food on your plate." "I want doesn't get." "Children should be seen and not heard." According to whom? Certainly not the children in the last example! This kind of statement is the expression of beliefs that can imprint themselves on the receiver for life. And what I have said in this paragraph is of course in my opinion!

GENERALIZATIONS

Generalizations exist when you take specific experiences and generalize them to make them true outside their particular context. In so doing you distort your experience.

Sometimes it is important to do this. You need generalizations as referents in language, otherwise you would have to go into a tremendous amount of detail when you speak. However, generalizations can still be misleading.

❏ I always catch a cold in the winter.
❏ No one ever tells you what is going on around here.

UNIVERSAL STATEMENTS

Universal statements consist of words such as no one, everyone, never, always, all, nothing. The speaker has generalized specific experiences to make them true in all circumstances. One way of responding would be to use the generalization back to them as a question:

❑ Always?
❑ No one?

Alternative ways of responding would be to challenge the detail behind the statement:

"She never listens to me."
"How do you know that?" or "Has there ever been a time when she did listen to you?"

These challenges reconnect the speaker with the reality of their experience.

STOPPERS AND LIMITERS

I was recently in discussion with a friend of mine who works as a personal assistant. In this role she provides administrative support for a team of senior managers. She had shown a high level of skill in her ability to coach and facilitate others. I was discussing the possibility of how she might use these skills to help the management team introduce the changes they had talked about.

"Oh, I can't do that," she immediately replied. At some level she had chosen to limit her potential in this context.

Can you imagine the managing director of a company or the head of a country saying "I can't" when asked to consider the future? They wouldn't last in that position for long.

Faced with "I can't," what can you say? "What stops you?" is one choice. This invites the speaker to identify and face up to the reality of the obstacles, imagined or otherwise.

"What would happen if you did?"

Another possibility is to ask, "What would happen if you did?" This is a very powerful question. In its own right it can empower people to go beyond the barriers they build for themselves. However, when you ask the question, pay attention to whether the speaker really answers it in their thinking and in their speech. You may find that they answer spontaneously with comments such as "Well, I just can't," indicating that they haven't really considered the question. However, if you ask the question in a way that encourages them to consider the possibility—"I know you can't but what would happen if you did use your skills to help the management team?"—then the other person has to imagine what that would be like in order to answer the question.

Eye movements, explained in Chapter 3, give you clues about whether someone is processing the question or not. If they answer with an unblinking, immediate "I can't," it is unlikely that they have processed the question. However, if they look away or even defocus, looking straight ahead, some processing is taking place. Once they have done that they have gone beyond the barrier.

What we know is that once a possibility is imagined it opens the door to its becoming reality. When you use this kind of question you are influencing the possibility of the idea becoming the outcome. Questions are powerful influencers because they invite the listener's mind to participate in finding an answer. Questions are inescapable.

Questions are inescapable

DRIVERS

Drivers are statements of need: "I have to finish this article," "I must tidy my desk," "I should go and visit my friend." None of these statements implies that the speaker really wants to do any of these things.

For most people "musts," "shoulds," "oughts," and "have tos" are accompanied by a feeling of tension. "I must tidy my desk." "I should go and visit my friend." These words are characteristic of "driven" behaviors, often driven by someone else even if that is someone from your past, a parent or a teacher perhaps. Maybe they were the ones who believed that you must keep your desk tidy.

Musts, shoulds, and oughts are accompanied by a feeling of tension

Outcomes containing words such as "must," "should," or "ought" lose their power because the words suggest outcomes that belong to someone else. Your true outcomes contain words such as "really want to" and "can." The words you use are an expression of your experience. They trigger very different types of feeling, which will in turn influence your potential and your ability to succeed in achieving what you really want.

Distortions are examples of language where the owner of the words has distorted their experience. It may be that they have made faulty connections between different parts of their experience.

BLAMERS

❏ You make me angry.
❏ This company demotivates me.

The owner of this sort of statement has given the responsibility for their state and feelings to others. They have become dependent on their environment and surrendered their choice to feel the way they want to feel. It is not that these statements aren't true; they are. But the speaker has allowed others to affect them.

The challenge:

❏ How is it possible for me to make you angry?
❏ How does the company demotivate you?

The question encourages the other person to consider exactly how that happens. Once they begin to understand the structure of this experience, they begin to have a choice. They may still choose to feel angry, but they will own that anger once they begin to say "I feel angry" rather than "You make me angry." Instead of giving power to others for their feelings they restore it to themselves.

PRESUMPTIONS

❏ I know why you did that.
❏ She only said that because she was annoyed with me.
❏ You're upset, I can tell.

These are examples of the speaker's presuming to know what others are thinking or feeling. They are interpretations, a form of mind reading. For example, it would be more accurate to say "You interrupted that customer before they had finished speaking and you kept your arms folded throughout the conversation" than "You were obviously annoyed with that customer." The former is specific whereas the latter implies a value judgment.

"How do you know that?" enables the speaker to reconnect their interpretation of others' behavior back to the behavior itself. It challenges the assumptions that the speaker is making. It encourages them to be specific in their observations and in their feedback.

Interpretation is when two statements are linked in such a way that they are taken to mean the same thing. The statement takes the form "This means that."

INTERPRETATION

I remember when I went for a job interview in London many years ago. When I left that interview, if someone had asked me what I thought about the interviewer I'd have said something like "He ignored me." What he actually did was swing his chair around and look out of the window each time he asked me a question. My belief at the time was: "He didn't look at me, he isn't interested in me for this job." What I didn't know then but discovered subsequently, when I joined the department, was that this was how he concentrated on conversation. In his perception he wasn't ignoring me at all.

Other examples of this are:

❏ You are speaking with a sharp tone of voice, you are obviously annoyed with me.
❏ My manager banged the door open. I knew I'd done something wrong.
❏ You are not smiling. You are obviously not enjoying yourself.

Challenge this pattern by asking "How does this mean that?"

❏ How does that tone of voice mean that I am annoyed with you?
❏ How does the fact that your manager banged open the door mean that you had done something wrong?
❏ How does the fact that I am not smiling mean that I am not enjoying myself?

MANAGE YOUR INTERNAL DIALOG

Use questions to challenge internal dialog

The language you use may be what you say openly to others. Equally, it can be what you say to yourself internally. You can use the precision questions described above to challenge internal dialog and in so doing change your feelings and your experience.

We are influenced by what we hear, not only what others say to us but especially what we say to ourselves in our own inner dialog. The questions we ask ourselves are especially significant, as our unconscious mind loves questions and will work on our behalf until it has found an answer. Remember those occasions when you have forgotten a person's name and asked yourself who they were, only for the name to pop into your head several hours later? Your unconscious was working on your behalf.

Your unconscious works on your behalf

However, it will only do as asked. If we ask our unconscious "Why did that job go so badly?" that is what it will search for and that is what we will get. And what we will very likely get as well is depressed! Whereas if we ask ourselves "What could I have done differently and how can I learn from this for the future?" then that is what we will get. With this we will move forward with learning for how to be more successful in the future.

By having awareness of the questions we are asking ourselves we can significantly influence the emotional state we experience. Our state influences our reactions and our reactions become habits—and habits determine our destiny. Surely it is worth learning how to manage our questioning skills?

PERSONAL CONFIDENCE

I was once asked by the technical director of a software development company to help him develop the presentations he was sometimes asked to give internationally. When he explained what he wanted, I discovered that it wasn't help with the design of the presentation, but help to manage his feelings beforehand. Typically he could not sleep well for at least three weeks prior to the presentation. He often felt physically sick on the morning of the presentation itself.

We began to explore the conversations he had with others and himself related to these presentations. What emerged was this:

"These presentations never go well. They expect me to manage the material and all the technical demonstrations. Giving

these talks makes me stressed. I know what people in the audience will think, they'll think this is all obvious. They'll want to leave. I can't relax. It will be the same experience all over again."

We discovered a series of deletions, generalizations, and distortions in his thinking. Over time we took each of these statements and challenged them in the following way:

His thinking	The challenges
"These presentations never go well."	Never? Has there ever been a time when one did go well? How well specifically do you want it to go? Which presentations specifically don't go well?
"They expect me to manage the material and all the technical demonstrations."	Who expects you to manage both? How exactly do you want to be able to manage the presentation? How do you know they expect you to manage both?
"Giving these talks makes me feel stressed."	How exactly does giving the talks cause you to feel stressed? How do you want to feel?
"I know what people in the audience will think, they'll think this is all obvious, they'll want to leave."	How do you know that? How can you be sure?
"I can't relax. It will be the same experience all over again."	What stops you from relaxing? What can you do? How do you want to experience this presentation? What would happen if you did relax?

Bit by bit we unraveled the complex web he had spun for himself. He gradually sorted out what he did want to achieve and how he could manage himself to do that.

Three months later I received this letter from him:

Dear Sue,

I have just returned from giving a presentation in Paris. It was a joy to do. I enjoyed the demonstrations and I particularly enjoyed the questions I got from the audience. The hardware didn't all work perfectly but I used this as an opportunity to show how quickly we could recover problems when they occur. You'll be pleased to know nobody left the presentation—at least not until the end! Most of all in the weeks prior to the presentation I slept well, in fact I think I can safely say my family were pleased to have me around. This was not the case in the past. I actually *enjoyed the run up to the presentation and I'm looking forward to the next one. Thank you.*

Yours peacefully
John

MANAGE YOUR EXTERNAL DIALOG

Many people have choice: Choice of who to use as our supplier, choice of who we remain with in a relationship, choice of whose method of presentation appeals to us most, choice of who we want to do business with. For the fortunate the choice is literally endless. So we need more than ever before to be aware of whether we are offering a choice to others that they find appealing.

Maybe you think that people choose you for how you look, for the products you offer, for the information you provide them with. You are wrong. More than anything else people choose you because of the influence you have on them. Stephen Covey, in his book *Seven Habits of Highly Effective People*, talks of the legacy we leave. It is our legacy, not our arguments or correctness, that determines whether others will come back for more. And our legacy is the effect we have on others with our actions and our words.

Just as we influence ourselves with our inner dialog, so we influence others with the words we utter. And because of the unconscious mind's love of challenge, our questions have a greater influence than our statements. Questions stay with us until we have the answer and questions that we ask of others will do the same. So awareness of the questions we ask is important in realizing what state we are inducing in the receiver of the question.

Questions stay with us

People do business with us, choose to be with us, or select us as their supplier more on the basis of the state we induce in them than any of the content we might offer. They don't usually realise that, but ask yourself who you would rather do business with: someone who leaves you feeling invigorated and inspired, or someone who leaves you feeling that the world is dark and hopeless and full of woe? Would you choose someone who leaves you feeling confident in yourself or

People choose us on the basis of the state we induce in them

someone who reminds you continually of what you do wrong?

To choose the most appropriate dialog, in line with our overall outcomes, we need first to be clear what outcomes we want to achieve—not only for ourselves but more so for the person with whom we are dealing.

Consider the following scenarios and imagine the effects of each of the behaviors, one in line and one out of line.

You want to bolster the confidence of a member of your team. They frequently come to you with questions:

a Give them the answer or encourage them to find an answer.
b Ask them how someone else in the department (who is good at this aspect of the work) would do it.

You want to encourage someone to do business with you in the future. You are talking about their situation, in which there are several problems.

a Tell them specifically about all the problems you have noticed.
b Ask them to imagine what it would be like if the situation were just as they wanted it to be.

You want to create a culture of learning in the organization by supporting a process of giving and receiving feedback. You are being given feedback.

a Explain why you acted in the way that prompted the feedback.
b Ask the giver of the feedback to explain what you could do for them to feel that you have learned from the feedback they are giving you.

There are no prizes for the correct answers. This is common sense, after all—but are you aware of how often you use your common sense? And more important than that, can you imagine what it would be like if you always acted on the common sense you know you have?

SHORTCUT TO CHALLENGING PERSONAL LIMITATIONS

Consider for a moment something you would like to do in the future but haven't done yet. It could be something simple and short term, for example:

❏ Clearing your desk.
❏ Writing a letter to a friend.
❏ Reading a book you have bought.
❏ Giving a colleague some information you promised.

Or it might be on a bigger scale, such as:

❏ Learning a language.
❏ Taking the holiday you have always wanted.
❏ Changing jobs.
❏ Starting a family.

a Which ones would you put into the category of "must" or "should" do? Which ones feel more appropriate when you precede them with words like "want to" and "can do"?

b Take one of the "musts" and one of the "can dos." In your mind, step into the "must do." For example, "I must clean my desk." What sort of feeling do you get when you say this to yourself?

c Now try on the "can do." For example, "I can learn French." Choose your own "I can" and repeat it to yourself. Say it in a matter-of-fact, encouraging tone of voice. How do you feel? Usually "I can" said to yourself in a positive way generates feelings of confidence and enthusiasm. It is a way of giving yourself permission, reminding yourself what you can indeed do.

SUMMARY

Recognizing and challenging deletions, generalizations, and distortions in your own and others' speech patterns will not only improve the quality of the way you communicate, it will improve your ability to choose what you really want from life. Skilled communicators have mastery over their language. The more flexibility you have over your language, the more

Skilled communicators have mastery over their language

potential influence you have over your experience.

Given that we have less and less control over the pattern of external events, the place where there is room for growth is within. In learning how to use technology we are looking constantly to save time and effort. And yet the contexts in our lives where we waste the most time are when and where we create an effect in others through our language that subsequently needs repair. If we become skilled in choosing language in line with our own and others' needs, we will save hours, days, months, and even years in some cases from the time it takes to achieve what we really want. How much new technology can offer you that?

Challenging deletions, generalizations, and distortions in language with rapport and when appropriate will reconnect you and others with your experience. These challenges are a way of restoring ownership and they are an elegant way of empowering yourself and others to increase the choices you have available to you. The skill of questioning is a way of clarifying and influencing relationships.

The room for growth is "within"

THOUGHT PROVOKERS

1 Take a piece of paper and write down your ambitions for yourself and what, if anything, gets in the way of your achieving them. Do a brain dump—whatever comes to mind write it down. Set yourself a limit of five minutes and keep writing whatever comes to mind in that time.

2 Reread the passage you wrote about yourself. What patterns can you detect? Use the questions set out in this chapter to challenge those patterns for yourself.

3 Test your own assumptions. Consider the following statements and note your immediate thoughts:

a A friend in a computer software company tells you they have a new managing director. She also says the MD is very young for the job. In your mind how old would they be?

b A colleague tells you he is moving companies and getting a significant pay increase. He currently earns $80,000 per annum. How much do you imagine the pay increase to be?

c Your boss tells you she has an urgent job for you to do. When do you imagine this has to be completed by?

d A friend tells you she has just bought an expensive new car. What price range would that fall into in your thinking?

e A colleague tells you he is going to take a long holiday. How long do you imagine that to be?

f A friend invites you for a long run. How long would that be?

Now ask a colleague, a friend, a member of your family or your boss the same questions. How do your answers compare?

4 To challenge the language patterns in the following statements, what questions would you ask?

a I can't change the way I am.

b No one can help me.

c I know they'll think I'm nervous.

d He did it deliberately.

e I'm annoyed because you are late.

f There is only way to give feedback constructively.

g My staff don't respond to my directions.

h This relationship isn't what it should be.

i I'm upset.

j You upset me.

5 Think of a situation recently where the outcome was dependent on what you said and you didn't get the effect you wanted. What did you say? How much time did it take you to resolve the issue (assuming it has been resolved)? What could you have said instead?

6 Now think of another situation that was strongly influenced by the words you used and where the outcome surpassed your expectations. How did what you said affect the outcome? How might you surpass your expectations in other contexts of your life in a similar way?

REFERENCES

Richard Bandler & John Grinder (1975/76) *The Structure of Magic, Vols* I *and* II, Science and Behavior Books.

Stephen R. Covey (1999) *The Seven Habits of Highly Effective People*, Simon & Schuster.

There existed a psychotherapist who believed that many of the problems people brought to him were characterized by the existence of fish in their dreams. One day a client came to him and was discussing the problems he had.

"Tell me," said the psychotherapist, "did you dream last night?"

"I might have done," replied the client.

"And tell me, in this dream was there a river?"

"I don't think so," replied the client.

"Well, was there any water, if not a river?"

"I guess there might have been."

"And was there a pool on the ground?"

"I couldn't be certain but it's possible," the client replied.

"And in this pool could there have been a fish?"

"I can't rule out the possibility that there might have been a fish."

"Aha!" said the psychotherapist. "I knew it!"

7

Hypnotic Language

"Tread softly because you tread on my dreams."
WB Yeats, "He Wishes for the Cloths of Heaven"

People sometimes express concerns about the "programming" part of the name neuro linguistic programming, which may be associated with manipulation and brainwashing. Given that NLP is a powerful tool, they are right to be concerned. My approach with business is to make the unconscious conscious, on the basis that through conscious awareness we have choice. I also feel this is in line with the business goals of empowering and developing individuals through awareness and choice.

It is interesting, then, that the truth is that we are programming other people and ourselves most of the time. We are manipulating our own and others' responses and we are brainwashing ourselves and being brainwashed just about every moment of every day. The problem is that without awareness and without training we tend to do it clumsily and often in ways that are at odds with what we really want to achieve.

In a group of which I was a member we were discussing an important meeting that we were due to attend. The group leader looked at us directly and said, "Don't be apprehensive..."

Our unconscious minds are obedient to commands—we seek out the commands in a sentence and ignore the rest. Embedded in the group leader's sentence was a very clear command: "Be apprehensive." I wasn't apprehensive until the

We are programming ourselves and others most of the time

group leader said this! If I say to you "Whatever you do, don't stop now," I have given you the instruction to "stop now."

I was out to lunch with my sons and on the next table were a mother, father, and immaculately dressed little girl, about four years old, in a beautiful pink chiffon party dress. She was remarkably well behaved throughout the meal. For dessert the father ordered her a huge chocolate milkshake, which arrived with a jumbo straw. As the waitress put the milkshake down in front of the little girl, her father said very clearly, "Whatever you do, don't blow down the straw." I leave it to your imagination what happened next!

We *need* to learn how we already use these hypnotic language patterns. By doing so we can learn how to be more respectful of ourselves and others in choosing language that supports what we want.

When John Grinder and Richard Bandler set out on their exploration of the structure of excellence, they modeled outstanding psychotherapists. One of the people they modeled was Milton Erickson. In studying Milton Erickson they learnt about the power of the voice and the influence of language, especially hypnotic language. The results of this work became known as the Milton Model. To quote from John and Richard's book *Trance—Formations*, the Milton Model provides the user with ways of being "artfully vague." Being artfully vague allows a communicator to make statements that sound specific and yet are general enough to be an adequate pace for the listener's experience, no matter what that is. This is the opposite of the model for precision explained in Chapter 6, which is designed to specify experience more fully. The Milton Model provides the user with a language structure in which just about all specific content is omitted.

The history of hypnotic language in NLP

Hypnotic language was used originally by psychotherapists for the following reasons:

Our unconscious minds are obedient

❏ It stimulated altered states of consciousness—trance.
❏ It allowed therapists to bypass conscious resistance.
❏ It gave space for the listener to make sense of the language in their own way and therefore draw on their inner resources.

❑ It avoided saying anything that might mismatch the specific meaning of situations for the listener and was therefore good for building rapport.

APPLICATIONS IN BUSINESS

If you think hypnotic language (trance-inducing language) is the preserve of psychotherapists, go to any regular business presentation and check out the trances that have been induced in the majority of the audience!

The workplace is already full of hypnotic language

I would first of all emphasize that this is not so much about introducing hypnotic language into the workplace—the workplace is full of it already, often inappropriately—it is, rather, about being aware of what language patterns we are using and choosing ones that fit our purpose and lead to a win/win situation. If you take a business report or presentation you are more likely to find that it already contains more hypnotic language patterns than anything else. The use of vague language (and it is more likely to be "clumsily" vague than "artfully" vague) avoids confrontation and challenge. If it is too vague for you to be sure exactly what it means, it is more likely to be ignored than challenged, and that for many people in business has been the safer option.

I quote from an article in a recent business magazine:

Therefore, in view of the absence of any objective evidence provided by the original proponents of the hypothesis, and the failure of subsequent empirical investigations to adequately support it, it may well be appropriate now to conclude that there is not, and never has been, any substance to the conjecture that people represent their world...

This is overwhelmingly hypnotically vague language and is taken from a report designed to highlight the ineffectiveness of NLP! Yet the author appears to be unaware of the patterns in his own language and the effect of those patterns on the reader.

What are some of the pitfalls we can avoid by learning about hypnotic language?

❏ We can choose when we want to induce a trance and, more significantly, when we do *not* want to do that.
❏ We can maintain and strengthen rapport by being aware of the effect of our words.

The managing director was discussing the style of coaching that he wanted the rest of the board to adopt. Although he believed he wanted to encourage a coaching style in the business, he had not let go of the desire to find a way to "coach" people to come to his conclusions! He repeatedly asked questions of the board as follows: "What would I have to ask to be sure that he [the person being coached] came to the right conclusion?" or "How can I say this to her so that she realizes what I want?" The effect of these questions was to irritate the other board members who wanted a freer, more open style of coaching. The emotions in the meeting became heated.

What the MD was doing was using questions that contained powerful assumptions. The assumptions were ones that other members of the board didn't share, but they didn't know how to unpack the questions in a way that allowed them to challenge the assumptions. This is a pattern of hypnotic language that I have explored later in this chapter.

So the reasons *for* using hypnotic language skillfully are:

❏ We can choose language that is in line with the outcomes we want to achieve.
❏ We can respect other people's unique interpretations of a situation, especially when we do not know the context.
❏ We can recognize when other people are using hypnotic language on us and we can then challenge that.
❏ We can create space in our language for others (possibly someone we are coaching) to draw on their own resources rather than relying on us for answers. In this way we can help build confidence and self-esteem.

AMBIGUITY

A delegate on one of my courses in Denmark was doing a coaching exercise. I was the subject for his questioning skills and he was exploring how I thought of my role in different contexts. He asked me "Who do you think you are" and was about to add "in your work context?" Because of the accent and the way he emphasized the words, I heard it as "[Just] who do you think you are?" The meaning I put on this was "What right do you have to think of yourself this way?" I am quite sure this was not the way that he meant it, but the fact that I put this meaning to it meant that it had a significance for me that was more powerful than the original. I began to appreciate the arrogance that I was communicating in the way I was being.

Ambiguity is an aspect of hypnotic language

Ambiguity is an important aspect of hypnotic language. It causes disorientation and creates space for the listener to create their own meaning, one that might take you much longer to discover at a conscious level. The significance of encouraging the listener to find their own meaning is that they are likely to have a higher level of commitment to any meaning they find for themselves than to any you might offer them.

EMBEDDED COMMANDS AND QUESTIONS

In the example at the beginning of this chapter I referred to the father who told his daughter not to blow down the straw. His sentence contained an embedded command: "blow down the straw." Our unconscious minds are very obedient and detect any commands in conversation and seek to fulfill them. So on hearing this the little girl was doing exactly as her unconscious mind believed it was being told to do when she blew down the straw.

Words shape our external experience

Words shape our external experience. When my husband's new boss told his team that they "must not lose the business with this client," he was offering their unconscious minds the structure of thinking that could lead to loss.

Words sculpt our inner world and subsequently shape our outer world. What we say to ourselves (our inner dialog) has an influence on what we see, hear, and feel. Similarly, our spoken words influence not only ourselves but also our listeners. It is vital that we take responsibility for the effect we create with our language if we want to maximize our influence. In other words, the meaning of our communication is indeed its effect.

(See Chapter 9 for more on this belief.)

We can embed positive or negative commands. Examples of positive commands might be:

❏ You can begin to *relax*.
❏ I have been wondering how you might begin to *see a way forward*.
❏ I don't know if you will *begin to feel motivated*.

And some negative ones that, when our unconscious minds find them, are stripped back to the command component:

❏ Don't *think deeply about what you might be learning*.
❏ On no account do you need to *be aware of what you are saying*.

You may already be starting to think about some of the inappropriate examples you have heard. For example, has anyone ever come to you and said "Don't *worry*, everything is going to be all right," when probably what they meant to communicate was "You can *put your mind at rest now*."

You can also embed questions as a way of gently prompting a response from your listeners:

❏ I am curious to know *what you would like to get from this meeting*
❏ I was just wondering *what you would like to drink*.

"You can put your mind at rest now"

Most people will answer the question without even realizing that they have not been asked a question directly. What they often experience is a respectful and allowing style of conversation. This style of questioning is entirely appropriate when dealing with someone who might feel very sensitive, say in an appraisal or coaching meeting or with someone who is feeling nervous in an interview where direct questions might be too unnerving.

Just this week on one of my courses I heard one delegate say to another (who wanted to develop a new relationship), "Does thinking like that make you feel more alone?" If they had been aware of the effect they really wanted they might have said, "Does thinking like that make you feel more connected?"

Alternatively they could have asked an open question: "How do you feel when you think like that?"

One way to help embedded commands or questions be received as such is to mark them out in some way in the way we present them. For example, we might pause before and after the embedded command or mark it out with a raised eyebrow or a hand movement. If our marking out is subtle it will be perceived but not consciously detected. The appropriate use of embedded commands and questions can be a graceful way of collecting information and a respectful form of influence. I know that with a little practice you can…

Embedded quotes get the message across

Embedding a quote in a sentence can be a very powerful way of getting a message across by bypassing any conscious resistance. For example, you might describe a conversation with one of your clients to another client by explaining that the first client had found it difficult to delegate responsibility. You might then explain that you said to her: "You will only realize your true potential when you learn to let go of control." You have in effect said what is in quotes to the person you are talking to now, but you have avoided taking responsibility for the message. The effect of this is that they cannot dispute the story and the likelihood is that they will take in the quote as if it applied to them without being able to challenge your right to offer it to them personally. This can be useful if you are dealing with someone whose preference is to dispute and mismatch what others say.

PRESUPPOSITIONS

You may have wondered while reading this how you can use these language patterns in your everyday work.

The previous sentence is a classic example of hypnotic language. It is a fact that you are reading this (unless someone else is reading it to you or you have found some other way of taking in the information in this sentence). And I have linked with that fact a response that I would like you to have, that is, wondering. And I am suggesting that you wonder about how you can use these language patterns in your everyday work. The question I have posed is how you can use these patterns.

Notice that I have therefore based this on the following presuppositions:

❏ That you can use these language patterns.
❏ That you can use them in your everyday work.
❏ That you want to use them in your everyday work.
❏ That there are such things as language patterns.
❏ That you are able to wonder about them.
❏ That you would want to wonder about them.

If you accept the introductory statement you are accepting all these presuppositions simultaneously. Presuppositions are a powerful form of influence. Used effectively they can accelerate your progress toward an outcome. Used ineffectively they will irritate and provoke your listener, even though your listener may not always be sure what it is that is having that effect. The value of learning about these patterns is that you can become aware of what works for you and for others. By having this awareness you also have the means to explain what is happening and the words to plan differently.

Presuppositions are very effective in training programs when you want a group to accept certain premises for their development. For example, If you want a group to learn how to give feedback to each other, rather than asking if they want to give feedback you ask *how* they will give feedback. You have given choice, but not over what you consider to be the non-negotiables. This is why in coaching it is so important to be aware of the language you use. There is a big difference between asking someone "*Can you* make a commitment to a next step?" and "*What* commitment can you make to a next step?"

To find out what is presupposed in a sentence and therefore not open to question, there is a simple test. Let's take a simple statement, "Colin mowed the grass." If we negate it, we have "Colin did not mow the grass." What is still true is:

❏ Colin exists.
❏ The grass exists.
❏ Colin could have mowed the grass.
❏ The grass can be mowed.
❏ There was an expectation that Colin might mow the grass.

> Presuppositions are a powerful form of influence

In the earlier example, when the manager asked "How can I coach people to come to the right conclusion?" he was presupposing that:

❑ There is a conclusion.
❑ There is a right conclusion.
❑ He has a right to coach people.
❑ He can coach people.
❑ He has the right to coach people to come to a right conclusion.

We can discover what control we are holding on to

This is powerful language when used by communicators who presuppose what they don't want questioned. Often the communicator does not realize what they are presupposing (especially when they are unaware or unskilled in the use of these patterns). Learning about presuppositions can help us to discover what control we are holding on to and what choices we might be able to let go.

As I was writing this chapter I became aware of an outcome that I had set myself, to decide which option of two key opportunities I was going to take for my future. I realized that I had presupposed that it had to be one or the other. With just this realization I discovered that the way forward for me was to believe that it did not have to be one or the other but could be both.

Some more examples of sentences and questions that contain presuppositions:

❑ You might wonder who is going to volunteer for this project.
❑ Do you want to sit down while we go through this report?
❑ You might ask yourselves which department will achieve their target first.
❑ How can I delegate in such a way that we devolve ownership in the business?

Some traditional sales closes include presuppositions, for example: "Do you want to place the order now or later this week?" For me this is an example of inappropriate and outdated use of presuppositions. One of the factors that determines whether a statement is appropriate or not is whether you have a right to assume the presupposition. Does a salesperson have the right to assume that you will place an order? I don't think so, which is why I would find this style of question offensive. However, I will not presuppose what you can believe about it!

Do you realize how much of this you are taking in unconsciously?

DISTORTIONS

I am opposed to smoking and one of my colleagues, who does not share my view, is aware of my feelings. We have had discussions about this where we both tried to convince the other that we were right. Recently I sent an email to this colleague talking about a fellow presenter whom I admire very much and had met for the first time. My colleague knows this person and responded by saying how much she admired him too and how caring this presenter was at all times, even in casual moments like a smoking break.

When I read this I felt an inner conflict and was not sure initially what that was about. Then I realized that my colleague was linking something with which I agreed (the admiration that I felt for the colleague) to something of which I did not approve (smoking).

What my colleague had done is a form of unconscious anchoring (see Chapter 12), which works very effectively if we want the two things to be linked together. However, if it is unecological for us to link the two together, the distortion leads us to experience the inner resistance that I felt when I read this email.

Nevertheless, as I describe in Chapter 12, anchoring is a valuable and naturally occurring tool. We can use it for ourselves and to support and coach others when we link something that is occurring or is true for them with something that we want them to respond to. For example:

❏ You are reading this sentence and you are wondering what other forms of hypnotic language there can be.
❏ You are taking in this information and you are exploring how

you can practice these patterns in ways that enhance what you do.

In these two examples it is the use of the "and" that has the influence by linking two components of the sentence together. What happens is that you get the listener into a "yes" way of thinking and without a break you present another (nonfactual) idea to their mind. It's a bit like getting someone to open the door to accept a parcel that they have ordered and while the door is open starting a discussion about the weather!

Other forms that this linkage can take:

Get the listener into a "yes" way of thinking

❏ As you sit here listening to what I am saying you can begin to wonder how what I say applies directly to you.
❏ While we talk this through in this way you can start to think how we might take this forward.

And a stronger form of this kind of linkage:

❏ Sitting here listening *will make you* aware of just how much there is to learn.
❏ Watching this presentation *requires that you* relax and concentrate fully on what we are saying.
❏ The way that you are breathing *causes you* to begin to relax completely.

My experience is that if the motivation behind your statements is a genuine win/win and is perceived that way by your listener, these kinds of statements will be accepted and will accelerate your progress toward a mutual outcome. If they are not—if they are, for example, being used to manipulate someone against their wishes—then although the listener may not know what is wrong they will sense it. They may get that "something not quite right," instinctive reaction to you or what you are saying.

Your listener may get that "something not quite right" reaction

---

MIND-READING

You might be wondering what I am going to say next.

I am mind-reading when I say that. However, if you *are*

wondering or if it is plausible that you *could be* wondering or might choose to, then it nudges you down that route. Mind-reading occurs when you act or speak as if you know the other person's internal experience. As with all the other patterns this can be helpful and an enriching experience or it can be patronising and disruptive. (And rather than presuppose that these are the only two effects it can have, you can also think what other possibilities there are!)

Some examples of mind-reading:

❏ You are probably asking yourself what you can do about this.
❏ I expect you will have an answer.
❏ I know what you will say if I tell you.
❏ Your next step is predictable.
❏ You might be thinking what your outcome might be.

I remember a car journey into London with a colleague. It was as if this colleague had just been waiting for the opportunity to tell me (without interruption) what they had on their mind. The conversation took the form of her telling me for most of the journey what I should do with the opportunities I had and with the business and what I must do for myself. The effect of this mind-reading and the powerful language of shoulds and musts was that I felt as if I was under fire. I was mentally exhausted and very relieved when we got to our destination!

SUMMARY

It is important for us to be aware of hypnotic language patterns. With this awareness we can choose the patterns we use with others and ideally choose those that most support us in achieving our mutual outcomes. With this awareness we can also be aware of what is not working and precisely select alternative ways of meeting our own and others' needs.

THOUGHT PROVOKERS

1 Take a piece of written communication that you have sent recently. It could be a letter, an email, a report. Select three or four sentences, especially ones in which you are making suggestions or recommendations. Negate the sentences and list the presuppositions on which you have based your statements. How many of those presuppositions were you aware of using and how many were used without conscious thought? What do you learn from that?

2 Identify someone with whom you experience a lack of choice in conversation. Write down some of the typical things they say to you. What (if any) hypnotic language patterns are they using?

3 Think of someone who typically resists any suggestions you make. Thinking back on the way you have put those suggestions, what options do you now have that might work more effectively to reach a win/win position?

4 Identify three situations where you believe that using hypnotic language would support you in achieving mutually desirable outcomes with another person.

REFERENCES

John Burton & Bob Bodenheimer (2000) *Hypnotic Language: Its Structure and Use*, Crown House.

John Grinder & Richard Bandler (1981) *Trance-Formations: Neuro-Linguistic Programming and the Structure of Hypnosis*, Real People Press.

Sidney Rosen (ed.) (1991) *My Voice Will Go with You: The Teaching Tales of Milton H. Erickson*, W. W. Norton.

Last night I watched a football game on television. One team wore their coloured jerseys indicating they were most likely the home team while the other team wore white jerseys. Neither team had a good win–loss record so the game seemed evenly matched. Most of the players were fairly new to the professional ranks except two on one team. I set this up this way to illustrate how beliefs influence outcomes. The team carries a belief about their ability to play effectively or not. Each individual on the team also carries a belief about his own competence. These may or may not be consistent.

What probably is true is that each of these players once carried very high beliefs about his own competence. No player could even be on a professional team if he did not once demonstrate his ability to win. And we all know beliefs precede and are consistent with ability. Maybe when he played college ball or maybe when he played in high school. But no doubt he once felt certain of his competence, he believed he could and would win. He knew and remembered how to win. Well in this game last night both teams demonstrated their current beliefs that differ from their past beliefs, they believed they could not use their competence. They seemed to forget what they believed about their ability and how to use it. The game illustrated very well the old adage, use it or lose it. Both teams tried to lose it.

So I began to wonder if all the players, except two, forgot their beliefs about their high ability and where might it be stored. One player had not scored a touchdown all year and this game was the 12th, amnesia at its worst. Yet sometimes when you look inside yourself it becomes very difficult to do so objectively. So much seems at stake that you lose some perceptual ability, you know?

So where is the objective, unbiased storage of beliefs containing high ability? It suddenly dawned on me, the ball! After all, who scored more touchdowns and field goals than any player? The ball! Who was present during each tackle or run and catch for a touchdown? The ball, wow! It contains such a rich storehouse of memories about how to play well, score and win. Just ask the ball because it knows how to score and win, it has done so for many individual players and teams and each scoring player carries something that knows how. Follow the ball and let it tell you how, guiding you to the score. To win you just need to have a ball.

Story reproduced with permission from Hypnotic Language by John Burton & Bob Bodenheimer.

8

Metaphor: The Key to the Unconscious Mind

"Engaging the book as a listener forced me to consider the awesome power of metaphor, and how thoroughly it defeats our attempts to contain it."

Kathleen Norris, The Cloister Walk

*I*n previous chapters we have explored how thinking patterns, e.g., visual, auditory, and feelings, influence the way we communicate and consequently the effect we have on our listeners. We have also considered how the meaning of our communication can go through a process of deletion, distortion, or generalization before it emerges as conversation with ourselves and others. The quality of this conversation has an impact on our experience. There is so much more going on in our thinking of which we are often unaware. NLP provides us with ways of accessing and utilizing much more of our thinking than if we only work with the conscious mind. One of the ways in which we can draw on this greater resource is through metaphor.

Metaphor is the essence of thought

Metaphor is the essence of thought, for example we may think of life as "a bed of roses," work as "a battle," our leisure time as "a feast of entertainment." One of my clients recently described himself as being "between a rock and a hard place." Whatever the metaphor, it emerges in the words and expressions we use and influences our own and others' experience of conversations and situations.

Metaphors permeate our lives. They are symbols for what our unconscious mind is saying. When we don't listen our unconscious steps up the signals until the message materializes in physical symptoms or illnesses. Our dreams are metaphors and a means of our unconscious mind finding a way to communicate with us. Our words are metaphors, sometimes containing what we want to communicate and sometimes communicating what we really mean but did not intend to communicate. The more we can learn to listen to the metaphors in our life, the more we can draw on the power of the unconscious mind.

Metaphors permeate our lives

The metaphors we choose are all powerful in the way we influence our experience.

"Metaphors and mental models are the tools we use to shape our realities."
    Michael Lissack and Johan Roos, The Next Common Sense

Metaphors thread their way through everyone's life, from the story at bedtime, through the parables in the Bible, to our everyday speech and the way we think of ourselves, our business, our life. Advertising is metaphor. Metaphors can be enchanting, enticing, and mesmerizing. Their effects may be enlightening and empowering when developed and recounted constructively. Used carelessly, however, they can be damaging and disturbing. And above all, metaphors are our inner reality. What is certain is that if we want to maximize our potential, we need to learn to listen and interpret the metaphors by which we live.

Metaphors can be enchanting, enticing, and mesmerizing

Metaphors may be single words, expressions, or stories. To understand how to construct and tell a story metaphor is to know how to influence with elegance and respect. Milton Erickson was a master of the metaphor. He was also a master of change. The methods he used to bring about change in therapy are just as powerful in influencing change in business.

Metaphor is elegant influence

The following is an example of one of his stories, told to explain the way he worked with his clients:

One day an unknown horse strayed into the yard of the farm where I lived as a child. No one knew where this horse had come from as it had no markings by which it could have been identified. There was no question of keeping the horse—it must belong to someone.

My father decided to lead it home. He mounted the horse and led it to the road and simply trusted the instinct of the horse to lead itself towards its home. He only intervened when the horse left the road to eat grass or to walk into a field. On these occasions my father would firmly guide it back to the road.

In this way the horse was soon returned to its owner. The owner was very surprised to see his horse once more and asked my father, "How did you know the horse came from here and belonged to us?"

My father replied, "I didn't know, the horse knew! All I did was to keep him on the road."

Generating commitment

This story illustrates not only the way Milton Erickson worked with his clients, but also the way most NLP is conducted today. By providing guidance only where needed, NLP respects the fact that everyone has all the resources they need to solve their problems. Given the space and encouragement to use these resources, you are more likely to find solutions that are congruent with who you are. These solutions are therefore much more likely to be ones to which you are committed and which therefore will work to produce the outcome you want.

When presented with a metaphor we make our own unique interpretation of it in a way that makes sense to us. Most significantly, it is our unconscious mind that makes sense of it and so metaphors bypass conscious resistance and embrace our unconscious. If you are faced with someone who will not intellectually consider what you are saying, try telling them a story, a parable for what you want them to learn.

A director of a company facing closure was confronted with the unenviable task of announcing to one of the divisions that they had to lose half of their workforce in the following two years. This meant making 2,000 people redundant. Everyone was apprehensive and tense. Rumors of the cutbacks had already spread throughout the site and it seemed unlikely that the employees would be willing to listen to what the director had to say, let alone participate in the implementation of the cutbacks.

The director cared about his employees and believed that there was a possible future if they all cooperated and thought together about how they could reconsider the future. He likened the business to a snowball rolling downhill, gathering more snow and momentum as it gained speed. He explained that there were two possible routes this snowball could take. One possibility was for the snowball to grow in size and speed as it rolled downhill, only to roll out on to the plain where it would melt and disappear. The other possibility was for the snowball to roll on down the mountain until it had become such a size and had such a speed that nothing could stop it until it reached the fertile valley at the bottom of the mountain. For him the fertile valley represented a revitalized business. "We can influence the path that snowball takes," he explained. They did.

More recently I was involved with a company whose directors talked in the following terms:

❏ Being in the firing line.
❏ Attacking the competition.
❏ Aiming at the target.

They described the workforce as the "troops." Employees in this company did not "step out of line," nor did those with any entrepreneurial style stay very long. I even saw a slide in one of their presentations headed, "We will fight them on the beaches." Fight whom, I wonder? It is important to question whether and how these metaphors fit with the network culture that is absorbing the business world, in which we need to learn how to help our customers to thrive, how to support our employees to grow, and how to flourish in conditions that are right for us personally.

Individuals and companies have metaphors that express their unique culture. The question is whether or not these are metaphors that support the culture and style they really want. The clue is in the language and behavior of individuals, as in the military example above. Not surprisingly, many of the older managers in this company had spent time in the forces. Now the company was searching for a way of developing a new style of leader who encouraged autonomy and cooperation. It was

Changing culture

time to change the metaphor that underpinned the culture of this company.

Listen to the language that colleagues and friends use. Have you heard these sorts of statements?

- ❏ I need to combat his response.
- ❏ We can overcome objections.
- ❏ We need to keep our heads down.
- ❏ On track to achieve what we want.
- ❏ Steaming ahead.
- ❏ We will carry no passengers.
- ❏ Everything in the garden is rosy.
- ❏ They are blooming.
- ❏ Business has died down.
- ❏ Life is a ball.

When you are aware of the metaphor by which you, friends, and colleagues live, you will be aware of the way you and they are thinking. Understanding the metaphor both in and behind the communication can help you make sense of an individual's experience. If you know someone who thinks in terms of overcoming objections, you may begin to understand any resistance they experience from their colleagues, staff, and customers. Imagine how you would feel if someone were attempting to overcome your objections!

Visual metaphors

Metaphors are rich in their ability to enhance communication. Below are some examples of visual metaphors drawn by course delegates to depict either the way they saw themselves then or the way they wanted to see themselves in the future.

These pictures provide a wealth of information, not only for the observers but also for the owners. Questions can reveal many implications of the metaphor that have sometimes been outside its owner's awareness.

When thinking about what metaphors are true for you, you may find that your unconscious mind pops an image or a thought into your head. Your unconscious mind is the source of your real hopes and fears. The more you learn to acknowledge what your unconscious tells you, the more you will have access to this powerful resource. Major breakthroughs in thinking are believed to have come about through the power of metaphor. It is held that Einstein discovered the theory of relativity as he lay daydreaming, imagining himself riding a sunbeam.

Your unconscious mind

"Metaphor and symbolism enable us to give form to those aspects of life which are the most mystifying; namely, our relationships, our problems and their solutions, our fears and desires, our illness and health, our poverty and wealth, and the love we give and the love we receive."

James Lawley and Penny Tompkins, Metaphors in Mind

THE STRUCTURE OF METAPHOR

Excellent communicators and influencers use metaphor to capture and hold attention. With metaphors they weave a spell.

"The present life of men on earth, O King, as compared with the whole length of time which is unknowable to us, seems to me to be like this: as if, when you are sitting at dinner with your chiefs and ministers in wintertime ... one of the sparrows from outside flew very quickly through the hall; as if it came in one door and soon went out through another. In that actual time it is indoors it is not touched by the winter's storm; but the tiny period of calm is over in a moment, and having come out of the winter it soon returns to the winter and slips out of your sight. Man's life appears to be more or less like this; and of what may follow it, or what preceded it, we are absolutely ignorant."

The Venerable Bede

Story metaphors

Metaphors are invaluable in situations when you experience some opposition or conflict: Metaphors can't be disputed. They can be a valuable tool in business presentations when you want to avoid or overcome resistance. In such cases the metaphor could be a story you develop to make a point or it could be an incident from your own experience, the most natural form of presentation in any context.

A metaphor respects the power of the unconscious mind by allowing it to reach its own conclusions. It is like a puzzle: the unconscious mind tussles with it until it reaches a solution that fits for you and the complex interweavings of memory, experience, knowledge, skills, beliefs, wants and needs, and sense of being and purpose that form you. Only our unconscious minds can effectively work with this level of complexity.

Unique interpretation

When I did my first NLP training I was impressed with all of the tutors, but especially with David Gordon and the stories he told. It was he who told the story about the couple swimming to Japan that I have included at the end of Chapter 15.

When I heard this story I struggled to make sense of it and eventually abandoned any attempt at conscious interpretation. Occasionally the story came to mind, but I still didn't make any real sense of it. Two years later I was listening to a talk about goal setting and the whole point of the story fell into place in a way that I needed to understand at that very moment. I wasn't ready to understand it two years earlier, but I was very ready at that point of my life.

The fascinating thing about a complex metaphor is that it makes sense in different ways to different people. Your unconscious mind will work out a meaning that fits for you. A metaphor respects your ability to learn what you need from what it offers. This is why it is not the custom to explain the meaning of a metaphor.

THE DOOR TO CREATIVITY

I recently had a meeting with a manager in the Mars corporation. I was impressed with the values and style they brought to the business. We were discussing the impact that Mars ice creams had on the ice-cream market in general, how it had raised the quality of ice creams, not only those of the company's own manufacture but of others too.

The manager I was talking to worked for a division of Mars that sold ice cream to countries including Africa, India, and the United Arab Emirates. One of the factors influencing the quality of the ice cream is the temperature at which it is kept. If this is too high, the quality of the ice cream deteriorates. In the UK there are strict controls on the conditions in which food produce must be kept, but this is not the case in some other countries. To guarantee the condition of the ice cream, Mars decided to provide those countries with freezers in which to keep it. The regulation temperature for ice cream in the UK is −18°C. The Mars freezers are set to keep the ice cream at a temperature of −25°C. The company owns these freezers and recognizes that to ensure the quality of the product it must manage the product environment.

Coincidentally, we were having problems with a hotel booked by one of our clients for a series of courses we were running. I applied the Mars thinking to the problems we were experiencing. The Mars situation acted as a metaphor for my experience with the hotel: The freezer was the environment for the ice cream, just as the hotel was the environment for the training. To ensure the quality of the training we needed to ensure the quality of the hotel, especially in one that we hadn't personally selected. The result has been that we now provide free training for the staff of the hotels in which we do the work. This is appreciated by the staff and of course helps to ensure the quality of the training: A win/win situation.

Subsequently I have generalized that metaphor to explore ways in which I can support all of my contacts—my clients, my colleagues, my suppliers, my "competition," and anyone else with whom I come into contact—to thrive. So a metaphor is a way of transferring learning both into other different contexts in your life and across contexts as a principle for your business.

Thinking metaphorically can generate many new and different ideas that will benefit you and everyone in your life.

Metaphorical thinking

SUMMARY

Metaphors have been with us in many forms for as long as we can remember. Stories in the forms of fairy tales, proverbs and parables are passed down from generation to generation. Metaphors are so rooted in our upbringing that for many people they act as an anchor for relaxation and involvement. As such, metaphors bypass any conscious blocks or resistance and slip into the unconscious mind. The unconscious mind responds to the challenge of the metaphor by finding a unique solution that fits the listener's experience and needs.

Metaphors are powerful and memorable. Many of the best speakers and leaders use metaphor as a way of communicating what they want to say. A skilled story teller is a skilled communicator.

Metaphors are also used in our everyday lives. The metaphors in an individual's or company's language provide many clues to the patterns by which that individual lives and the culture of the company of which they are a part. By learning how to construct and recount metaphors, you will be learning how to open your listener's or reader's mind to new possibilities and choices. And by learning how to listen to the metaphors that our unconscious minds give us, we learn to use our internal wisdom and to develop our coherence so that we become more of who we are truly meant to be.

THOUGHT PROVOKERS

1   If you were to draw a metaphor for yourself, what would you draw? As you read that question you may have noticed that a picture popped into your mind. What was it?
   ❏ What does this represent for you?
   ❏ What are the characteristics of this metaphor?
   ❏ What are its strengths?
   ❏ What are its weaknesses?
   ❏ How are the elements of the image connected?
   ❏ What does this signify?
   ❏ What is missing and what does that signify?
   Show the drawing to someone else and encourage them to ask you questions about it. Their questions may give you insight into

the deeper significance of the metaphor for you.

2 What metaphors would you use to describe:
   ❑ Your career?
   ❑ Your relationships?
   ❑ Your social life?
   ❑ Your past?
   ❑ Your future?

   How do the characteristics of the metaphor manifest themselves in these areas of your life? For example, if you say "Life is like a dream," what does that mean? Is it unreal? Dreams can be intangible. Dreams have many meanings and the purpose of them can be unclear. There are pleasant dreams and nightmares. Explore the possibilities of the metaphor for you.

3 Think of a situation that you would like to influence. It could be a presentation, a meeting, or a discussion with one of your colleagues. Develop a metaphor that you can use the next time you are in this situation.

4 Think now of the company that you manage or work for. Is there a metaphor that expresses itself through the language and actions of the employees? Set yourself the task of identifying any metaphors that you hear being used in your company or in the companies of any of your customers during a particular day.

REFERENCES

James Lawley & Penny Tompkins (2000) *Metaphors in Mind: Transformation through Symbolic Modelling*, The Developing Company Press.

Michael Lissack & Johan Roos (2000) *The Next Common Sense: An E-Manager's Guide to Complexity*, Nicholas Brealey Publishing.

I hired a carpenter to help me restore an old farmhouse. After he had just finished a rough first day on the job, a flat tire made him lose an hour of work, his electric saw quit, and now his ancient pickup truck refused to start. While I drove him home, he sat in stony silence. On arriving, he invited me in to meet his family. As we walked toward the front door, he paused briefly at a small tree, touching tips of the branches with both hands. When opening the door, he underwent an amazing transformation. His tanned face was wreathed in smiles and he hugged his two small children and gave his wife a kiss.

Afterward he walked me to the car. We passed the tree and my curiosity got the better of me. I asked him about what I had seen him do earlier.

"Oh, that's my trouble tree," he replied. "I know I can't help having troubles on the job, but one thing's for sure, troubles don't belong in the house with my wife and the children. So I just hang them up on the tree every night when I come home. Then in the morning I pick them up again. Funny thing is," he smiled, "when I come out in the morning to pick 'em up, there aren't nearly as many as I remember hanging up the night before."

9
Metamessages

"Within this thin wafer of bread is caught up symbolically the labor of plow and of sowing, of harvest and threshing, of milling, of packing, of transportation, of financing, of selling and packaging. Man's industrial life is all there."

Wilford O Cross, Prologue to Ethics

How often have you heard someone say "But I've told you this already!" when you have not understood, remembered, learned, or acted on something that was said? How often have you blamed the other person in these circumstances?

If we want to get our message through and maintain long-term collaborations and partnerships, we need to understand the strategies of the people with whom we are dealing. Their ways of learning, understanding, and remembering may be very different from our own. If we think someone has understood just because we have told them something, we can be in for a big surprise, for example, if we find out that an essential part of their strategy for understanding relies on their seeing what we are saying as opposed to being told.

And when we do begin to discover what others need from us, we need the flexibility to respond in ways that they recognize. This does not mean that we have to compromise who we are; we can be true to our values yet develop the flexibility to demonstrate those values in ways that generate cooperation and respect.

We need the flexibility to respond in ways others recognize

I entered a local café. The food is excellent, the coffee good. The venue is attractive and the service is usually fast. However, when I stopped there for an early morning coffee the waitress did not smile or greet me. As soon as she had taken the order she returned to talking to one of the other waitresses. She was the same with other customers. Although so much else about that café is excellent, the overall impression I got that day (and other days) was that customers weren't important.

So you might get 99 percent of what you offer right, but to provide the support, service, friendship, and even love that really shows you care in the way that the other person will recognize, you need to know how to get 100 percent right. You need to know how the message you are giving matches (or not) the perceptions of those on the receiving end of you and your business. If you get the match right, it is increasingly likely that people will choose you as the person or business with whom they want to trade, and keep on choosing you for the future.

People will choose you

This overall impression is the metamessage—the message that is the sum total of all that we are doing (and not doing) that is creating an impression on other people.

A metamessage is what is communicated but not said. Because it is what is *not* said, it is often the things of which we are unaware that create this overall impression. In this chapter we are going to explore these "things" and how you can become more aware of them. In this way we increase the chance that we do indeed communicate what we mean to communicate.

A metamessage is what is communicated but not said

You may have experienced some of the following:

❏ Being surprised when you discover that someone has got the "wrong" impression of you.
❏ Discovering after an event that the way you thought you had come across was different to the way you had been perceived by others.
❏ Feeling annoyed with someone because they did not understand what you intended.
❏ Being surprised that something you asked someone to do was not done or was done in a way that you didn't want.
❏ Finding that people react to you in a way that you don't want.

❏ Hearing "secondhand" what someone thought of you but was unable to tell you directly.

It is our behavior and not our intention that affects other people.
You may, of course, experience the counterpart to these:

❏ Having planned the response you want from others, you get exactly that.
❏ You receive consistent feedback on how you come across to others and it is in line with how you want to be perceived.
❏ When you ask or discuss with others what you want them to do, by and large what you get is what you expect.
❏ Sometimes you don't come across the way you would want, but you know it and people are able to tell you this too.
❏ You are able to elicit and receive feedback openly and honestly and you do so.
❏ The feedback you get from others is in line with what you have sensed to be true before they even tell you—there are no surprises.
❏ People say of you, "What you see is what you get."

Some years ago when working with a multicultural team I was fascinated by the way the different members of the team interacted with their respective colleagues. In particular, I was intrigued by the German manager who spoke to everyone else in an extremely forthright way but did not allow others to finish when they spoke to him. In one of the feedback sessions I took him to one side and explained that I thought he was being inconsistent with his listening skills. I explained that he gave the impression that he wanted others to listen to him and yet at the same time was giving the impression that he did not want to listen to others. He looked me straight in the eyes and said with a very strong tone of voice, "That is exactly right. I don't want to listen to them—I do want them to listen to me!"

There are a number of potential scenarios.

1 **Our perception of what we are communicating is different to others' perceptions of what we are communicating and we are unaware of this. We "think" we are communicating what we want.**

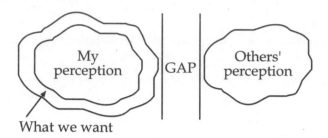

In this scenario we will have problems with others. We may not understand why or how they react to us in the way they do. And they probably have difficulty dealing with us and explaining why they feel the way they do towards us. The issues I address in this chapter can help to give you the awareness that can bring the different perceptions into line.

2 **Our perception of what we are communicating is the same at that of others and it is not what we want.**

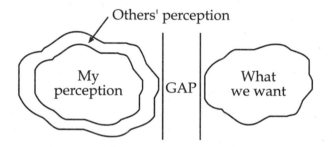

In this case we know what others think of what we are doing and that is not the impression we want to create. Awareness is better than no awareness, nevertheless. What you can do in this scenario is to decide whether you want to create a different impression. If you do, the way forward is through increased flexibility. All of the other chapters in this book are about increasing your flexibility. Work through the chapters in Part II, Model Yourself with NLP. Go through them in order. If you follow the guidelines, you will find that with each one you bring the perception of you increasingly into line with what you want it to be.

3 Our perception of what we are communicating is the same as others' perception of us and it is what we want.

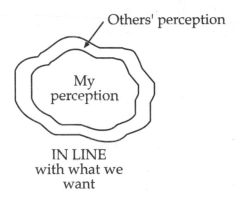

Others' perception

My perception

IN LINE
with what we
want

This is the ideal. This is the desired state of increasing our awareness of our metamessages so that we know what we are communicating, we are aware of how that is being received by others, and it is in line with our desired outcomes.

THE BELIEFS BEHIND "HEALTHY" METAMESSAGES

If our desired outcome is to be giving out "healthy" metamessages, in other words to be creating the impression we want in other people, there are certain beliefs that support this.

First, *the meaning of our communication is the effect that it has.* If we blame others for their misunderstanding of what we intend, we are not going to influence successfully. When we blame others we let go of the possibility of increasing our awareness, our sensitivity, and our flexibility. What we get is a direct result of what we do, what we say, and the way that we do both.

The meaning is the effect

To believe that the effects of what we do are a direct result of what we are doing is to be open to continuous learning. Everything that happens to us, every reaction we get, is the effect of what we are doing and the way we are doing it. The opposite of this is when you hear someone saying things like "That's her fault" or "That's your perception" (as if it is wrong) or "Not my problem" (when someone reacts to you in an adverse way).

Secondly, *everyone has their own unique perception of the world.* We can go so far as to say that there is no reality, there is only

Perception is all there is

perception. We filter what we experience through our various senses and we do this in ways that are unique to us. This does not make one person's perception right and another person's perception wrong; it merely makes them different. We are different in many ways. If we are willing to explore and learn from this difference, we ultimately learn how to cooperate and live together. We learn to accept other people for who and what they are.

When we are faced with a difference in our perception and that of others, very often the natural reaction is to seek out other perceptions that match with our own. In this way we can confirm our map of the world, but it does not lead to new learning. Only by going against some of these natural tendencies and being open to learning from difference can we develop and increase our influence.

FACTORS THAT CONTRIBUTE TO METAMESSAGES

Everything is a metaphor and as such carries information about the whole. It is the sum of the parts that communicate a metamessage about our intentions. If we want to get the "right" message across, we need to know what message each of the parts communicates, as well as the overall impression of the sum total of these parts.

FACTOR 1 ENVIRONMENT

Our environment is part of the metamessage, and it is often the first port of call for new contacts of our business.

I enter the offices of a potential client, a marketing company. Everything is light and bright. The dominant colors are yellow and natural wood. An elegant, modern flower display stands in the corner of reception. Beyond reception I can see clearly into the open-plan offices. Everyone's desk is the same, but everyone has their own personal effects. The receptionist smiles and asks if I would mind taking a seat while she gets the person I am booked to see. While I am seated, everyone who comes past asks me if I am OK and being looked after. There are sweets in the shape of fish in the bowl beside me and a stack of the latest magazines. I feel I could happily sit in this reception area for the rest of the afternoon.

I was later to discover that there is total openness in this company—The Yellow Submarine—to ideas and especially to feelings. Not much goes undisclosed. The board members were some of the most willing to open themselves to personal feedback that I have ever met. There is no difference between the desks of the managers, the board members, and anyone else in the business, and there is a real sense of equality. Everyone is part of the "crew."

We approach the office premises of our new client. It is a standard, new, purpose-built block on an industrial estate. We enter the reception area and immediately notice that this company has chosen to use space differently to many others with similar buildings. There is an open waiting area with richly textured and deep colored sofas. The receptionist is seated behind a highly polished wood reception desk with a high front. She greets us courteously and asks us to take a seat while she calls our contact. We sink into the soft sofas and notice that there is a PC with which we can access introductory information about the company. On the walls surrounding us are annual photos of the complete team of company employees.

This company—Intuitive Systems—has been chosen as a model of excellence for others in its field of software development. It is outperforming most of its competitors and achieving steady growth. It has the style of a family company and tremendous loyalty from all its employees. I felt welcomed and at home with this company and I was flattered to have been asked to work with it.

An interesting contrast to these experiences was the following one, a visit to a site of a company with which we were already working.

I had not been to this site before, even though I had worked with the company for a couple of years. I had difficulty finding it because the sign depicting the company name was obscured. When I eventually did find the entrance, I turned in and was stopped at the police security box and asked for identification. Once I was cleared, the security officer directed me to a building that I could barely distinguish at the back of the site. Seeing my puzzled look, he suggested I follow the car in front of me. The road went through an expanse of wasteland, which I assumed had once supported the manufacturing plants. I arrived at a building at the far side of the site. It had a new façade on the existing building behind it. I entered the reception, which resembled a doctor's waiting room of old with a sliding glass screen between me and what I assume was the reception office.

This latter company had been devolved from its parent company and was faced with the challenge of changing its outdated practices and finding a competitive new way of working that would help it build its business into the future. It was seeking to attract new clients, new business partners, and new suppliers.

And what about the following description of the headquarters of Yahoo!, a web portal?

In the front foyer, a visitor is greeted by a life-size papier mâché Elvis and trapezoidal sofas and chairs in the official corporate colors, purple and yellow. The curiosities that lie beyond include conference rooms named after the biblical plagues (Blood, Hail, Frogs, Locusts, Boils, etc.) marathon table-hockey games in the lunchroom, and a possible glimpse of the company's cofounder, David Filo, in distress jeans and T-shirt, and barefoot.

The founders of Yahoo! are renowned for doing what they really want irrespective of other demands on them. They have resisted some of the marketplace's aggressive tactics, for example they have a policy of only placing one banner advertisement per page and not using popup ads that have to be clicked away before you can access the page you want.

All environments tell a story

Our environment is an expression of who we are. At this very moment I sit overlooking a valley in the Dordogne in France. All the windows and doors are wide open and nothing impedes the view of the landscape of which we are a part. I have space and quiet in my surroundings.

All environments tell a story. Our surroundings are an expression of decisions we make, compromises we have agreed to, goals we have achieved, desires and obligations. Look around you now. What does your environment say about you? In what way is it a metaphor for who you are? What message does your environment give to people who come there? Do you know?

Anything outside of us constitutes our environment. This may include the buildings, the style of the offices, the surrounding area. However, it also includes the materials used by the company: the stationery, for example, and the way letters are written and addressed.

I received a letter from one of my long-standing suppliers on which my name was misspelt and which arrived in a window envelope with an address label stuck over the window.

I cannot be sure what this means or why the company has done it unless I ask. Nevertheless, it forms an impression. I make unconscious judgments about the company based on these details, just as I make judgments based on someone's nonverbal behavior. For example:

- ❏ *Is it losing the personal contact it has had with its customers?*
- ❏ *Is it watching costs or cutting corners by using up old supplies?*
- ❏ *Is it unconcerned about its image or unaware of how it may be perceived by its customers?*
- ❏ *Is it careless?*
- ❏ *Is it cutting corners in the training of its staff?*
- ❏ *Is it under such pressure that it is losing touch with the details of the business?*
- ❏ *Doesn't it care about its customers?*
- ❏ *Are staff failing to communicate with each other within the business?*

Every detail reflects something of the inner workings of that company. As Peters and Waterman said in A *Passion for Excellence*, coffee stains on the flipdown trays of an airplane mean the company doesn't do its engine maintenance right.

Ultimately the details are an expression of the person who heads up the organization. The external signs are a statement about how they communicate their values and what those values are. The external signs are also an expression of the relationships the leader has with the people who work with them. The external symbols point to the coherence or internal conflicts that may exist within the individual and therefore within the company.

Some notable examples of symbols that had a positive influence on me include:

- ❏ The "welcome home" card sent by the holiday company.
- ❏ The latest equipment on the desks of every employee.
- ❏ The comprehensive directions sent to guide me to the company premises.
- ❏ The bowl of fruit on the table in the meeting room.
- ❏ The Japanese Koi in the pond outside reception.
- ❏ The speed and personal style of the online chatroom designed to answer any queries I have on the company's website.

Some that created an altogether different impression:

- ❏ The windowless rabbit-hutch offices of the company development staff.
- ❏ The dead flowers in the vase on the reception desk.
- ❏ The marble staircase down to the senior managers' parking bays and the scuffed rubber one that proceeded to the floors reserved for the cars of the rest of the staff.
- ❏ The rubbish behind the desk of the airline check-in counter.
- ❏ The "difficult to see over" height of the reception desk.
- ❏ The streaks on the coffee cups.
- ❏ The security guard on reception building a matchstick boat!

FACTOR 2
HOW WE DRESS

A few years ago I went to an image consultant. I was curious to know how these consultants worked, as we were planning a form of image development as part of the work that we doing at that time, and I was also looking forward to some personal feedback. I wore what I thought was one of my best outfits. I was interested when the consultant, Chenube Roy, asked me what messages I wanted to give the world in the way I dressed and looked. I was impressed by this question, which dispelled the myth that all image consultants worked purely with what was on the outside. It provoked some thought and I replied: "Openness and a slightly sexy image." She looked at me in my calf-length skirt and high roll-neck sweater. She tugged at the large man's handkerchief that was poking out of my pocket, pulled a face of disbelief, and said "Really!" That was some of the most useful feedback I have ever had on my image.

What we wear communicates messages about what is important to us, both generally and in the moment when we picked that jacket or that suit out of the wardrobe.
One of my friends always wears clothing that has some unusual detail about it. Often it is the stitching that is different to the norm or it may be that there is an aspect of the design of the garment that is unique. It is never very obvious, but if you look carefully it is always there. What he wears says a lot about his personality and what is important to him.

Each of the following situations has something in common. In each case, the overall message that the managers were giving was at odds with their stated goals for the situation. As the old expression goes, "It's not what we say but the way that we say it," as well as what we don't say and what we don't mean to say but that slips out of our mouths almost unknowingly.

The managing director was responding to feedback that the staff wanted to meet with him informally more often than was the case currently. He usually did a "walkabout" at Christmas time, rarely more often than that. Having decided to get round and meet with people more often, he arranged to talk to groups of staff at the factory site. He wanted to be sure to get to see everyone, so he planned the time that he would spend with each group. When he started each group session, in order to help himself stick to the time he told them that he could only spend 10 minutes with them. The impression this gave far outweighed the real intention behind the talks.

A senior manager was invited to talk to one of the business teams to hear their ideas for taking ownership of some of the business issues. They felt they could support the directors' strategy for devolving decision making by forming project groups to make recommendations and decisions to improve the business processes. This senior manager was very much in favor of the objective of increased ownership and involvement in

**FACTOR 3
THE WAY WE BEHAVE
TOWARD OTHERS**

strategic issues throughout the business. However, each time a team member suggested an area with which they might get involved, the manager responded by saying that the directors were already looking at this issue. When a team member said they were unaware of this, the manager replied by saying that clearly they (the directors) needed to improve their communication with the company. The result of this was that team members stopped making suggestions for how they could assume ownership.

I had organized a series of feedback meetings with staff in a company in which I was doing some leadership training. The managing director, who was very much a champion for this training, had insisted that he come along to the meetings too. I invited the staff to give me open and honest feedback so that we could apply the learning from the first phase of the training to the next phase that was about to begin. Each time someone made a comment, the MD justified or gave reasons to explain the issue raised. If someone gave feedback that he perceived as negative, he defended the aspect of the training on which they were commenting. Eventually the staff stopped giving feedback.

FACTOR 4
THE WAY WE
DEMONSTRATE SKILLS

Aligning our behavior with our desired outcome is not only the most powerful form of influence, but a way of teaching to the unconscious minds of our listeners/observers.

A director wanted to introduce a new feedback scheme into the company, one where, instead of waiting for the twice-a-year appraisal, staff were encouraged to give and invite feedback continuously. He was due to present his thoughts for the scheme and the training that he felt would be needed at the board meeting that afternoon. During the morning he specifically and informally gave feedback to several of the members of the board in such a way that they found it easy to accept and were almost unaware that they had received "feedback" as such. Unconsciously this director was planting the seed that feedback can be an informal, everyday process.

Skilled trainers know that if they want to teach the principles of a topic—let's say "rapport"—they teach it first to the unconscious minds of their audience by doing it before they talk about it. For example, in the previous teaching session they would be very explicit about the way they build and maintain rapport. When they come to teach rapport as a topic, the unconscious minds of the people in their audience register that they know this already, because they have had a recent reference experience of what it is all about. They need never know this at a conscious level, but the metamessage is, "You know this."

Alicia was about to be promoted to the position of salesperson and was both excited and apprehensive about this. She had some very sophisticated relationship-building skills, but she was concerned that if she had a run of rejections she might lose her determination to persevere. She recognized in other situations in her life that sometimes when she was not winning she gave up.

Several of her colleagues were telling her how she could deal with this. Essentially they were telling her what they would do. However, one colleague remembered that Alicia was a good runner who frequently took part in marathons and had talked about her strategies for finding energy to keep going when she "hit the wall." The next time she talked of her concern about how she might handle rejections if she experienced them, he asked how she found the tenacity to keep going when she was running. It was as if a light bulb had gone on as she realized that she did already have (albeit in a different context of her life) the strategy for keeping going when things got difficult.

The advice that Alicia received from the majority of her colleagues is typical of how many people respond when they hear someone talking about problems—they told her what to do. However, the metamessage in doing this can be received as "We have the answers to your issues" and "You don't have the resources to solve this." Conversely, the metamessage of the colleague who helped her to find the strategy from within her own experience was, "You have all the resources you need within yourself already." This is an empowering way of responding to Alicia or anyone else with a personal issue for which they have not yet found a solution.

Teach first to the unconscious minds of your listeners

FACTOR 5
THE WAY WE MEET OUR
OWN OR OTHERS' NEEDS

David was a renowned chatterer in his department. This was OK to a point, but in recent months he had been beginning to disrupt his colleagues' concentration and work. His manager had spoken to him on a number of occasions about the need to let others get on with their work, but this had had little or no effect. As a desperate measure the manager had now instructed existing and new employees to the department not to speak to David during peak work times. Not to be deterred, David now often left the department to chat to people from other departments who met at the coffee machine. Sometimes he went to reception where he chatted with the receptionists. Managers from other departments started to complain. David's manager called him into her office on each occasion and spent several hours talking and seeking to coach David on the effect of his behavior.

The metamessage that the manager was potentially giving to David was, "Each time you disrupt others' work I will spend time with you—in fact more time than I spend with anyone else in the department." Without realizing it, the manager was playing right into David's hands (although he was not consciously aware of this) by giving him even more talk time than he was managing to get for himself.

FACTOR 6
OUR BELIEFS

I hope that you have experienced the company of someone who believed in you totally, someone who believed that no matter what you did you would always win through OK. It would not have mattered what that person said to you or how they said it, because through it all their belief would communicate itself to you in the form of the metamessage, "You have the ability to succeed in whatever you do." When I worked in ICL I had a manager that believed in me in this way. He gave me projects that I did not know how to do when I started them, but I learned the skills and the belief in myself as I worked my way through them.

Conversely, you may have experienced the company of someone who did not believe in you, someone who believed that you either did things for ulterior motives or were just lucky when you did succeed, and who seemed always to be waiting for your next mistake. Even if those people did praise or encourage you, if they did not believe in you and what you were capable of then that would cut through the behavior with the metamessage, "You are not OK."

My guess is that you respond to people according to what you think they believe about you. What we give others is often what they choose to connect with. Of course, the converse is true—what we get from others tells us a great deal about what we are choosing to connect to within them.

SUMMARY

A metamessage is the sum total of many factors, including:

❏ The timing of what we say.
❏ The environment in which we say it.
❏ The medium we use.
❏ What we wear.
❏ The extent to which we use the language and the preferred senses of our target audience.
❏ What is not said.
❏ What is presupposed in what we say.
❏ The metaphors we use.
❏ Our beliefs and the way we communicate them.
❏ Our awareness and sensitivity to others' needs.

All of these elements and more add up to an overall message that is "read" by the unconscious and sometimes the conscious minds of our listeners.

By understanding how the elements of our metamessage fit together and how they are filtered by the people with whom we are dealing, we can begin to establish the influence we are having in everything we do.

THOUGHT PROVOKERS

1   Look around you now. What is present in your surroundings? What characterizes your environment? Is it inherited and if so what decisions have you made either to accept it or change it? How is your environment a metaphor for the patterns you run in your life? How is your acceptance or influence of your surroundings symbolic of the decisions you make concerning the other bigger systems of which you are a part—for example your team, your organization, your family?

2   Visit your company as if you were an outsider. If possible, walk in the footsteps of someone who is entering your company as a guest or a visitor. Pay attention to those things to which you notice them paying attention. What are you drawn to? What do you hear? What values and impressions do these things give and how are they characteristic of patterns in the culture of the company? Notice especially how the space is used, how open or closed the area is, how easy it is to make contact with those people you want to reach, what is the decoration, and what accessories are there? What state are the surroundings in? What are people saying?

3   Invite feedback from your visitors to establish what they notice in their first impressions of the company. Ask them what they paid attention to and what significance they placed on what they saw, heard, and felt. Ask them what impressions they formed instantly and to what extent these impressions changed subsequently, especially what contributed to these impressions.

4   Consider all the actions you have taken so far today. What have you been an example of to others?

5   Think of someone you witnessed recently whose words were at odds with their actions. What effect did that have on you?

6   Think of someone whose words were at one with their actions. What effect did that have on you?

7   Someone whose self-esteem you would like to help boost asks you if you think they are right to stand their ground in respect of a decision they have made. What do you say?

8   What is the metamessage in the story opposite?

Not long ago I read a newspaper article describing the behavior of a schoolboy who had become so unruly that teachers were recommending that the headmaster expel him. The boy bullied other children, swore at teachers, and was usually involved in a fight at least a couple of times a week. The teachers had tried every form of punishment and detention they could think of but the boy would not conform.

Eventually the headmaster summoned the boy to his office and gave him an ultimatum: "You have this choice—either you accept the offer I am about to explain to you or you will be expelled." The boy said nothing.

The headmaster carried on, "This is the offer. You are to agree to bully once a week, to swear a total of five times a day (this was a lot less than the current behavior), and to fight once."

Programming

"It's about people, the rest is technology."
Communications company Ericsson, quoted in The Next
Common Sense

The process of coding talent is known as modeling. When you step into someone else's shoes and reproduce what they do and the results they achieve, you are modeling. Modeling involves reproducing the same sequence of thinking, language, and behavior patterns as your subject. To do this, you may also need to take on (albeit temporarily) their identity and beliefs. In effect, to use a computer metaphor, you are eliciting the program code needed to demonstrate the talent and you are running the program as and when you want it.

Reproducing excellence

The purpose of modeling talent in business is to reproduce excellence. If you want to reproduce the success of an outstanding salesperson, manager, or presenter, modeling enables you to do this. Equally, if you want to reproduce the way a successful, enterprising company or individual presents themselves through a remote medium such as the World Wide Web or email, you can do this too. If you want to discover how some people are able to thrive in the context of a network economy, you can learn how they do this so that you can do it for yourself.

These top performers will run mental and physical programs of which they are unaware and which will almost certainly not be in any book on standard selling techniques, management models, or presentation skills. The programs they run may be specific to the industry, the client, or even the place and occasion. Excellence, as such, is context specific. You may discover that parts of their program add little or no value and are redundant and that yet other parts can be developed. By discovering and developing what you learn you can not only reproduce the skill that that you are modeling but you can tweak and enhance it so that you can achieve an even higher level of skill than the original.

Excellence is context specific

NLP is an active process. It is a form of research into what works with the purpose of enabling us to reproduce and enhance success in ways that are unique. The more you model excellence, the more you discover. NLP operates at a higher level than most traditional training in the sense that it enables us not just to learn what works but *how* it works. The process of NLP offers ownership and discovery and enables you to learn how to learn. By embarking on a process that is NLP, we not only learn how to learn but increase our ownership and personal discovery in the whole process of personal and business growth.

Learning how to learn

10
Modeling

"It is rare that one cannot learn from another or from life's experiences, if the effort is made. Perhaps that is the secret of achieving a peaceful society; searching for each other's unique and special knowledge."

I f someone can do it, anyone can do it. That is the basis of modeling. Modeling is concerned more with the how than with the why. There is a joke that NLPers don't introduce themselves by saying "How do you do?" but "How do you do that?" Modeling is a state of curiosity and selflessness. It is a desire to listen, watch, respect, and learn from others as well as ourselves. Modeling is an interest in process over content.

Modeling is a state of curiosity

When my son sent emails from his travels around the world, I was initially interested in what he had to say, what he was doing, where he was, and where he was headed for next. My husband, however, was really interested in how my son's ability to communicate what he was doing matured as he traveled. His use of words and expressions developed a style and richness that we had never noticed before. On one occasion we got a copy of an email that went out to all his friends as well and I learnt things that no email addressed "dear Mum" was ever going to reveal. I was astonished at some of the content and said to my husband, "Just read what he is saying!" My husband replied, "Yes, but look at how he is saying it!"

THE IMPORTANCE OF MODELING

Modeling is one of the most important skills we need today. More than ever before, we need to be self-reliant in the way we learn, develop, manage ourselves, take initiatives, and cope with constant change. Even though you may work for a large organization, the chances are that no matter how much support you receive, you either already are or most certainly will be expected to be self-reliant in the way you respond to the challenges you face. There are few easy options at work and the pace is such that others are busy looking after themselves.

We need to be self-reliant

However, the good news is that most people have barely scratched the surface when it comes to drawing on their inner resources and few really know how to do this. Modeling is the answer. It is not just a technique, it is a lifestyle, such that wherever you are and whoever you are with you can be learning and growing.

Modeling is a way of achieving lifelong learning and true personal fulfillment. It is a way of respecting the unique talents that we all have.

Modeling is life-changing

I recently watched a TV program showing how the IQ tests that were once used for college selection in one part of the US discriminated against the young black population. These people did not score well on the qualities measured. However, a researcher discovered that when they experimented with another test that measured very different aptitudes, the same population excelled. The implication of relying on the original test was, in one of the boy's own words, "We have no option but to make a living by going on the streets and selling drugs." By introducing the new test the researchers were opening doors to education for this previously neglected group of people.

There are powerful implications in the yardsticks we use to "box" people into what is acceptable and what is not. Modeling goes way beyond a new test. It respects the fact that whatever talents we have are of value and can be directed toward our own good and for the good of others. To learn to model is to explode the myths of IQ stereotypes. It is to learn to respect and allow everyone their rightful place in the world. As the quote at the beginning of the chapter suggests, maybe our ability to model is the key to a peaceful society.

In the business context, we need to be exploring previously untapped resources. We need to learn from what every individual has to offer. If we do what we always did we get what we always got—a recipe for business suicide. So modeling opens up a completely new world in how we recognize potential and, more significantly, release it for the good of everyone.

Sitting by Nellie

Modeling can take many forms. Some of your most fundamental skills will have been learned by modeling others. Babies and young children are expert modelers. Only when they start learning by more traditional methods do they begin to lose this skill. Some traditional methods of schooling train out of us our most natural learning talent. "Sitting by Nellie" was the method by which many employees were taught to do their work. This only worked well if Nellie was a model of excellence or if the new employee was smart enough to know what worked and what didn't. Unfortunately, it often resulted in the reproduction of bad practice.

If we do what we always did, we get what we always got

You can model anything; people are excellent in many different spheres. You can, for example, have excellence in the ability to:

❏ Generate commitment and respect.
❏ Motivate yourself and others.
❏ Sell and influence.
❏ Achieve a personal best in sport.
❏ Listen.
❏ Speak a language fluently.
❏ Communicate using the latest technology.
❏ Network.
❏ Lead and inspire.

Equally, you can have excellence in your ability to:

❏ Get depressed.
❏ Sulk.
❏ Lose your temper.
❏ Remain untouched by emotion.
❏ Procrastinate.

- ❏ Worry.
- ❏ Resist change.
- ❏ Respond aggressively to others.
- ❏ Panic.

By modeling any of these you can develop a conscious awareness of the process, and with conscious awareness you have a choice, which is to continue the same process or to do something else. Merely the process of studying what we are doing and how we are doing it lifts us to a level of detachment in which we can choose what we do and, more importantly, what we continue to do in the future.

With conscious awareness you have choice

Many companies now have a system of mentoring whereby members of staff, as part of their development, are allocated to a more senior or more experienced employee in order to learn from them ("sitting by Nellie" relabeled). All too often, the success of this system hinges on the experienced employee's ability to impart their skills. Often they don't know their most powerful skills nor how they use them. If, however, the learner is equipped with NLP modeling skills, they can elicit the skills they need to learn irrespective of the awareness and skill level of their mentor. The subject being modeled can also benefit from this process by learning from feedback on how they structure their experience. With this awareness they can achieve greater consistency in the skills they have.

Mentoring

My very first full-time job was as a computer operator in the glass-manufacturing firm Pilkingtons. I had never worked on a computer before and I was allocated to Geoff to follow him around and learn what he did. Occasionally Geoff would explain what he was doing, but more often than not he would just do what he did (and at that time operating the computer sometimes meant a bit of engineering and a bit of fixing programs that crashed in the middle of the night when the programmers weren't around to sort out the problems). Geoff was very good at all of these things, but he wasn't very good at explaining to me what he did nor how he did it.

You can apply the process of modeling to yourself. You might, for example, want to reproduce an ability or skill that you have

Transferring a skill

in some areas of your life or work, in order to use it in other contexts. Let's suppose you are influential when dealing with colleagues but don't have the same level of influence with clients. You could model yourself in order to discover the difference between the two, so that you can use your influence in whatever context you choose.

One company that employed a telephone marketing team could not understand why there was such inconsistency in the results it was getting with some of its telemarketeers. With some clients they were very successful and were able consistently to convert a call into an appointment, but with others they struggled to get past the first few minutes of the conversation. What the company discovered when it modeled what was happening with these calls was that the telemarketeers were building mental images based on what they had heard from others in the company about the different groups of people they had to call.

One of the biggest differences between the successful calls and the unsuccessful ones was connected with the mental image the caller had in their mind as they made the call. For those that were most successful the caller imagined the recipient of the call in a light room, brightly lit. The image was vivid and in color and they imagined the other person as smiling. (This was entirely in their mind as they never saw the people they phoned.) For the ones that were unsuccessful the callers typically imagined the recipient of the call as being in a dark room, the image was defocused and gray in tone, and the person had a serious expression on their face. All this before they had even dialed the number!

By modeling the successful mental strategies they were able to train the previously less successful marketeers in these thinking techniques. The average conversion rate of call to appointment increased significantly.

STRATEGIES

We achieve the results we do through the programs we run in our minds and in our actions. Just as computer programs are a sequence of codes, so personal programs are a sequence of mental and behavioral codes. When you walk, talk, drive, read, or laugh, it is unlikely that you think consciously about how you do these things. The programs that make them happen are managed on your behalf by your unconscious mind. These programs are known as strategies.

Nevertheless, if you want to model excellence either in yourself or in other people, your aim is to elicit both these unconscious strategies as well as the conscious ones that enable you to do what you do. When you have the strategy for how someone manages their experience, you have the key to reproducing that experience for yourself.

When a chef produces a gourmet dinner, not only is he following a recipe for the ingredients, he is also following a recipe for thinking and behavior. He may, for example, have an image of what he wants the dish to look like accompanied by the aroma of the final meal. He may also be concerned with timing and the look and feel of the ingredients. He has a unique way of achieving the result.

I watched a program on BBC television in which companies were invited to put their business up for overhaul. One of these programs featured Mo's corner shop. This was a typical corner shop, packed full of thousands of different product lines, many of them beyond their shelf life and many almost impossible to find easily on the cramped shelves. So Mo applied to the BBC team of experts to have them redesign his business. He was under threat from the big supermarkets nearby, so not only did the BBC team want to increase the efficiency of the shop but they also wanted to find ways to differentiate Mo's shop from these bigger competitors.

The expert team set about reorganizing and relabeling the products on the shelves. They installed self-clean, maintenance-free bread ovens to supply daily fresh bread. They introduced a new stock control system and eliminated the 80 percent of products that had not sold for years. And they went into Mo's office, where they found that his method of personal organization was to use three-year-old diaries (or older), cross out the days, and overwrite them with the current year's days and dates. So the office came under the experts' scrutiny and revision as well.

Unconscious strategies

After all of this and much more, Mo was left with a completely overhauled shop. The time needed to find and buy items had been cut by at least 50 percent and his customers were delighted with the changes. But what about Mo? He was delighted too, although he appeared at times to be a little bemused. This was not surprising really when you start to deduce what must have been going on in his head or, more to the point, how *it was going on in his head. Mo's shop was an expression of his internal structuring. His shop and everything about him were a mirror to his internal experience.*

The methods used by the BBC team (the results of which were wonderful, in the short term) are the methods used by so many businesses wanting to update and bring about a culture change. The remedy so often seized on is to change the environment. How many businesses and shops have you seen go about a facelift in just this way? Yet the facelift that would really make the difference is the inner facelift. This is what modeling is all about. By modeling what was going on in Mo's inner experience, we can deduce not only how he has got what he has got but also, to take it one step further, what he might need to change in his inner world to really make a difference.

DECISION-MAKING STRATEGIES

We have strategies for making decisions such as what to have for dinner, where to go on holiday, how to plan our day. There is a pattern to the way we do this.

For example, the way I decided to write this book was:

1   I saw others (close friends) write a book.
2   I imagined myself writing a book.
3   I asked myself repeated questions over time about what the topic would be and how I would do it.
4   I looked and listened for examples of how others did this.
5   When eventually I could clearly see myself writing a book (even down to seeing the context in which I would write it), I got a feeling that the time was right.
6   I committed myself by telling people what I planned to do.

Understanding a strategy gives me choice about how and when I use it. Equally, if someone wanted to influence my decision about writing, it would help if they understood my strategy rather than trying to impose their own.

Suppose you identify that your partner in negotiation has a strategy that involves:

1 Creating a picture of what they want (visual).
2 Asking themselves a question about the viability of that outcome (auditory).
3 Getting a feeling of certainty that this is what they want (feelings).

By matching this strategy you will be helping and influencing their decision-making process. Let's say their outcome was to ask for promotion to a new job. You could match their strategy by saying:

Matching strategies

1 "Imagine what it would be like to approach your boss, to see yourself with her clarifying your future" (visual).
2 "Ask yourself if that is a feasible thing to do" (auditory).
3 "And you will instinctively know whether this is the right approach for you" (feelings).

It is important to remember that if you ask someone "How do you do that?"—if you ask them consciously to recall their strategy—it is unlikely that they will be able to give it to you. They may either say "I don't know," or they will tell you what they think they do. This is rarely the same as what they actually do. To elicit a strategy, the person you are modeling needs to be doing or reliving the experience that you wish to model.

To find out more about how to model a skill, see the shortcut at the end of this chapter.

MODELING IN BUSINESS

Modeling in business has led to significant breakthroughs in the way that skills are taught. Traditionally, companies used standard training programs to teach standard skills. More often than not, trainees were left to their own devices to adapt these skills to their unique environment. There are unique patterns that work in one company, one department, or one market segment, and that will not work in another. Modeling enables you to elicit these context-specific patterns in order to reproduce excellence in a place of your choice. By choosing the people who excel within your organization, not only will you be able to reproduce their levels of success, you will also be able to help those same people achieve greater consistency in their own performance.

Consistency in performance

When PricewaterhouseCoopers wanted to reproduce the outstanding performance of some of its top project leader coaches, it decided to use NLP to model the strategies that worked. It selected its outstanding performers and I was invited to model them to find out how they do what they do. I watched them in action working with groups of trainees and talked with them about their beliefs, their values, and their sense of identity and purpose.

What emerged was a consistent pattern for the ones who achieved results significantly above the norm. All had a quality of selflessness, a purpose that was beyond themselves, and all had values that included love and care for others. At the level of behavior they were all skilled in the way that they used metaphor and visionary thinking. And they were so dedicated to meeting the learning needs of their trainees that if they did not do that to their satisfaction (in one case especially) this resulted in the coach's temporarily feeling physically sick. (I did not necessarily want to others to have to reproduce that!) However, once we knew what some of the key pieces were in the strategies (and there was much more), I was able to present this to others who had not yet achieved the same level of excellence.

Refining the strategy

The joy of modeling is that you can refine the model by testing which elements add to excellence and which detract or make no difference. By taking away one element at a time, you can determine how this affects the overall result. This enables you to generate the most effective model, which you can use to teach others, including the person you modeled.

This process applies when modeling anything, whether an individual, a team, or a complete organization. The skills it takes to sell a luxury car are quite different from those it takes to sell a software package. The skill required to motivate a group of production line workers is quite different from that needed to motivate advertising account executives. The skill needed to communicate face to face may be very different from that needed to communicate via the World Wide Web. The skills you need in the rapidly unfolding Information Age are vastly different to those that might have stood you in good stead in previous times. Modeling enables you to uncover the uniqueness of the model, the quality of the inborn talent, and the natural skill.

Modeling enables you to uncover natural skill

A client of mine said, "This modeling is the secret weapon for today's business if everyone but knew it." It is easy to access the strategies you want, although it is not yet usual practice to do this in business. Any individual or organization that employs this kind of thinking is still going to be well ahead of the game for several years to come.

We can find useful strategies behind any behavior. It is the process of what we do that is always valuable, even if the content is not. We need to look at all the behaviors we use to uncover the strategies that lie behind them. By doing this we can find that even behind some of our weaknesses we have strategies that are invaluable used in the right context.

There are useful strategies behind every behavior

Take the example of someone who sulks. I know of people who can sulk for hours, days, weeks, and in some cases years! This might not seem a valuable skill to have, but behind the sulking lies the strategy of maintaining one emotional state for a period of time. In this context it is a negative skill, but suppose this same person wanted to maintain a state of confidence or motivation and had not succeeded in doing so. Where do they look for the answer? Not to self-help books and not to other people—what they want is what they already have. They have the strategy for maintaining a state, all that they have to do is transfer that strategy to another emotional state. In the rest of this section we are going to explore how to do this.

There are companies that are modeling already. Examples of business modeling projects include the following:

❏ A major car manufacturing company encouraged its employees to invest time in their personal development. It funded everyone to learn something new on one condition, that it was not to do with their work. Some people learnt a new language. Some learnt how to play a musical instrument. Some took up a new sport or hobby. Whatever they did, they did because they wanted to. This was a smart move on the part of the company. What it was doing was strengthening its employees' strategies for doing for what they really wanted (outcome thinking) and for learning. One of the goals of the organization at this time was to be a learning organization, in which learning was a fundamental part of the culture, and the strategy it adopted was a powerful way of achieving this.

❏ A marketing company decided it would model the way that the founders of the company brought in new business. Until this time no one else in the company had the same consistent level of success in the way they did this.

❏ An IT manufacturing business modeled the way that one of its leaders successfully negotiated between the different cultures in the business after a merger.

❏ A building society modeled the way that one of its directors inspired those who joined the business.

The point is that modeling is a very different way of thinking and working to the past. Giving people in a company the skills to model is giving them the means of generating ways of finding solutions to any situation they encounter.

A BENCHMARK FOR EXCELLENCE

The result of much of the modeling that has taken place has been the discovery of certain patterns of excellence. I offer this benchmark for excellence with caution. It is not fixed, it continues to develop. I offer it as a shortcut to excellence today, but tomorrow who knows?

THE ELEMENTS OF EXCELLENCE

I use the term excellence to mean individuals and organizations who consistently achieve the goals they set themselves. It covers especially people and organizations who are achieving goals that not only benefit themselves but also people and organizations beyond themselves—whose goals are not just for personal wealth but for richness of life. People and organizations who achieve excellence in this way do the following:

They pay attention to the role they play in the larger system of which they are a part. They have a purpose to contribute to this bigger system in a positive way, to add value. Richard Branson, for example, seeks to create systems of fair trading in the markets in which he operates. There is increasing resistance to businesses that trade only for their own profit and a growing move toward those businesses that respect the environment and take an ecological approach to the way they trade. Companies that sustain their success over time are now the ones who can network and create genuine win/win scenarios with their employees, clients, and suppliers, as well as anyone with whom they have contact.

Systems

They have a commonly held and understood mission or identity. If it is a team or organization, this mission will be an expression of what each team or company member really wants and truly demonstrates in their moment-by-moment behavior. Successful startup companies, for example, are ones whose motivation is their passion for the work. Just as a strong sense of self is the basis for individual confidence, so a coherent mission is the base for a solid and attractive business.

Mission

The founder of Yahoo! says that he does this work because he loves it, even previously when there was no money in it and he believed there would never be a significant financial return. The business is an expression of his personal identity. This company is now valued in billions of dollars.

They hold and live out beliefs of excellence. They believe that:

Beliefs

❑ Each person is unique and it is important to respect that difference.
❑ Everyone makes the best choice available to them at the time they make it.

❏ There is no failure, only feedback, and consequently we are always learning if we choose to think this way.

❏ Behind all behavior is a positive intention if we want to find it.

❏ The significance of our communication is not in its intention but its effect.

❏ There is a solution to every problem.

❏ The person with the most flexibility in thinking and behavior has the best chance of succeeding.

❏ Mind and body are one and each influences the state of the other.

❏ We have all the resources we will ever need within ourselves right now.

❏ We learn by doing, reviewing, theorizing, choosing, and acting again—learning is an active process.

❏ Knowledge, thought, memory, and imagination are the result of sequences and combinations of ways of filtering and storing information—they are strategies we have developed, often unconsciously, to deal with life as we have experienced it.

❏ If we do what we have always done we will get what we have always got, so if what we are doing is not working we need to do something different.

❏ Our influence comes from within ourselves.

❏ The only person in the world we can change is ourselves.

These beliefs are explained in detail throughout the book and some particularly in Chapter 14.

Capabilities

People and organizations who achieve excellence are also capable of:

❏ Sensitivity toward themselves and others. They are able to recognize changes in their own and others' states and respond to those changes. They consistently put themselves in the shoes of the people with whom they are dealing, in order to know and take responsibility for the effect of their communication.

❏ Flexibility in being able to change what they are doing and how they are doing it when what they are doing isn't working. As a comparison, for years people in some market sectors have been taught a specific sales procedure—10 steps to selling double glazing, insurance, a car. Probably even worse are salespeople who don't use any steps at all. How different it is when you are dealing with someone who employs both sensitivity and flexibility in the way they approach and respond to you.

❏ Thinking in outcome terms and dovetailing their outcomes with those of others so that they achieve a win/win situation, meaning success for everyone involved.

❏ Building lasting relationships and strengthening the networks that surround them.

❏ Learning continuously from everything that happens to them, no matter whether it is initially seen to be good or bad (the result is that they turn everything to "good").

❏ Being interested in and curious about what is happening around them and the people they meet, and demonstrating this in the way they are open to what they can learn from others.

❏ Acting and speaking on a day-by-day basis that lives out their mission, their beliefs, and their capabilities. By watching and listening to them it is evident what their mission, beliefs, and capabilities are. Their behavior is congruent, consistent, free of mixed messages. They operate on a set of principles that forms the basis of everything they do.

Behavior

❏ Changing their behavior so that they continually increase their flexibility while remaining true to their values.

❏ Asking questions in a way that allows them to learn from themselves and others.

❏ Asking for feedback and giving feedback when they have permission to do so.

❏ Enacting the behavior they want from others so that they lead by example.

❏ Recognizing that their environment and their appearance are an expression of who they are and what they think and getting feedback to find out if that is true for them.

Environment

❏ Taking responsibility for influencing their environment so that it supports the outcomes they want to achieve.

❏ Respecting their environment and always leaving it "better" than the way they found it.

SHORTCUT TO MODELING A SKILL

NLP is a process of modeling and the rest of this book explores the details of how you can do that with skill and professionalism. This shortcut is an introduction to that process. It is what we do already but often unconsciously.

1 Identify the skill that you want to model and reproduce. Be specific in the definition of that skill. For example, you may know someone who can:
   ❑ Get and hold the audience's attention within seconds of the start of a presentation.
   ❑ Make decisions.
   ❑ Wake themselves up in the morning without the aid of an alarm clock.
   ❑ Set realistic time targets that they consistently achieve.
   ❑ Start the day in a positive frame of mind.
   Decide specifically what skill you want to reproduce and in what context you want to be able to use it.

2 Select a person, or people, in the company whom you consider demonstrate excellence in the skill. Choose the top performers. Be sure you understand what you mean by excellence. Define excellence in terms of the results that your model of excellence achieves. Define excellence in terms of what you see, hear, and feel when this top performer is displaying this skill.

3 Observe your model in action to identify the following:
   ❑ What specifically they do and how do they do it.
   ❑ Any subtle behavior patterns—watch their eye movements and their nonverbal behavior.
   ❑ How they manage their environment.
   ❑ Their language patterns—which filters do they use?
   ❑ What beliefs and values they demonstrate and express.
   ❑ How they communicate a sense of identity.
   ❑ What purpose they seem to or say that they fulfill?

4 Question your model. First, ensure that they associate into an experience when they are using the skill you wish to model. When you are certain they are associated (they are imagining themselves using the skill), be sure to phrase your questions in the present tense to keep them associated, e.g., "What are you seeing?" "What are you saying to yourself?" and so on. You are interested in the

"what" and the "how" of what they do and not the "why."
Check out their thinking at each of the logical levels. For
example, you can ask them:

❏ "What are you aware of in your environment?"
❏ "What are you saying and doing?" (Useful to compare this
with what they are actually said and did in your
observations.)
❏ "What are you thinking?" (Watch their eye movements,
which will give more information about their internal
strategy than their conscious answer to the question.) If
you notice them using visual eye accessing cues, for
example, ask them, "What do you see?"
❏ "What are your capabilities?"—one of them will be the
skill you are modeling.
❏ "What is important to you at this time?" (This is to elicit
values.)
❏ "What do you believe?"—about yourself, about others,
about the situation.
❏ "How would you describe yourself?" (What is your identity?)
❏ "How do you connect with other systems of which you are
a part?"

Get feedback throughout to ensure that your subject is
comfortable and happy with the way you are going about this.

5 Have someone else model the skill and compare your
findings with theirs.

6 Now reproduce the thinking and behavior patterns of your
subject so that you take on their strategy.

7 Test your model by taking away one element at a time as
you use it. If the element isn't key to the process it won't
make any difference. In some cases taking away an element
may even enhance the process.

8 Do the results that you achieve match the results that your
model achieves? If they do you have been successful; if
they don't, go back and find out what other elements make
a difference.

9 Note down the strategy so that you can continue to use and,
if appropriate, develop it.

SUMMARY

The applications of NLP grow every day. It has been used to find out how famous leaders generate commitment and passion. We have used NLP to find out how they think, how they use language, and what subtle changes in their body language influence the responses they get. We have studied skilled negotiators, people who can discuss the most sensitive of issues and lead the discussion to an agreement that gains the commitment of all involved. We are also using NLP to model the successful startup companies in the world of high technology.

Sport has given a great deal to business thinking in recent years. An understanding of how top athletes excel enables us to grasp the components of self-motivation and take those principles for ourselves.

There are many, many more examples: Salespeople who can relate to their customers' unexpressed needs, presenters who can put over information in a compelling, motivating way, consultants who by the most elegant of questions can trigger off profound change. How do they do it? With NLP we are learning and we can continue to learn the answers.

The skills and techniques explained in the later chapters of this book are the result of modeling excellence. When you engage in NLP you engage in a powerful learning process that continually evolves. This is continuous improvement

The result of modeling is conscious competence, a mastery of the skills you have and the skills you want to have. With practice these skills and ways of thinking become a part of your unconscious competence; you don't have to think about them, they become a natural part of who you are. In its simplest form NLP is a process you have been using all of your life. In its most sophisticated form it is a way of generating excellence in everything you do, as an individual, as a team, as a company.

Some people have shied away from NLP because of the passion with which others have proclaimed its benefits. Nevertheless, some of the concerns about this enthusiasm and zeal are to do with the power of the technique. It works. It does indeed make a difference.

THOUGHT PROVOKERS

1 In what unique ways do you add value to:
   - ❏ Your family?
   - ❏ Your role in your business?
   - ❏ Your friendships?
   - ❏ The community of which you are a part?
   - ❏ Life?

2 Think about the events you have planned for the rest of this week. Are there any about which you don't feel too confident or happy? Think of someone you know who could handle these events in the way you would like to. Step into their shoes and imagine yourself handling these events as if you were that other person.

3 Which people have been the main influences on the way you are today? What is it about each one that you have incorporated into the person you are?

4 Who would you most like to resemble in skill or in style? Is there a colleague or a friend whose style and skill you admire? Imagine how you might come to resemble them.

One day a man was tending his garden, which bordered the desert in Arizona. Dusk was descending and he heard in the distance the sound of motorbikes. A gang of Hell's Angels rode up, attacked him, tied him to the back of one of the bikes, and drove him into the desert. There they left him barely alive as night fell. The man survived the night and began to regain consciousness as the sun appeared above the horizon.

He knew that the sun in the desert means certain death. Without food, water, or shelter he stood no chance of survival. Then at his side he noticed a small bush. He crawled underneath and curled up using the little shade there was to protect himself from the burning rays of the sun. He felt despair—no one knew where he was.

Just at that moment he saw a falcon landing on the branch of the bush. To the man's amazement the falcon spoke and asked, "Can I help you?"

Shocked, the man replied, "I am dying of thirst, my mouth and tongue are swollen. To survive I need water."

"Look behind you," said the falcon. "There is a snake. Follow

the snake, for it knows where the water seeps out of the rocks. There you will be able to drink."

The man returned to the bush, and the next day the falcon came back. "How are you?" the falcon asked.

"I have drunk but I need food to survive—water alone is not enough."

"Stay quiet and wait until the antelope passes by. When it does, follow it—it can show you where the cactus plants are whose flesh you can eat."

Sure enough, when the man followed the antelope he found food and was able to eat. Feeling fitter, he returned to the bush and once again the falcon arrived. "Can I do anything for you?" it asked.

"Yes," replied the man. "Although I have drunk and eaten I still need salt to survive. How can I get the salt I need to live?"

"Have no fear," replied the falcon. "The fox also needs salt. If you follow the fox you will see where it finds the rocks to lick that will give you the salt you need."

The man did as the falcon said and the next day returned to find that the bush under which he had sheltered was burned and charred. "What will I do now?" asked the man. "I have no shelter, I will burn to death."

Then the man realized he had been out in the desert each day following the animals. He had learned how to find food, water, and salt. He knew how to survive. He noticed the rich colors of the sky as the sun dipped low on the horizon, the blues, the purples, and the gold of the sun itself. He heard the exquisite songs of the birds in the distance and he felt an inner peace and joy.

"Shall I show you the way home?" asked the falcon.

The man thought for a moment and then said, "I think I'll stay a little longer."

11

Strategies for Successful Living

"We have different gifts, according to the grace given us."
Romans 12:6

We are creatures of habit. Our lives follow patterns that we take with us wherever we go. I remember a phone call from someone I had met on a course. He explained, "I just wanted to tell you that I am going through a bad patch in my life. My relationship with my partner was not working out so I decided to finish it. And I have been very unhappy in my job so I have decided to resign. And I wanted to tell you that on top of all that I have decided to leave this country—I am fed up with the climate and the culture here." And he thought that he would not take his patterns with him!

It is our patterns in thinking and behaving that create our response to our circumstances, *not* the circumstances themselves. It is only by becoming aware of these patterns or habits that we can begin to choose the life we want. Running away from what we don't want is not the answer. We remain the constant that creates our circumstances, unless we choose to look within to uncover and review those patterns that are making our lives what they are.

STRATEGIES FOR SUCCESS

These patterns and habits are known as strategies in NLP terms. A strategy is a sequence of thoughts and behaviors based on a set of beliefs and a sense of self. We all have characteristic elements in our strategies for both our resourceful and unresourceful states. We have learned strategies that can work for us or against us. Once we are aware of what we are doing when our lives are going well and what we are doing when our lives are not going well, we have choice. By making the unconscious conscious in this way we eliminate the need for judgment and through awareness we create freedom.

We have learned strategies that can work for us or against us

"Those able to realise that the thinking of today is about strategy and communication rather than technology alone will be able to run rings around the pure technologists."
Peter Small, The Entrepreneurial Web

Harry was concerned with his response to some of the people in his organization. He was aware that he treated some people with respect and courtesy at all times and yet with others it was all he could do to contain his frustration and aggression. He knew that the former was the way he wanted to be with everyone, not only because of his values as a human being but also because it made good business sense.

When he talked about the people he treated with respect (who were also the people with whom he learned the most), he looked directly at me and he talked about himself using "I." All his gestures were close to his chest (his heart). When he talked about the people with whom he had difficulty, he stopped saying "I" and said "you" or "one" instead. He indicated these people in his thinking by pointing to them in the air as if they were up and to his left, away from him. When he talked about the people he respected his whole face softened, he spoke in a relaxed manner, and his whole demeanor was one of ease. When he spoke of the people with whom he had difficulty, his voice as well as his facial muscles hardened and his body state was one of tension.

Peter wanted to find a way to get some personal space in his life. He ran a successful business and he worked almost without

a break from the time he arrived in the morning to midnight each day, taking work home with him. Sometimes he even worked until one or two o'clock in the morning. When he thought of how he wanted to spend his time with his family his whole body relaxed. His speech slowed and he paused between sentences. Also when others asked him questions he paused thoughtfully before he answered. When he started to think of the problems, which was often, he began to interrupt others leaving no space between sentences, either his own or those of others. His speech accelerated. His patterns in behavior, especially his spoken behavior, were his patterns in life.

Our every move, every gesture, every intonation and speech pattern reveal the patterns we run in our lives as a whole. Peter's lack of space in speech was a perfect metaphor for the lack of space in his life. We cannot not communicate our issues to the world at large, but we can learn to listen to these issues so that we can coach ourselves and others.

THE GROOVE IN THE WELL

At our home in France we have a well dating back to the seventeenth century. There is a groove in the front of the well where the rope to lower and raise the bucket has been pulled for all these years. It would be difficult to get the rope positioned in any other place than in this groove—the rope naturally defaults to the groove.

The rope defaults to the groove

It is the same with our patterns. Once the groove is cut, the easiest choice is for us to do what we have done before. Unfortunately, this is not a recipe for success in business. You may be familiar with the expression "if it ain't broke don't fix it." Today it is more likely that if it ain't broke it is probably redundant! We don't get many second chances—we take our chances or our chances pass us by.

What we need increasingly to be able to do is to cut new grooves for ourselves, and to do so daily, so that we are continuously making new connections in our behavior and our thinking. To do so we need first of all to find the behaviors that we want and then we need to practice them until they become a natural choice. We already have these alternative choices in our repertoire. We just need to note when we are behaving in a way that is in line with how we want to be and mark it out (anchor it) so that we can access it when we choose.

A delegate on one of my courses who had lived a fairly depressed life and was often in a down state said, "If there is one thing that I have learned with NLP it is that if I ever experience a resourceful state, anchor the bugger!"

CODING STRATEGIES

Before I started to write this morning, in my head I saw the title of the chapter I was going to work on. I pictured any writing I had done to date on this subject. I asked myself what was important to me about this subject right now in my life and how I was using this topic for myself today. I remembered images of situations where I had used this topic to make a difference for myself and I also began to imagine (by picturing them) situations that might occur during the day that would be helped by my paying attention to this theme. I began to feel associated and experienced a sense of satisfaction. As I allowed that to develop, it became a feeling of eager anticipation of what I could say when I sat down to write. I started to create some of the sentences and examples I would use.

The above is a strategy.

Yesterday I was feeling tired. My husband used what I considered to be an emotive word in something he said to me. It was an emotive word because for me it was an anchor for feelings of inadequacy. I heard the word and started to repeat what he said to me over and over in my mind. I told myself that he "should" not have said that and began to imagine ways in which I make a point to him in conversation. I imagined him avoiding this indirect feedback and started to feel annoyed. I remembered (by picturing them) situations in the past (that didn't involve him at all) in which I had had similar feelings. The feelings intensified. He spoke to me again. I snapped back.

The above is also a strategy.

The ability to stand back and recognize our strategies is the ability to transcend limiting states of mind.

Strategies consist of much more than thinking patterns; they consist of the way we structure our beliefs, our values, our sense of purpose, our sense of identity, and more. However, if we start with a simple approach to modeling our thinking strategies, we can code the elements. For example, we can have any of the following elements in a strategy:

❏ An image that we see externally—Visual/external—V^e
❏ An image in our mind that we remember—Visual/internal/remembered—V^{ir}
❏ An image that we create in our mind—Visual/internal/construct—V^{ic}
❏ A sound that we remember—Auditory/internal/ remembered—A^{ir}
❏ A sound that we construct—Auditory/internal/ construct—A^{ic}
❏ An inner dialog—Auditory/Inner dialog—A^{id}
❏ A feeling that we experience physically—Kinaesthetic/external—K^e
❏ An emotion that we feel—Kinaesthetic/internal—K^i

I have frequently used my cycling as an example of modeling and one of the significant learnings for me was to learn how to match my husband's hill-climbing techniques. To model a skill we have to want to do it and believe we can do it. I most certainly wanted to learn this skill as I so frequently got left behind on the hills—and some of the hills in France are very long! I also believed that I could do it. I had learned to cycle on the flat as well as my husband and I firmly believed that at a minimum I could at least learn to keep up with him.

The strategy I had been using was to see a hill approaching (Visual external), tell myself "Oh no this is going to be a problem" (Auditory internal dialog), picture how difficult it was going to be (Visual internal construct), start to feel frustrated with myself (Kinaesthetic internal), and go round that loop until I got off the bike or lagged behind feeling pretty fed up! So the sequence was:

The ability to transcend limiting states of mind

$$V^e \rightarrow A^{ic} \rightarrow V^{ic} \rightarrow K^i \rightarrow$$

Then I decided to model my husband's strategy and started by watching him. I noticed that he didn't look up at all, he looked down at the pedals or the ground all the time (Visual external, although a different visual external to the one I had been using). He maintained a regular rhythm with his pedaling (Kinaesthetic external). That was all I could get by watching him. I tried these bits of the strategy and it made a difference. I got up the hill at a consistent speed, but it hurt! I was aware of the pain in my thighs all the way up.

So I then asked my husband about his strategy (I didn't use those words). I told him what I thought I had discovered about his strategy and he confirmed that was what he did. However, he added some new pieces that I could only get by questioning or by watching his eye movements. When he looked down he said he did indeed watch the pedals but only fleetingly—he listened to the regular rhythm of the pedals as they turned (Auditory external), he said something to himself like "That's good" (Auditory internal dialog), and he felt satisfied (Kinaesthetic internal). So I asked him about the pain and he said that yes, he felt pain (Kinaesthetic external), but he told himself that the more pain he felt the fitter he was getting (Auditory internal dialog) and he felt good about the pain (Kinaesthetic internal).

This was quite a different strategy from the one that I had been using and there were some key pieces I had not picked up the first time round. His strategy coded was:

$$V^e \rightarrow A^e \rightarrow A^{id} \rightarrow K^i$$ and anywhere in there if he became aware of pain he would insert a loop $(K^e \rightarrow A^{id} \rightarrow K^i)$

I have just returned from a cycling circuit with my husband that included several hills and we made it to the top at the same time for most of them—I even got to the top first on a few!

WHY IT IS IMPORTANT TO LEARN HOW TO MODEL

If your work depends in any way on your ability to influence others, to do this with excellence you need to know how to model. We all have strategies for how we learn, for how we make decisions, for how we buy, for how we motivate ourselves… The list is endless. So if we want to influence ourselves or others, we can only do so if we use the relevant strategy. If you are already good at influencing and you have never come across the concept of modeling, then you probably do this unconsciously. However, we cannot leave these skills to chance and intuition— we need to be masters of our trade. The more skillful and respectful influencers know how to detect the strategy of the person with whom they are dealing and how to use that strategy to adapt their communication to suit the individual.

We need to be masters of our trade

For example, if you want to help someone make a decision and you have learned that their strategy for decision making involves them creating an internal image, then asking themselves a question in order to get an internal feeling that lets them know the decision, you can adjust the way you summarize your discussion with them. To match their strategy you can say, "Imagine the scenario in the future (you might be more specific here if it is appropriate) (Visual construct), and ask yourself how is this going to make a difference to you (A^{id}), and you will sense that this is the decision that fits for you (K^i)."

At the end of Chapter 20 I describe a very elegant use of a learning strategy by Robert Dilts (one of the leading creative developers of the use of NLP) to help a boy who had been described as learning disabled spell complex words and regain his belief in his ability to learn. If you are a manager you need to know the strategies of the people who work for you to enable them to reach their true potential. If you are a parent you need to know the learning strategies of your children to help them be the individuals they are meant to be. If you are a salesperson you need to know the buying strategies of your customers. If you are a member of a team you need to know the motivational strategies of your fellow team members. There really is no end to the contexts in which this is important in your dealings with others.

There is no end to the contexts in which this is important

This also applies to yourself. If you want to write you need to know your best writing strategy. If you want to motivate yourself you need to know your motivation strategy. I have just received an email from someone who uses NLP to help himself improve the quality of his life after being diagnosed with

Parkinson's disease. When you know your own strategies you can use them, modify them, develop them, transfer them to other contexts in your life, and if you wish replace them.

TOTE

You may be thinking that I am introducing the concept of gambling to modeling! Far from it—modeling is a way of ensuring certainty and consistency in the results we achieve. The TOTE I refer to here is not the betting kind but stands for Test→Operate→Test→Exit.

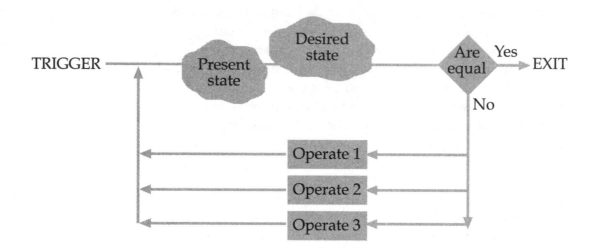

The principle is that our behavior is driven or motivated by an outcome and we recognize when we have achieved our outcome by a unique set of evidence criteria (i.e., what we will be seeing, hearing, and feeling when we have achieved the outcome). We are constantly comparing our present state to our desired state to find out if they match. When they do match we know that we have reached the exit, i.e., we have achieved our outcome. If the present state does not match the desired state, we have to do another operation to discover if that makes a difference.

We are running TOTEs throughout our lives comparing where we are with where we want to be and taking actions to bring us closer to the exit and eventually to the exit itself. An interesting observation from modeling leaders in business over many years is that they keep going until they have reached a successful exit, whatever it takes, whereas others who do not naturally emerge as leaders exit, but at an earlier point than their original outcome determined.

In effect when I was modeling my husband's cycling I was running a TOTE. I knew what the exit was: for me to reach the top of the hill either at the same time as my husband or before him. And I wanted to have enough breath to keep on cycling at the same rhythm. After my first pass at cycling my state did not match the desired state, so I knew that some of the operations in the TOTE were missing. That prompted me to question my husband.

The key here is not just to ask the person you are modeling. What they think they know and what they really know are two very different things. It is key to have the subject imagine that they are doing the act you want to reproduce. Alternatively, you can have the person actually do the thing you want them to model. In my case I could not keep up with my husband long enough to ask the questions and talking was not a part of his strategy. So by questioning and watching for clues as he talked about his strategy, I got the remaining operations that enabled me to exit the loop.

What they think they know and what they really know are two very different things

Essentially the TOTE is a feedback loop designed to prompt you to find what you need to achieve your desired state. Key skills for successfully navigating the TOTE in order to be able to model are sensitivity to what is happening, a willingness to learn from feedback, and the flexibility to do or learn something different when what you are doing is not working.

Our days are a series of TOTEs. Some repeat every few moments, some every few hours, some perhaps every few days or weeks. And there will be some TOTEs that only repeat every few years or maybe longer. The value of knowing someone over time is that you are in a position to learn about the TOTEs with a longer time frame.

Living by TOTEs

By modeling we discover the structure by which we and others are getting results. By choosing qualities that we admire and that get results we value, we are able to model how we or others get those results. And in the process of doing that we are valuing the structures that we uncover, even if some of them are currently being used unproductively.

When my son was reprimanded for unofficially getting himself down to Southampton on a school trip to join his friends and finding a place to stay, he was in trouble for not doing this through the official channels and for not letting anyone know where he was. However, what he was doing was showing great initiative and determination to get to where to where he wanted to be. This same son has traveled round the world and is now working in Australia.

SHORTCUT TO DEVELOPING A STRATEGY

I discussed earlier in this chapter the concept of cutting a groove. We cut grooves that result in resourceful states and we cut grooves that result in unresourceful states. Given that the states to which we give our attention are the ones most likely to be strengthened, this exercise is about identifying a strategy that leads to a resourceful state so that you increase the likelihood of having consistency in your ability to choose this state when you wish.

1 Identify a resourceful state that you would like to experience when you choose, one that you have experienced before. For example, it might be a state of confidence, enthusiasm, or motivation.
2 Wait until the next time you have this state. (You could alternatively go back in your thinking to associate into a time when you had this state previously.)
3 Be aware of what it is like to be in this state—what are you seeing, hearing, saying to yourself, and feeling?
4 What was the trigger for the state—what set you on a sequence of getting to this state?
5 What happened next—what did you see/hear/say to yourself/feel? (If you are not sure just keep the question "What am I doing in my thinking?" in your mind each time you experience the state.
6 Write down the sequence of thinking patterns so that you can check it out again the next time you experience it.
7 Test to see if you can create the state without the usual trigger. If it doesn't work, keep tracking what happens when you do get the state so you can find the missing pieces.
8 Keep the question "How am I doing this?" in mind.

SUMMARY

One definition of NLP is that it is the study of the structure of subjective experience. We all experience external events, but what we do with them is subjective. If we want to reproduce the results that we recognize in ourselves or in others, then what we can study is the structure of that subjectivity. Not only can we then learn how to reproduce those skills, but we are respecting the uniqueness of our individual interpretations of life. If we can learn how to respect individual culture, maybe we can begin to do the same in the world at large.

THOUGHT PROVOKERS

1   Write down what you think is your thinking strategy for each of the following:
   ❑ How you get up in the morning.
   ❑ How you respond to feedback.
   ❑ How you decide when it is time to stop work.
   ❑ How you decide to buy something.
   ❑ How you learn.
2   Identify any TOTEs that you recognize you often run successfully (familiar behavior or thinking loops for which there is an exit that matches your original desired state).
3   Identify any TOTEs that you recognize you often run unsuccessfully (familiar behavior or thinking loops for which there is an exit that does not match your original desired state). This will be something that you recognize you consistently try to achieve but where you repeatedly get frustrated in the process of doing so.

REFERENCES

Robert Dilts (1996) *Strategies of Genius*, Meta Publications.
Robert Dilts (1998) *Modeling with* NLP, Meta Publications.
Stephen Wolinsky (1991) *Trances People Live*, Bramble.

Two monks came upon a girl struggling to cross a river. One of the monks offered to carry her across and the girl accepted, so he picked her up and waded to the other side of the stream where he put her down safely.

When the other monk joined him he remonstrated with the first monk, "I cannot believe that you carried that girl. It is against all our principles. You know that we are not allowed to touch or even think about women. And yet despite that you carried this young girl in your arms!"

The first monk looked at his brother and replied, "Yes, I did carry the girl. The difference between you and I is that I put her down when I reached the other side. You are still carrying her!"

Part II
Model Yourself with NLP

O nce you have explored the elements of NLP, the exciting part is putting those skills together in many different ways to achieve the results you want. One of the principles of the way NLP is taught is that it starts with yourself.

An example of Influence

A woman took her son to see Mahatma Gandhi, who asked what she wanted. "I'd like you to get him to stop eating sugar," she replied.

"Bring the boy back in two weeks' time," replied Gandhi.

Two weeks later the woman returned with her son. Gandhi turned to the boy and said, "Stop eating sugar."

The woman looked surprised and asked, "Why did I have to wait two weeks for you to say that?"

"Two weeks ago I was eating sugar," Gandhi replied.

With NLP we can learn to recognize the structure of our own strategies—we can model ourselves. By first learning to model ourselves with NLP we become a model of the principles that influence those around us. For example, once we have learned how to set compelling goals for ourselves, we are more able to facilitate compelling goals for others.

"Example is not the main thing in influencing others. It is the only thing."

Albert Schweitzer

WHAT WORKS?

The techniques in this section are derived from modeling people who are excellent in their ability to lead themselves. By learning these skills you will reinforce the self-leading skills you already have and develop new ones that suit your unique circumstances.

More and more it is entrepreneurial style and skill that are emerging as significant for this new age. Whether we work for ourselves or an organization, we need more than ever before to be able to lead ourselves. NLP is a way of creating your own sense of direction, of harnessing the resources that are naturally yours, and of influencing others to collaborate with you.

The topics included in this part of the book follow a natural sequence for self-leading.

Tap into your inner potential: Anchoring

The first of these is Tap into your inner potential: Anchoring. This is an approach for enabling you to access your personal resources when you want them. In particular, anchoring is a way of managing your emotional state. The ability to choose the best emotional state to suit your circumstances is one of the most powerful and yet most overlooked skills we can have. When you can choose your state you can choose your techniques and the kind of influence you want to bring to any situation.

Align yourself: Neurological levels of change

When—and only when—you have the state you want can you build on that by ensuring that you are the example you want to be. You may not be able to control external events, but you can control the way you respond to them. We each have values and beliefs that drive every move we make and every word we utter. Sometimes those beliefs and values are what we want them to be and sometimes they are not. Before we can ever think of how we might influence others, we need first to think of how we want to influence ourselves. And it is not just beliefs and values but our sense of identity and purpose in life that provide the example that unconsciously influences others to want to be a part of what we represent or not. Chapter 13, Align yourself, deals with all the elements of influence. By thinking through not only how you are but what you might want to change at each level, you can generate an aligned state where every part of you is working toward the same outcome. When you achieve this state of coherence you can achieve your maximum state of success, influence, and satisfaction.

When technical skills are equal, it is the person, the team, or the company who has the greatest belief in themselves that will win through. The quality and nature of our beliefs override our technical knowhow. If we believe we can, then we can. Those people who have mastery in their ability to lead themselves share certain core beliefs. Chapter 14, Write your own lifescript, explores these beliefs, their increased significance today, and ways in which you can try them on for size to influence yourself.

Chapter 15 is Achieve what you really want. People who consistently achieve their goals have a way of imagining those goals as if they already have them. They are able to harness the power of their unconscious mind to work for them to realize goals in ways that are compelling. You can learn how to do this for yourself by following the steps in this chapter.

It is interesting to contrast the elements of this approach with some of the standard objective-setting approaches used in business. The difference between NLP approaches and many of the techniques that have been taught previously is that NLP provides us with the tools to find out what really makes the difference. How often have you learned techniques on training programs only to return to work and resume your normal practices after a day or two? If the techniques worked then you would probably continue to use them. If you apply all the elements of outcome thinking, as with all other NLP techniques, you will begin to achieve what you really want.

The above skills and ways of thinking are at the heart of self-leading. By starting with ourselves our example is in line with our words and our actions. Although I would say that you could dip into this book at any point, when it comes to applying the principles *you* are the beginning and the end.

Write your own lifescript:
Beliefs of excellence

Achieve what you really want:
Well-formed outcomes

12

Tap into Your Inner Potential: Anchoring

"Let the foundations thereof be strongly laid."

Ezra 6:3

We need to be able to manage our emotional state

A s I write here in France with my son sitting outside in the sunshine, the song "Dancing in the Moonlight" is playing on the radio. That music has become a regular part of our time here together this year. I suspect that particular track will be a reminder to me for years to come. The music is now an "anchor" for a very special time and the very good emotions I have attached to this period. And the value of associating the music to this time is that I will not only be able to recall the events we have experienced when I hear it, but I will also re-experience the emotions I feel right now.

Leading starts with the ability to lead ourselves. To do this we need first and foremost to be able to manage our emotional state. Not only is this the first step but it is probably one of the most important steps and yet surprisingly it is omitted from many leadership models. Any glitch in emotional state leads almost inevitably to a less than resourceful response to situations. If we feel irritation, guilt, anger, frustration, doubt, or self-consciousness, the result will be less than we are capable of and will be unlikely to be a win/win. In contrast, feelings of ease, confidence, forgiveness, acceptance, inspiration, and amusement are states that are much more likely to lead to us giving of our best, whatever the context.

Different states lend themselves to different circumstances. For example, a state of trust in my ability is the best state in which I can cycle. A state of thoughtful meditation is the best state for me to write, and a state of amused self-assurance is best for me when giving a talk at a conference. We can learn to recognize and choose which states work best for us in those situations when we want to give of our best. And once we have the state we want, the challenge is to hold on to it when it is threatened by circumstances outside our control, particularly if those circumstances are less than desirable ones.

When leading ourselves and others, we need to be able to stand firm and hold on to our convictions and our beliefs when everything around us may seem to be changing. Leaders are typically people who have this capacity to stand firm and stand alone. Leaders intuitively know how to anchor the emotions and the confidence in themselves that they need.

Anchoring is a process of learning to hold on to the states that are crucial to success. It is a way of choosing the emotional state we want and finding a way of accessing it when we choose. An anchor is a stimulus: It may be a sound, an image, a touch, a smell, or a taste that triggers a consistent response in ourselves or someone else.

The ability to use anchors in NLP enables us to:

❑ Access the resources (feelings and states) that we want when we want them.
❑ Replace unwanted feelings and thoughts with desirable ones.
❑ Gain control over our emotions.
❑ Keep on course when going through periods of intense change.
❑ Positively influence the response we trigger in other people.
❑ Experience the day as we want, no matter what is happening in our work and life.

You already have anchors that work for you. For example, think of the associations you have with:

❑ A favorite piece of music.
❑ A special perfume.
❑ A specific touch.
❑ The taste of a memorable meal.
❑ The view of a special place.
❑ Someone who is close to you.
❑ The memory of a particular time in your life.
❑ The anticipation of a future event.

We have anchors that work for us as well as anchors that are unproductive

It is also likely that you have anchors that are currently counterproductive.

ANCHORS CAN MAKE OR BREAK OUR DAY

Consider this scenario.

You get up and look out of the window. It is cloudy and wet and your heart sinks a little. You think about the day ahead and anticipate your first meeting. You know the person you are meeting and you start to feel a bit heavy as you think about how you expect this meeting to go. You think about the journey you have to make and you begin to imagine how difficult that can be and the sort of delays you might experience. You wish it were still the weekend and slightly dread the week ahead.

En route to the meeting you get stuck in delays and begin to feel tense and irritated. You can feel yourself fidgeting as you wait for the delays to clear. You get to the meeting with little time to spare and it goes much as you expected.

You arrive at your place of work and there is a stream of messages to deal with, some of them marked urgent. You start to feel stressed. The phone rings and you hear the voice of a colleague whose calls you dread, as he seems only to tell you problems. The day continues in a similar way and you arrive home in the evening with a headache and feeling tired.

Now consider this:

You get up and look out of the window. It is cloudy and wet. You are glad you didn't have this weather over the weekend—you

can let yourself concentrate on your work now. You think about the day ahead and anticipate your first meeting. You know the person you are meeting and you decide to pay more attention than usual to the outcome you want to achieve from this meeting. You start to get quite excited about the possibilities for the future. You think about the journey you have to make to get to this meeting and make some contingency plans in case there are any holdups. You also plan how you can use the traveling time to good effect.

En route to the meeting you get stuck in delays, but you realize there is nothing you can do about them so you use the time as you had planned to think of other things. You think about the weekend and how good it has been and how resourceful you feel now because of it. You get to the meeting with little time to spare and it goes much as you expected—you are well on your way to achieving not only the outcomes that you set yourself but also ones that you had not anticipated.

You arrive at your place of work and there is a stream of messages, so you decide to work through the urgent ones and put the rest out of your mind until you have got through the other high-priority issues for the day. This helps you to focus your thinking. The phone rings and you hear the voice of a colleague who seems frequently to talk to you about problems—you are privately amused at how someone can center their attention on the negative aspects of life so consistently. You listen with empathy and he seems to become more positive over the duration of the call. You feel very fortunate to have the work you have and to be surrounded by people who make your days so rich and entertaining. You arrive home tired but satisfied with the day and ready for a relaxing evening.

Our days are governed by the associations we have chosen (often unconsciously) to make with the various kinds of events we encounter. We make associations throughout our lives—the question is whether they lead to the kinds of outcome we want for ourselves or whether we are making our lives a misery because of what we are choosing to think about our circumstances. Given that what we choose to think is one of the single most powerful influences on the outcome of a situation, this is one of the most significant ways in which we can

We make associations
throughout our lives

influence how we experience our lives and what we get as a consequence of our thinking.

The anchoring process is a vital way in which we influence how we lead ourselves from within. We can choose the experience we have in life, irrespective of external circumstances.

MAKING ANCHORS WORK FOR YOU

The previous examples demonstrate how we sometimes use anchors in ways that trigger unresourceful states, such as depression, anger, frustration, or unhappiness. These are states that typically limit our subsequent behavioral choices. Let's suppose you are a person who sometimes gets stressed. You might ask yourself, "How do I get that way?" This is a far more useful question than "Why do I feel this way?" Asking the "how" question raises awareness of the structure of the experience, as opposed to reinforcing the reasons for the state and consequently the state itself. When you ask "how" you might discover that you just keep on thinking what might go wrong! We can be very skilled at generating unresourceful states for ourselves without realizing what we are doing. Most of our limitations are self-taught.

How, not why

We were invited by a manufacturing company to explore the staff's resistance to the new appraisal scheme. We discovered that previously the only time a manager typically sat down with a member of their staff was when they perceived a problem. Any discussion between a manager and a member of staff was usually a critical one. It was no surprise, then, to understand that the staff would be reluctant to welcome any scheme that promoted a discussion with their manager! The managers were unwittingly linking (anchoring) discussions about problems with the appraisal scheme.

Taking control

By using anchors hand in hand with outcome thinking, we can begin to take control of the effect we have on ourselves and others. For example, we can decide first of all how we want to feel in key situations such as:

❏ At the start of a presentation.
❏ Being on the receiving end of aggression.
❏ When we have to tell someone they have been made redundant.
❏ When delegating an area of work to a new employee for the first time.
❏ In a meeting when our point of view is different to that of the majority.
❏ When we get some tough feedback.
❏ When we are faced with unexpected change.
❏ When all the technology we rely on fails us.

Similarly, we can decide what effect we want to have on other people, when for example:

❏ They are entering a discussion with us.
❏ We are delegating jobs to them.
❏ They have feedback to give to us
❏ We are asking them for a decision.
❏ They receive an email from us.
❏ They check into our website.
❏ Someone makes contact with our company.
❏ They receive a call from us.

We have the ability to influence our own and others' responses in a way that is resourceful, one in which we have confidence and choice about what we can do.

ANCHORING A RESOURCEFUL STATE FOR YOURSELF

Let's start by considering how to generate the state you want for yourself. The process of anchoring involves linking a specific sight, sound, or touch with an experience that is present, i.e., a situation into which you are associated. The linking process subsequently enables you to use the anchor to reaccess that same experience when it can benefit you in another context.

PROCEDURE FOR ANCHORING A RESOURCEFUL STATE FOR YOURSELF

1 Choose a place that is free from distractions and make yourself comfortable.

2 Decide on a state/a feeling that you have experienced in your life that you would like to be able to access when you choose.

3 Choose an anchor that you can use whenever you want to access this feeling. It must be something precise and easy to use. For example, you could use the little finger and thumb together on your left hand.

4 Now recall the memory of a time when this feeling was at its strongest for you. Check that you are associated into this experience, that you are seeing it as if through your own eyes and not as an observer watching yourself. If you can see yourself in the picture as opposed to seeing it through your own eyes, you are dissociated. It is only in the associated state that you can really experience the feelings and therefore anchor them. The concept of association/dissociation is explained in Chapter 3.

When you are completely associated, pay attention to what you see. What colors can you see? Are they bright or pastel? Is it clear or hazy? Notice the quality of what you see and any other distinctions. What do you hear? Is it loud or quiet? What is the location of the sounds? Are there voices, are you speaking to other people? Listen to those sounds and anything else you hear. While you see this scene, allow yourself to experience the feeling of being there until that feeling is strong and enveloping for you. As you do so, touch your little finger and thumb together for as long and only as long as you feel these sensations intensely. When you have experienced the feeling and the touch of your finger to thumb, release that touch. Shake yourself or move in some way so that you bring yourself back to the present, which is called breaking state.

5 This touch has become the anchor for the feelings. Repeat the process several times until you know there is a strong connection between the touch and the feelings.

6 Test the anchor. Think of something else and as you do so touch your little finger and thumb together in precisely the way you did when you were setting up the anchor. This is called firing the anchor.

What happens? If you have set up the anchor effectively you will recall the scene, the sounds, and the feelings of the memory as if you were there. If this doesn't happen, keep practicing. It may be you weren't fully associated when you set the anchor. Check that you use exactly the same anchor to recall the experience as you used to set it up in the first place. The sensations in an experience tend to rise and fade. Set the anchor just as the experience is reaching a peak, and remove it as soon as or just before the feelings begin to fade.

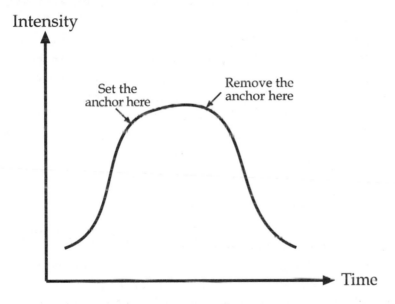

7 Now think of a future situation where you would like to have the feelings you have anchored. This time as you imagine the situation in the future, fire the anchor. What do you see, hear, and feel now? When you do this successfully you are transferring your desired feelings, your resourceful state, to another and in this case future context.

Learn first to do this for yourself so that you can recall the resources you want when you want them.

Remember the key factors in anchoring:

Key factors in anchoring

❑ Fully associate into the experience before you set the anchor.

❑ Make the anchored experience intense.

❑ Use a distinct and specific anchor that is easily reproduced.

❑ Set the anchor just prior to reaching the most intense part of the experience.

Use exactly the same anchor to recall the experience. In this example we used a touch as an anchor, but an anchor can be anything as long as it meets the above criteria.

TAKE RESPONSIBILITY FOR YOUR EFFECTS ON OTHERS

Exactly the same process works for anchoring others as for yourself. You cannot always easily know exactly when the point of greatest intensity has occurred for someone else in order to know when to set the anchor. You rely on your ability to detect from their external behavior exactly when this occurs. By building rapport you will learn to detect when this peak state is occurring. Otherwise the process is exactly the same as it would be if you were anchoring yourself.

STEPS FOR ANCHORING OTHERS

1 Ask the other person what state they want to have in a particular situation. Ask them to identify a time in the past when they had that state.

2 Decide on the anchor you are going to use and get yourself positioned so that you can use it easily.

3 Ask the other person to step into the time when they had the state they want now. Help them to associate fully into that experience by asking them about the quality of what they see, hear, and feel. Use present-tense questions to encourage them to associate into the experience, e.g., "What do you see?," "What do you hear?," "What are your feelings?"

4 Invite them to experience fully all the sensations of being there so that they intensify the experience. Do this by exploring with them each of their senses in this experience: visual, auditory, feelings.

5 Pay attention to them so that when you know they are reaching the peak of that experience, apply the anchor. Apply it for as long as they experience the feeling intensely.

6   As soon as the intensity of the feelings begins to diminish (again, you need to calibrate them to establish when this occurs), stop applying the anchor and bring them back to the present. You can repeat these steps a few times if you want to ensure that the anchor and the state are associated.

7   Test by applying (firing) the anchor. If the anchor works you will see the person reproduce all the external behaviors of the state once again. If this doesn't happen, go back and repeat the process, checking for full association, intensity of the experience, and accuracy of the anchor.

8   Now test the anchor in a future situation. Ask the other person to identify a future situation in which they want to have the anchored state. Ask them to imagine that future situation and as they do that fire the anchor. Watch what happens. If the anchor works you will see them manifest the same external responses to the anchor in this future situation. Eventually they will be able to think of the future situation and get the state automatically without having to fire the anchor.

You are anchoring other people all the time. The question is, are you anchoring them in resourceful or unresourceful ways?

BUSINESS ANCHORS

In a company for which I worked some years ago, there was a team meeting every Friday afternoon. This unfortunately was when most of the team felt at their most tired, but it was the only time we could all get together. Naturally, most of the team wanted to make decisions quickly so that we could leave early and go home. Harry, one of the team members, often had very creative and constructive ideas. However, when he started to speak, he would raise a difficulty with what had just been discussed. This was a consistent pattern for him. The result was that virtually every time he opened his mouth the rest of the team seemed to groan inwardly and usually ignored or attempted to quash the point he was making. Harry had effectively anchored this response just by opening his mouth!

Can you imagine how different performance appraisals would be if managers were measured by the state in which they left their staff at the end of the discussion?

The examples of anchoring we used earlier in this section, e.g., touch, aren't so available in a business setting. It isn't always part of the culture to touch others in this way. It is necessary to be a little more creative with the anchors you use to enable others to access resourceful states.

Examples of anchors you can use in business are:

❑ A word or words that you would not use regularly in conversation, said with a specific volume and tonality.
❑ Use of space. This can be employed to good effect in a presentation, where you can anchor different information and responses to you by standing or moving to different parts of the room.
❑ A posture or movement that you would not naturally make in discussion.

Use anchors with integrity

My experience is that using anchors in this way only works if you use them with integrity, in a way that fits with other people's outcomes. I believe that if you attempt to use them manipulatively, in a way that is out of line with the other person's outcomes, that other person will sense this, often intuitively, and subsequently block it.

STEPS FOR ANCHORING A RESOURCEFUL STATE IN A MEETING

1 Identify the state you want to anchor in the other person that will support the achievement of your mutual outcomes. This might, for example, be a state of confidence, decisiveness, or happiness.
2 Decide what anchor you will use, a particular word or a specific gesture or posture that can be noticed by them in some way (very likely unconsciously).
3 When the other person naturally demonstrates the desired state, use your anchor. You will probably need to do this four or five times.
4 If the discussion gets to a stage when this state would be valuable and is not naturally occurring, fire your anchor. Notice what happens. If you have been successful in setting the anchor, then the other person will demonstrate the state.

SWITCHING STATES

There are many different ways of using anchors. One easy way is to use a technique called collapsing anchors. This is a way of reconciling two states, for example an unresourceful state and a resourceful one. You could do this when you want to lessen an extreme negative state and achieve one that is a blend of the two, so that you don't lose the unresourceful state but experience it in a way that is manageable. The consequence of collapsing anchors is that you will achieve a third different state to the original two that is in someway a mix of the originals—a cocktail of the two that has a different taste to either.

One of the simplest ways to do this is to use the knuckles on one hand. With the extreme end of your righthand index finger, touch specific knuckles on your left hand. If it is easier for you, reverse the way you use your hands in this exercise.

1 Decide on an unresourceful state that you want to work with in this exercise. It might be, for example, a state of anxiety, stress, lack of confidence, or frustration.

2 Associate into this state so that you are re-experiencing it and anchor it by touching your index finger to the first knuckle on the other hand. Test the anchor until you know it works. Only access this state briefly.

3 Choose a different state altogether, a break state. This might be thinking about something funny or just something that requires thought, like saying your phone number backwards.

4 Choose a resourceful state, one of confidence, calm, or security, for example. Associate into a time when you had this feeling. When you experience the intensity of this feeling, anchor it by touching your second finger to the second knuckle on your other hand.

5 Test the anchors in the following sequence:
   a Break state.
   b Fire the first anchor.
   c Break state.
   d Fire the second anchor.
   If either of the anchors fails to work, repeat the sequence of resetting them.

STEPS FOR COLLAPSING ANCHORS

6 Now apply both anchors simultaneously. You will feel some confusion as the two states sort themselves out into a new, integrated state. If the less resourceful state is still a strong part of the subsequent state, go back and choose and anchor an even stronger resourceful state. Repeat the process. You may also find that it helps to fire the anchor for the resourceful state for a second or two before also firing the anchor for the unresourceful state.

7 Now think of a future situation, one that typically in the past would have triggered off the unresourceful state. What happens as you think of this situation? If the collapsing anchors technique has worked, the unresourceful state will not exist any more.

Some of these techniques may seem quite formal at first, yet these processes are ones that we are slipping into and out of through a typical day. What we are doing here is breaking them down into their constituent parts in a similar way to how we might learn to drive a car. However, once you master the skill, you can begin to use it more informally. For example, if you find yourself slipping into a state of unresourcefulness, you can learn to step quickly into a resourceful one. Recall a time when you felt particularly resourceful and reaccess those feelings by associating yourself once more into that situation.

You can learn to step quickly into a resourceful state

Eventually you will find that even the process of switching from unresourceful to resourceful becomes automatic. Your unconscious mind makes the switch for you without your even having to think about it consciously. You will have "hard-wired" the strategy for resourcefulness by learning to chain anchors.

CHAINING RESOURCES

Sometimes the gap between the unresourceful state and the resourceful one that you would like in its place can be too wide to step from one to the other in one go. In such cases it is useful to learn to move through a series of anchored states to lead yourself gradually from the least resourceful to the desirable state. It is worth emphasizing there that it is also important to know when to stay in what might at first seem to be an unresourceful state. The risk of always creating a pathway out of what we believe to be "unresourceful" states is that we fail to value the richness of diversity, the beauty of all emotions.

The beauty of all emotions

Staying in a state or moving to another is a choice. If the gap is a wide one—from, for example, a state of extreme stress to one of total relaxation—you might want some interim steps. You might choose to go from stress to concern, then from concern to neutrality, and from there to mild amusement, and then finally to relaxation. In this case you would be chaining anchors so that you are creating a pathway for yourself from one state to anther. By learning the chain each time you experience the first undesirable state, you will automatically move down the path that you have created for yourself.

STEPS FOR CHAINING ANCHORS

1   Decide on an unresourceful state that you want to work with in this exercise. Choose a state that you want to replace with another much more resourceful state, but one that you recognize is a significant distance from the first undesirable state. You might choose an initial state of something like anxiety or stress or depression. The replacement state might be something like calm, relief, or ease with yourself. Check that the replacement state is one that is truly desirable as a replacement whenever you experience the first.

2   Associate into the first state so that you are re-experiencing it and anchor it by touching a part of your thigh. (You are going to use places in line down your thigh to access each of the subsequent states until you get to the resourceful one.) Only experience this first state briefly (there is no need to stay there too long). Break state.

3   Choose a next intermediary state, for example irritation, but something much less intense than the first state. Experience this state and when you are fully associated into it, anchor that on to a point a bit further down your thigh. Break state.

4   Choose a more resourceful state, one of confidence or security for example. Associate into a time when you had this feeling. When you experience the intensity of this feeling, anchor it by touching a point further down your thigh again. When you have done this successfully, break state.

5   The number of intermediary states you need will depend on the intensity of the first state and the gap between the first and the destination state. Repeat this process until you have anchored all the intermediary states and the final destination state.

6   Test the anchors to make sure that they all work, being sure to break state between each one. If any of them are not yet fully anchored, return to experiencing and anchoring them until they are.

7   Now fire the first anchor and when you are fully in that first state, fire the second anchor simultaneously and as you experience that second state approaching its peak, remove the first anchor and, continuing to hold the second one, fire the third one. (You are always linking each state with the next one in this way.) As the third one builds, remove the second anchor and fire the next one. You should experience yourself moving through each state in turn and as you do so you are connecting them together in a chain.

Do this until you have reached the destination state. When you have the destination state, fully remove the previous anchor and fully experience this final resourceful state. Break state. This is important so that you when you repeat the whole process to check that it works, you want to ensure that you end on the destination state and don't loop it back to the unresourceful state that you started with.

8   Repeat step 7 until you have the states chained together.

9   Now fire the first anchor. If you have chained the states together successfully, you will go through the chain you have created for yourself and automatically move through the states, finishing at the destination state.

It is not that we don't do this already—we do. However, without thought and care we tend to create chains that either are not very efficient (e.g., it takes longer than it needs to get out of an unresourceful state), or we have created chains that take us to places potentially even less resourceful than the one we started with. How often have you begun a day feeling a little gloomy and then got frustrated with yourself for doing that, which led to your getting annoyed and then stressed and so on? How much more desirable is it to find that if you do get into a state of confusion, for example, you can lead yourself to state of curiosity, inquiry, and finally understanding and insight?

I believe that putting yourself into a resourceful state is a vital precursor to most situations. You can learn to recognize which state is most useful to you, for example in:

Hard-wiring the strategy

❏ Giving and receiving feedback.
❏ Solving problems and being creative.
❏ Being assertive.
❏ Listening.
❏ Tackling work that you would not naturally be motivated to do.
❏ Spending time with your family.
❏ Making a presentation.
❏ Dealing with customers.
❏ Writing.
❏ Going on holiday.
❏ Starting the evening.

More traditional training will teach you what structure to use, e.g., how to structure appraisal, how to handle objections, how to plan a presentation. NLP teaches you how to generate the state that triggers the resources and style you need to achieve what you want.

ANCHORING INSIGHT

One of the characteristics of NLP is that it can accelerate your ability to learn. NLP is about how to manage change skilfully and powerfully. If you can manage and facilitate change, you can learn.

SHORTCUT TO ANCHORING RESOURCEFUL STATES

1 Decide on a trigger that you want to use the next time you experience a state you want to anchor (a specific touch/a word that you say to yourself/an image).
2 Give yourself an internal alarm so that the next time you experience a desirable state (which might be quite unexpected), you get a prompt to anchor it. You could do

this just by asking your unconscious mind to remind you with a thought of anchoring when you are next in a desirable resourceful state (no matter how fleeting).

3 When you are at the height of the desirable state, use your anchor to "fix" it.

4 If it occurs more than once, use your anchor each time you are at the height of the emotion to strengthen the effect of the anchor.

5 Think of occasions when the state you have just anchored might be useful to you.

6 The next time you are in a situation when you feel this state that you have anchored might be useful to you, fire the anchor.

SUMMARY

Anchors are a natural occurrence. You have many associations already established, some individual, some connected with other people. Most of these will have occurred by chance without any forethought. Some association anchors will be helpful, supportive, and rewarding for you; some will not. The process of anchoring enables you to choose the associations you want both for yourself and for others. Mastering the skill of anchoring means learning to lead yourself by managing your state of mind. It also means taking responsibility for the effect you have on other people.

This chapter has set out a few of the ways in which you can apply the anchoring techniques, but you will find that anchoring is part of everything you do. Begin to explore how you can use these anchors creatively as a way of enriching your day-to-day living and making your involvement with others a constantly rewarding experience.

THOUGHT PROVOKERS

1 What state do you typically have in the following situations and what state would you like to have?

Situation	Current state	Wanted state
Giving a presentation		
Saying what you want		
Refusing personal requests		
Appraising or being appraised		
Going for an interview		
Exercising		
Dealing with aggression		
Having your ideas challenged in public		
Add your own situations		

Choose one of the above situations and use either the self anchoring, the collapsing anchors, or the chaining anchors technique.

2 Write down the state that you would like to generate in yourself and in others in the following situations.

Situation	Own state	Desired state in others
Appraising others		
Giving feedback		
Explaining what you want		
Clarifying technical information		
Running or contributing to meetings		
Add your own situations		

Use either of the anchoring techniques to experiment with generating a desired state in yourself and in others.

3   Write down the states that you would like to have when dealing with each of the following people and the state you would like them to have:

Person	Your desired state	Desired state for them
A member of staff		
A colleague		
Someone in your family		
Your best friend		
A friend		
A customer		
A supplier		
Your partner		
Someone else		

Use either of the anchoring techniques to experiment with achieving these desired states.

4   Develop a list of anchors that you could use in your everyday situations. Check they meet the outline for an effective anchor, i.e., that each one precise and easily reproducible, and that it can be used uniquely to anchor a specific resource.

5   How has your day been so far? What anchors have you used that have worked for you/worked against you?

6   Read *An Evil Cradling* by Brian Keenan as an example of someone who chose what he made of extreme circumstances.

Many years ago there was a sailor who had traveled to many different countries around the world. He had been to many places and seen many different sights. One day as he was sailing across the seas he came upon an island and decided to rest there for a while. He moored his boat on the shore and began to look around. All around the island was a beautiful white beach and behind the beach was dense tropical jungle. All was quiet until...

He thought he could hear a faint noise in the distance and tilted his head to listen. He sensed it came from within the jungle and walked closer. Sure enough, once again he heard this faint noise in the background. He started to hack his way through the foliage in order to make a pathway. The more he moved inland the louder the noise became. He continued to cut his way through until eventually he reached a clearing and there in the middle of the clearing he saw an old man sitting cross-legged on the ground.

The old man had his eyes closed and was chanting "Mo, Mo, Mo" in long, soft tones. The sailor stood and watched and listened. "Mo, Mo, Mo," continued the old man. Eventually the sailor approached the old man and tapped him on the shoulder. The old man turned slowly around and smiled.

"Excuse me," said the sailor, "I think you have made a mistake. I think you should be saying 'Om, Om, Om.'"

"Oh," said the old man, smiling. "Thank you so much," and began to chant, "Om, Om, Om."

The sailor felt pleased with himself and made his way back to his boat. He began to sail away, and when he had sailed for a while he felt a tap on his shoulder. He turned around, surprised to see the old man, who said, "Forgive me for interrupting your journey. Could you please remind me what the chant should be?"

The sailor, in a state of shock, said, "Om, Om, Om."

"Thank you so much," said the old man and walked back across the water to the island.

13

Align Yourself: Neurological Levels of Change

"Conscience is that ability within me that attaches itself to the highest standard I know, then continually reminds me of what that standard demands. If I am in the habit of always holding it in front of me, conscience will always indicate what I should do."
Oswald Chambers, My Utmost for His Highest

We live in a complex, unpredictable world. We can no longer rely on plans and predictions. We are called to work in ways that are entirely different to the ways of the past. The only part of the system on which we can potentially rely is within ourselves. And yet this is the part of the system that for many people lies largely untapped. We have to trust and believe that if we are true to ourselves, our outcomes will unfold in line with that truth.

Our outcomes unfold in line with our truth

When I wrote the first edition of NLP *at* Work I said that to achieve our goals we needed to be able to imagine and feel them, and this still holds true. However, I have seen a new and different style of achievement develop in the last five years. This relies more and more on our ability to allow outcomes to unfold. We have to be able to walk forward with faith into a world that is chaotic and abstract and allow the opportunities to present themselves. What we do need to be able to do, however, is to be so aligned, so true to what we believe, that we are in a position to seize these opportunities when they occur. Our example is our reputation. By being aligned with ourselves we find that we attract the opportunities that fit with the direction in which we want to move.

It is as if we are sportspeople playing a game. We don't know where the next ball will come from nor how it will come. But we manage ourselves so that we have a strong sense of the outcome we want to achieve and are always in a state of readiness and flexibility to seize the chances as they present themselves.

"Mastering complexity means not letting complexity get the better of you. It means having a coherent viewpoint to guide action in spite of the confusion, uncertainty, and ambiguity that are introduced by the swirl of events and interactions going on around you. The mastery we are alluding to is that of the craftsman and not that of the M in MBA. The ability to act coherently in the face of complexity, and to do so on an ongoing basis, is the hallmark of a true master."

Michael Lissack and Johan Roos, The Next Common Sense

This personal best or congruence is increasingly one of my main aims in my NLP training and consultancy. By having a personal sense of direction, resolving inner conflict, and managing personal change, we can move toward a state of alignment or coherence. When we have this state we are at one with who we are there is little or no conflict or stress. We approach the best we can be.

We can move towards a state of alignment

While writing this chapter I have been watching the Tour de France cycle race. Yesterday Lance Armstrong outcycled all other cyclists in the field to take the yellow jersey (worn by the overall leader on time at any point in the three-week race). Only a few years ago Lance Armstrong was diagnosed as having cancer in just about every part of his body and given a negligible chance of survival. Not only did he fight his way through the cancer, but he fought back to regain his fitness to cycle and win the Tour de France, one of the most grueling sporting events in the world, not once but twice and is now on course to win it for a third time. When he started on his cycling career he was not a popular rider; because of his arrogance and aggressive tactics he became a target for the French press. However, through his illness and astonishing recovery he has learnt a purpose in life.

He cycles to make people aware of cancer. He cycles for his wife and his son and his expected twins.

Armstrong's cycling style is influencing other cyclists worldwide. His key adversary Jan Ullrich yesterday crashed off the side of the road, and it is the custom not to take advantage of the misfortune of an adversary. Lance Armstrong followed this custom to the letter and took one foot out of its pedal to wait for Jan Ullrich to catch him up. As he overtook the leading cyclist Laurent Jalabert, a French favorite who had shown great courage to lead through the mountains all day, Armstrong indicated for Jalabert to accompany him to the finish line. (Laurent Jalabert indicated that if he could he would have.) This morning the headline in the French press is "Armstrong—Ace of Spades—Ace of Hearts." They describe his performance as that of a virtuoso.

Lance Armstrong is cycling with purpose, with a total sense of his identity as a world-class cyclist, with principles and beliefs not only about his sport but also about what is possible when everything seems to be lost. He is showing principles of integrity in everything he is doing and demonstrating a skill in cycling that is artistically outstanding—he dances in the pedals. His influence is assured for posterity, not only in the world of cycling but in the world at large.

Just as a company can work more effectively if each of the teams within it cooperates and works toward the same goal, so an individual can function more effectively if each of the "parts" is cooperating with the others. This kind of aligned state can be achieved by dealing with change at a number of levels. I will explain in this chapter how to achieve this state of alignment so that you can obtain this coherent, aligned state for yourself. And I will explain what strategies to use at those times it slips away from you. Other chapters also address this integration of parts, notably Chapter 18 on resolving conflict.

Robert Dilts, one of the leading international NLP trainers, has developed a model for change that was originated by Gregory Bateson, anthropologist and author of *Towards an Ecology of Mind*. This model, the logical levels of change, provides a powerful framework for discovering how to achieve alignment.

Purpose — *What purpose does this fulfill for me to do this?*

Identity — *What is my sense of self? How might this change?*

Beliefs and values — *How does this fit with my beliefs and values?*

Capabilities — *How can I do this? What skills do I need?*

Behavior — *What can I do? What action can I take?*

Environment — *How does this affect my environment?*

THE DIFFERENT LEVELS

You can use this model to clarify your thinking about yourself, your team, and your company. I recommend you start by applying the model to yourself. Change comes from within; once we have our mental model aligned we are in a position to manage our external environment. In fact, my experience is that once we have inner alignment our external environment starts to shape itself to fit with that.

PURPOSE

The level of purpose is sometimes described as the level of spirituality. Although this term can have a religious connotation, what it refers to here are the larger systems of which we are a part. Understanding the spiritual level for ourselves means understanding the interconnections between us and the bigger systems. At this level, we are exploring what value we bring to those bigger systems of which we are a part. For example, we might consider a bigger system to be any of the following:

❏ Our family.
❏ Our marriage or partnership.

❑ Our team.
❑ Our community.
❑ Our company.
❑ Our faith.
❑ Our world.

It might be a temporary bigger system like:

❑ The group we are meeting with today.
❑ The client with whom we are interacting right now.
❑ The dynamic between us and the staff in the restaurant in which we are eating.
❑ The people on the train on which we are traveling.
❑ The people in the queue in which we are standing.
❑ The family members we are with right now.

By paying attention to this level we can become aware of the way we are always adding value by being who we are, no matter the system we happen to belong to at that time. This is our highest level of unconscious influence. This is the level at which most people make decisions about whether you are someone with whom they want to do business, live, collaborate, make a long-term business commitment, and so on.

In modeling companies that have achieved long-term success and are able to develop and grow, we discover that one of the characteristics setting them apart is their attention to the system of which they are a part. They are companies with missions that are ecological, i.e., they cooperate and contribute to the bigger system. For example, if it is a travel company it is one that pays attention to its effect on the culture of the countries with which it does business. If it is an information technology company it is one that thinks about and plans the impact it wants to have on the future culture and world at large through the development of technology.

Lentern Aircraft manufactures aircraft components. It is a traditional manufacturing family business and as such has been subject to all the pressures of the manufacturing industry in the 1990s and now the millennium. Yet this company, through the drive of the managing director especially but with the backing and commitment of all of his fellow board members and senior management team, has committed to challenging the way it works continuously so that it is living out values of learning, care, integrity, fun, and honesty. It has empowered champions of this learning to take the principles out to everyone in the company who wishes to learn about it.

Lentern has a reputation for being a company that is good to work for. Clients, suppliers, and competitors increasingly ask employees what they have got that is making such a difference (because they would like some too).

The unconscious value you add to the bigger systems of which you are a part is your most significant form of influence. Stephen Covey, in his book *Seven Habits of Highly Effective People*, refers to it as your legacy. And the legacy does not have to be only what you leave when you die; it is what you leave when you leave a meeting, leave a room, leave a company

Peter is employed on a contract basis by a fast-growing startup company that attracts the best people and can afford to be choosy in who it selects to work with. He has been involved in a number of projects and it seems likely that he will be contracted by the company for the foreseeable future. Whenever Peter is at the company premises (he often works from his home), he seems to lift the energy and spirits of everyone with whom he comes into contact. He is now having to turn away some of the increasing requests that he gets to work onsite with the developing teams.

Our purpose is lived out through the kind of person we are. Identity/mission defines our sense of self and contains statements describing how you think of yourself as a person, "I am" statements, such as:

IDENTITY/MISSION

- ❑ I am a successful person.
- ❑ I am an optimist.
- ❑ I am a shy person.
- ❑ I am practical.

What you have coded within yourself in this way is central to who you are. It is quite different for me to say I write articles and books (a behavioral statement) than to say "I am an author" (an identity statement).

This level can also provide a means of thinking about the key roles you fulfill in your life, e.g., wife, mother, consultant, author, cyclist, provider. I am these things no matter where I am and who I am with.

A company's mission statement defines the identity of the organization, the unique nature of its business, and encompasses purpose, i.e., what it does for others. For example:

My mission is to support and develop the leaders of today to make a positive difference in the world.

This is a visionary mission and expresses the uniqueness of the business and the person who is running it. It is different to the mission statements that appear on so many financial statements: We want to be number one in the car hire business. We want to be the best web developers in Europe. These are self-based mission statements and are generally meaningless to both the employees of the business and their potential clients.

BELIEF SYSTEMS AND VALUES

Our belief systems are shaped by our purpose and identity and, conversely, they support who we are and what we give.

Our beliefs are views about ourselves, other people, and situations that we hold to be true. They are emotionally held views not based on fact:

❑ I believe that people in general can be trusted.
❑ I believe that I can learn from any experience I have.
❑ I believe that the customer's needs are the heart of business success.
❑ I believe that integrity is the key to a successful business.

For a company these would be the beliefs on which the company and the way it goes about its business are founded. They only function as beliefs if the everyday behavior of management and employees is an expression of these beliefs. For this to be the case, the beliefs need to be ones that are drawn from the organization's employees. Ones picked from a textbook on management because they sound, look, or feel good won't work and are more likely to lead to increased dissatisfaction if the everyday behavior contradicts the published beliefs. However, where they do match, the result can be a major contributory factor to the cohesion and congruence of the organization.

"Coherence results from people feeling that the actions required of them are consistent with their own sense of purpose and identity and that of the organization of which they are a part. This feeling can only occur when the values and guiding principles embodied by the corporate purpose and expressed identity align with how the person defines and embodies their sense of self."

Michael Lissack and Johan Roos, The Next Common Sense

Our beliefs function in the form of values against which we make decisions throughout our life. These are qualities that you hold to be important to you in the way you run your business and live your life, for example:

Values

❏ Honesty.
❏ Openness.
❏ Integrity.
❏ Fun.
❏ Learning.

Some very interesting new values are emerging in some of successful startup companies, such as:

Emerging values in successful startups

❏ Generosity.
❏ Charity.
❏ Abundance.
❏ Relationships.
❏ Spontaneity.

We each have our own interpretation of what these values mean and how we know they are met. It is important not only to have values but also to know specifically how you will recognize that they are being satisfied.

For companies the same principles apply to values as to beliefs. They only function if they are indeed the values of the employees and management of the organization, if the covert and overt values are the same. An agreed and meaningful set of values provides a code of practice for how to go about the business. Having this leads to a culture of autonomy and ownership, where employees take initiatives and decisions and maintain a company style and set of principles. This way of leading a business is vital to release the creativity and innovation of all the people in the business and those who deal with that business. Those companies who are what Peter Senge calls "transparent," meaning that whatever point of contact you have with the company the same values shine through, are those that attract customers, suppliers, collaborators, venture capitalists, and contractors who want to do business with them. Transparency communicates certainty, to which most people are irresistibly attracted.

Taking time out to clarify purpose, mission, beliefs and values, and subsequently a code of practice for all employees has to be one of the best investments a startup company can make. It is also a sound foundation for established companies that have lost their way and want to inject new life into the business.

CAPABILITIES

Capabilities are increasingly becoming known as competencies. They are resources you have available in the form of skills or qualities, such as sensitivity, adaptability, flexibility, outcome thinking.

Many organisations are paying increasing attention to competency-based training and development. It is important to recognize that this is only one of the levels of change. What we can learn to do through modeling is to recognize unique capabilities, not only those that happen to be on a company's appraisal list. No matter how comprehensive this list, it can only serve to box people into predefined categories. The opportunity for forward-thinking leaders is to recognize and celebrate everyone's unique talents. More than that, it is a characteristic of leaders that they can and do recognize the unique qualities of the people who work for and with them as well as the people with whom they do business outside the

Forward-thinking leaders recognize and celebrate unique talent company. Natural leaders model naturally! And they can detect qualities such as:

Natural leaders model naturally

❏ David has the ability to ask multi-level questions and he indicates this by making a layering movement with his hands while he is speaking.
❏ Lin has the ability to make instant rapport the minute she is face to face with anyone.
❏ Kevin has the ability to observe and comment on his own behavior (and joke about it) while he is in conversation with someone.
❏ Colin can scan a screen of code and intuitively know where the bugs are.
❏ Nick can take a new idea and put himself in the shoes of the people who need to learn this idea in the business and work out the practical implications of that in how it is to be presented to them.

When I was working with people in the stores of one company I noticed that whenever I asked a question one of the packers, Mike, looked consistently left and to his side. It was a very marked preference in his eye-accessing cues. I had the opportunity to talk about the group's social interests and this eye-accessing cue became even more pronounced. I was able to comment on this (I had explained eye-accessing cues as part of a company-wide training program) and I discovered that Mike had a great interest in music. Not only that but, rather bashfully, he said that he could hear a piece of music and remember it exactly. (His eye-accessing cue was auditory remembered.) I commented on what a remarkable skill that was and he looked astonished and explained that he had always thought it was weird so had kept quiet about it!

I wonder just how many skills are buried in this way. When we are in alignment with ourselves we release the best of our abilities.

We can release the best of our abilities

When Goran Ivanisevic entered the Wimbledon tennis championships in 2001 he was not considered to have any chance of doing well, let alone winning. However, his belief in his purpose and himself gave him the influence to persuade the panel to let him enter the tournament on a wild card. His passion was intense. His purpose was to give something to a country that had been torn apart with conflict. Even during conflict in Croatia, he believed that his best contribution was not to take on the identity of a soldier but to inspire through his identity as a tennis player. He played every point as if it were match point. And he won the Wimbledon title in a final that will be remembered as one of the best finals ever if not the best.

BEHAVIOR

All of the previous attributes—purpose, identity, beliefs, values, and capabilities—show themselves in everything we do. Our behavior is what we do and say. It is what the world around us can see and hear us doing. All of my beliefs and values are apparent in every word I write, both the beliefs that I say and live out and those where I am not aligned.

You can think of behavior as the tip of the iceberg, the bit of you that is above the surface, whereas purpose, identity, capabilities, beliefs, and values are internal thoughts and feelings.

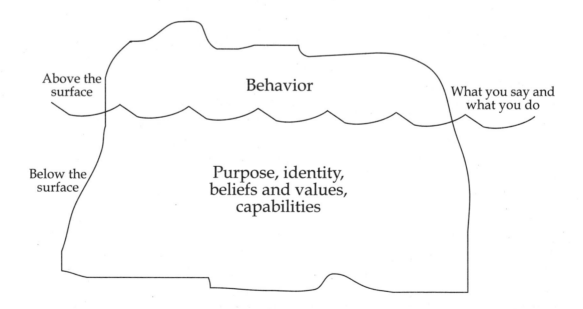

Above the surface

Behavior

What you say and what you do

Below the surface

Purpose, identity, beliefs and values, capabilities

Examples of behaviors:

❏ Asking questions.
❏ Saying what you want.
❏ Losing your temper.
❏ Writing out your goals.
❏ Giving feedback.
❏ Folding your arms.
❏ Smiling.
❏ Blushing.
❏ Running.
❏ Making eye contact.

Most people have a characteristic pattern of behavior that supports their achieving what they want and a pattern of behavior that can sabotage it.

Martin is a very caring leader. He is open to feedback and acts on what he hears. He laughs a lot, especially at himself. He is skilled at creating visions for the future and when he does this he looks very definitely up and to his right. He asks precise questions to be sure he has understood what others are telling him.

However, Martin can also sometimes dominate the conversation by taking much more airtime than anyone else in the meeting. He does this when he is feeling angry and his upper lip pulls back taut across his teeth. At the same time his behavior becomes muddled—he starts to answer his own questions and run different kinds of questions and comments into each other without a gap. He looks down and to the right when he feels this way. He interrupts others and he will not be interrupted.

Behavior can also be reflected in the personal development plans you set yourself:

❏ I will write down my priorities at the start of every day.
❏ I will read about a new aspect of technology every week.
❏ I will learn a new skill by practicing it every day.
❏ I will ensure I listen by summarizing each meeting I attend.
❏ I will agree and write up on the flipchart outcomes for each meeting I hold.

❏ I will check that all emails I send have the effect I want.

A company has everyday behavior that is characteristic of the company as a whole or of departments and teams within the company. For example:

❏ The sales support team handles customer queries efficiently and promptly.
❏ Staff keep you waiting and blame others in the company for any mistakes.
❏ Employees in the company take initiatives and make decisions on the spot.

Behavior can also be represented in the style of development plans the company sets itself:

❏ We will respond to phone calls within three rings.
❏ We will build quality into everything we do.
❏ We will empower people to make their own decisions.
❏ We will update our web pages every day so that they are always current.

It is as important to know how to be specific with our behavioral plans as it is to know when and how to "chunk up" to the higher levels for strategic or negotiating reasons. What is most important is to know the difference between the two kinds of levels. The temptation for many people is to explore the content, which is typically the behavioral content, of what is being said or of what is happening.

ENVIRONMENT

Finally, our environment defines the contexts in which we demonstrate all of the above elements. Environment refers to everything "outside" ourselves: the place we work, the economy, people around us, our business, our friends and family, our customers, and also includes what we wear. What we think about as being in the environment is also a measure of how much we take responsibility for what happens to us. For example:

❏ If we say "It's a tough world out there," this suggests that we put some of the power and influence outside ourselves.

❏ Equally, talking about "they" ("They won't let me" or "They don't tell me," see Chapter 6) gives the same impression.

"All travel is, after all, a journey in time and in mind. Like many people I believe that physical landscapes are a mirror of, or perhaps a key into, our inner landscape, It wasn't simply chance or good luck that brought us to Chile. The silent messages from the images on the hillside and those unearthed from the desert had assured me of that."

Brian Keenan, Between Extremes

THE INFLUENCE OF THE LEVELS

Gregory Bateson pointed out that in the processes of learning, change, and communication there is a natural hierarchy. The rules for changing something on one level are different to those for changing on a lower level. Changing something on a lower level could, but would not necessarily, affect the higher levels. However, changing something on the higher levels would always change things on the lower levels.

For example, if I want to influence my own or someone else's behavior, I would need to make an intervention at least at the level of capability. So if someone says that they can't do something (at the level of behavior), and I respond at the level of behavior by saying something like "Do it this way," I may have fixed the issue but that is all—no learning or no cure will have taken place. To effect lasting change I would need to intervene at a higher level, which might be to show the person *how* to do what it is they can't do (at the level of capability) or to challenge their beliefs about what they are capable of.

Businesses so often make the mistake of attempting to resolve an issue by taking action to deal directly with a deficit, for example loss of a customer prompts costcutting exercises, shortage of business triggers skills training, and so on. We need to learn to shift levels so that we intervene at a different and higher level than the one on which the issue presents itself. Such is the nature of NLP.

There is a natural hierarchy of change

Give a man a fish and you feed for him a day. Teach a man how to fish and you feed him for life.

SUSTAINABLE CHANGE

Your thinking about yourself at the higher levels will determine your thinking and behavior at the lower levels, whereas, for example, your behavior may or may not influence your beliefs at the higher level. As in the examples of behavior earlier in the chapter, companies that only pay attention to behavior when trying to introduce a new culture of quality, for example, find that the change isn't sustainable unless they also address the higher levels of beliefs and values. In order to bring about change it is necessary to work at least one level above the one you want to influence.

If you do have someone who does not manage their time effectively to enable them to do their job well, sending them on a course to learn how to use an organizer may not be the answer. One manager realized that for one of his team the issue was not just a behavioral one, but that the person did not value or believe in the use of time in the same way that this manager did.

Characteristically, NLP training works at the higher levels. Many change models are to do with beliefs and identity. Although NLP does include teaching of techniques, the emphasis is on using capabilities such as sensitivity and flexibility to make these techniques work. Much NLP work can be done without knowing the content of the problem or the issue at hand. This distinguishes it from many other forms of training. NLP training operates on the philosophy that:

People have within them all the resources they need to achieve what they want.

NLP training is generative and to do with learning about learning and thinking about thinking. For this reason alone, it has a rightful place in an increasingly complex world where we need to find our own personal formulae to lead ourselves.

REACTIVE OR PROACTIVE?

Imagine yourself in the following situation.

You have been working on a new project for your company for the last six months. It is now nearing completion and all the results have been achieved to plan. You believe that the results of this project are an important contribution to the future of the company. You are pleased with the contribution you personally have made and expect that the launch of this project will boost your promotion prospects. Two weeks before the launch the directors announce a major company reorganization. They announce that all projects started within the last year are to be put on hold awaiting any further decision by the board. You and the rest of the project team feel very disappointed and disheartened.

Which of the following would you be more likely to do?

- ❏ Accept the situation and feel upset.
- ❏ Get inwardly annoyed.
- ❏ Complain to others around you about the way you have been treated.
- ❏ Hope that someone else takes action to change the decision.
- ❏ Ask for a meeting with your manager to discuss the decision.
- ❏ Accelerate the completion of the project so that you can announce its readiness for launch.
- ❏ Leave the company.

What else might you do? Are you reactive or proactive in the way you respond to events in your life? Puppet master or puppet? What is it that distinguishes those who influence their own destiny from those who leave their fate in the hands of others or to chance?

Steve's conversations centered around what he and others did. For example, he would measure the strength of people's friendships towards him in terms of what they would do for him. Equally, he expected them to judge the level of his friendship by the type of actions he undertook on their behalf. He was self-

employed and considered himself lucky each time a new large contract "turned up." He was never entirely sure what the source of the next contract would be. He was influenced a great deal by the climate. When the weather was sunny and warm he generally felt more optimistic, whereas when it was cold and cloudy he often felt depressed.

Steve is affected by day-to-day behavior and the environment. He is reactive.

Linda is quietly self-assured. She is very skilled at listening to other people and reflects before she answers or acts on what they say. Her posture is very upright, balanced, and symmetrical. She knows what is important to her and has strong beliefs but does not impose these on anyone. In fact, she has a very nondirective style of being with other people. She is flexible in her behavior so if what she is doing is not working she tries something else until she finds a way that is effective. If things go wrong she takes stock of the situation and decides what she really wants to do. She gives the impression of being at peace with herself most of the time and she is an attractive person to be with. People enjoy listening to her speak.

Linda's strength comes from within herself. She is proactive.

Attention to lower levels

If your attention is directed mainly to the lower levels of change in Dilts' framework you will be thinking about how you and others behave, in the environment. You will be affected by changes in other people's behavior and changes in the environment. If the weather is sunny it may cheer you up, if it is dull and wet you feel down. This tends to lead to a more *reactive* way of dealing with life. A company that concentrates on the lower behavioral and environmental levels will be more likely to respond to "the competition," rather than moving toward its own vision of the future.

Carla had a very clear sense of identity and mission. She knew what she wanted to achieve and what was important to her. She believed that people could be trusted and that if anyone behaved aggressively towards her it was not meant toward her personally, but was more a statement of what they were feeling inside. She believed that she could learn from whatever happened. She even took times of recession as an opportunity to learn how to approach work and customers differently.

Proactive behaviour requires you to focus on the higher levels of spirituality, mission and identity, beliefs and values. The more able you are to operate independently of other people's behavior and changes in the environment, the more proactive you become.

Attention to higher levels

"You carry your own weather around with you."
        Stephen Covey, Seven Habits of Highly Effective People

For example, if you believe that people can be trusted, even if someone lets you down it is likely that you will continue to maintain that belief and see the incident as a one-off aberration.

Here are some examples of how different people think about themselves.

A Overall I think I've been very lucky, both in my career and in my personal life. I've always been employed and now self-employed; amazingly work always seems to turn up. My personal life has been less smooth and though I have many regrets, especially with regard to my children, I have experienced much happiness. I enjoy being and feeling fit, and I enjoy my work, demonstrating skills that I have and spending time with my kids.

B I am a girl who knows what she wants and how and when I am going to get it. I have decided to become a physiotherapist. I have researched into this and even had some experience in it. This work is right for me and I'm right for it. I'm a happy person who loves helping people. I get along with anyone and everyone, a feature of myself of which I am proud.

C I find it very hard to write about myself, maybe because I am quite a shy and inward person. I don't really like to let people know how I am feeling. I also know that I am a very negative person. I lack confidence in myself so therefore I never believe in what I do. I would like to be more positive in my attitude toward life and I wish I had the ability not to worry and to be more relaxed.

A talks mainly about issues at the level of behavior and capabilities. This person is more likely to be affected by the behavior of other people, by situations, by the results he achieves. A's style is likely to be reactive. B, on the other hand, discusses herself in terms of her identity. This is a person who knows what she wants and gets it, a happy person, someone who is proud of herself. This understanding and clarity about her identity will permeate everything she does and the way she perceives her experience.

The writer of C, however, describes himself as a shy and inward person who doesn't believe in what he does and who wishes he could be different. Even though he is sure about his identity, it generates behavior that he doesn't want and would like to change. It is certain that no matter what others do to tell him he is capable and he need not worry, his beliefs about his identity will override this.

So the writers of B and C are independently proactive but in quite different ways, whereas the writer of A, whose attention is more at the lower levels, is likely to be significantly affected by day-to-day changes in behavior and environment.

Getting a balance

You may be happy as you are. If, however, you are like the subject of C who wants to change, it is important to identify at what level you can make this change. For him the overriding comments were at the level of identity and belief: "I am quite a shy and inward person," "I never believe in what I do." One does not necessarily have to lead to the other. He could, for example, remain shy and inward and yet believe in what he does. For him to achieve the changes he wants, he will need to bring about change at the level of identity or spirituality.

For the subject of A, however, it would depend on whether he wanted to change. If he felt he was unduly affected by behavior and environment and wanted to develop greater independence, he could pay attention to levels of capabilities, beliefs, and identity.

WHEN WE GO OUT OF ALIGNMENT

I don't know anyone who has a coherent state of alignment at all times. What matters more is that the incidence of this state is increasing for you and that you know what to do when you are not in this state.

You may recognize you are out of this state when your circumstances affect you adversely, when you are preoccupied with a negative internal dialog, when your focus is on problems, or when you feel stressed, tired, or upset.

Are you experiencing any of the following right now?

❑ A family disappointment or upset.
❑ An unexpected change in your work circumstances.
❑ An uncooperative colleague or friend.
❑ A change in health.
❑ A surprise in the market sector in which you operate.
❑ A gloomy forecast.
❑ A personal conflict.
❑ An unsatisfactory outcome in your work.
❑ A home move.
❑ A major work challenge.
❑ A relationship problem.

It is possible that you have one or several of these. It is when these kinds of issues occur that our alignment is most challenged. Often the combination of such issues can trigger an unproductive pattern of thinking and behavior It is at these times when it is of most value to be able to hold on to a state of alignment. It is when we are tested that our true values and principles come through. The question is whether they are the ones you want to come through.

The more familiar you become with what you want to be important for you at each of the levels and the more you remind yourself of this, the more likely you are to be able to regain your alignment (and maybe not even lose it) in times of challenge and stress.

STEPS TO PERSONAL CONGRUENCE

By becoming aware of your thinking at each of these levels you will start to influence the process of personal alignment. The next step is to decide what you want to be true for you at each level. By working your way through the following questions, over time you will begin to develop a sense of personal congruence.

❑ **What is the system of which you are a part/would like to influence?** What contribution do you make to the bigger systems of which you are a part? What contribution do you want to make? (Other ways of thinking about this question would be to ask: What legacy do you want to leave? What added value would you like to give?

❑ **What is your identity/mission?** Thinking about identity and mission can sometimes take months or even years to clarify. Begin by writing down what you think they are. How would you describe yourself? What is your purpose in business, in life? There are many exercises that can help you think about this. Some examples are included in the thought provokers at the end of this chapter. Consider also what roles you feel you fulfill in life and those you want for yourself no matter what the circumstances.

❑ **What are your beliefs and values?** Be honest with yourself. Write down the beliefs and values that you actually operate to, rather than the "good," textbook words. Think about the decisions that you make on a day-by-day basis. What are the factors on which you make those decisions? What beliefs do you hold about yourself/other people/your family/your job/your life? Ask other people who know you what they believe you stand for. What do you want to stand for?

❑ **What are your capabilities?** Establish your true capabilities. These may be demonstrated not only by what you do in your work but by what you do outside that work. You may not be the best judge of your capabilities. Elicit other people's views on what they might be. What unique set of skills would you like to be able to realize from within yourself?

❑ **What do you do?** What is your everyday behavior? It is often others who can give this feedback most accurately. Do a self-perception and contrast it with others' perception of how you behave. Identify the behaviors that are characteristic of you, the things you say and do. What is characteristic of you when you are at one with yourself and when you are not? What would you like to be characteristic of you at all times?

❑ **What is your environment?** Where and when do you do the things identified above? What would you say are the external influences on you and your life? What does your appearance say about you—today? Every day? How is your physical environment a metaphor for who you are? In what contexts would you like to be able to make a difference?

Just the process of becoming aware of what these things are for you will give you more choice about whether you hold on to them or not. Awareness leads to choice. The person who wrote paragraph C earlier in this chapter, describing himself as a shy and inward person, has subsequently experienced significant shifts in his self-perception. He felt that the process of writing out the paragraph highlighted some of the patterns in his thinking about himself that he didn't like and wanted to change. This person has developed confidence in himself, has been appointed to a position of responsibility, and is generally much happier with life and himself. The way forward may not always be as straightforward as that, but it is surprising how often it can be much simpler than we let ourselves believe.

Awareness leads to choice

1 Choose something that you know to be true of you when you are aligned and that you can imagine easily. It might be a behavior, a value, a belief, or it might be something that makes you feel good when you wear it. It helps if you have anchored this aligned state previously, but this is also a way of doing that.

2 Imagine that the levels are stretched out in front of you. In effect, imagine that you can see the diagram on page 211 set out before you. You can do this sitting down or you might find it easier to walk through the levels as if they were marked out on the floor. Start at the level that you can imagine most easily and begin to walk up the levels, allowing yourself to imagine how you are and how you want to be when you are at one with yourself. Take whatever time you need to do this and allow whatever comes to mind to do so. This is not something you can do absolutely consciously or intellectually. Allow your unconscious mind to guide you.

SHORTCUT TO PERSONAL ALIGNMENT

You may find that the higher you go in the levels the more abstract your thinking becomes. You may be thinking in metaphors. Once you have reached the level of spirituality, turn around and look back down the levels with this sense of overall purpose. Now walk back down bringing this sense of purpose with you and explore each of the levels again, reminding yourself all the time of how you want to be.

SUMMARY

Proactivity is one of the fashionable words in business today. And although there is no right and wrong about proactivity and reactivity (we need some of both), there is undoubtedly a need for proactive leadership in an increasingly chaotic world. There is no longer any time to wait to follow others' lead. And there is no way that you can truly plan if what you are doing is waiting to see what move others make before you make your own. The logical levels of change model provides us with a means of understanding the patterns of proactivity and reactivity.

People who are clear about their purpose, identity, beliefs and values, and whose attention is centered on these levels, will be more independent of changes that occur at the levels of behavior and environment and more proactive in relation to them. People who are less sure of these levels in relation to themselves and whose attention is more at the lower levels will be affected and will react to their own and others' behavior and changes in the environment.

Think of sport as a metaphor for business. What creates outstanding performance in cycling or tennis or any other sport is what creates personal and business success.

There are many NLP techniques designed to bring about change at each level and some of these changes may be best brought about with the help of an external facilitator. However, by becoming aware of your thinking and beliefs at each of these levels and by beginning to question and challenge those you want to change, you will begin to influence your personal balance between proactivity and reactivity.

THOUGHT PROVOKERS

1 Consider the following aspects of your life. How close are you in each of these areas to the way you want to be? In the column headed "Ideal" give each a mark out of 10, where 10 signifies this is exactly as you want it to be and 0 indicates it is not at all as you would want it. In the column headed "Reactive/ proactive" rate yourself in terms of how actively you are influencing each area. 10 indicates you are, in your view, entirely proactive in the way you are influencing this area to bring it up to the ideal. 0 indicates you are waiting and hoping (or you've just given up).

	Ideal	**Reactive/Proactive**

Your job
Your social life
Your friends
Your skills

You will be building up a picture of where you lie on the reactive–proactive scale. Even if you have what you consider to be an ideal situation, or close to it, you may find that you actively influence that situation to keep it that way.

It can be useful to get other people's feedback on how they perceive you on this scale. It can be easy sometimes to delude yourself, for example into thinking that being busy is the same as being proactive, when in fact what you are doing is having little influence.

2 Take a few moments and imagine you are applying for the work you really want to do. Write a paragraph about yourself which, in your view, describes what makes you uniquely you.

3 Ask a colleague or friend if they will answer the following questions in the order given.

A What is characteristic behavior for you? (Behavior)

B What does your environment say about you? (Environment)

C What unique skills do you demonstrate and might demonstrate? (Capabilities)

D What is important to you about what you do and what values do you communicate to others by doing what you do? (Values)

E What do you believe is true about you and those around you that enables you to do what you do? (Beliefs)

F Who are you? (Identity)

G What value do you add to others by just being you? (Spirituality)

> How easy did they find it to answer the questions? Was it easier at the beginning or at the end? How did the quality of the communication change as you progressed through the questions? Each question corresponds to one of the logical levels of change. The ease with which your partner answered the questions can be an indication of how familiar that level of thinking about themselves is to them.

REFERENCES

Gregory Bateson & Mary Catherine Bateson (2000) *Steps to an Ecology of Mind*, University of Chicago Press.

James Collins & Jerry Porras (2000) *Built to Last: Successful Habits of Visionary Companies*, Random House.

Stephen R. Covey (1999) *Seven Habits of Highly Effective People*, Simon & Schuster.

Paul Z. Jackson & Mark McKergow (2002) *The Solutions Focus: The SIMPLE Way to Positive Change*, Nicholas Brealey Publishing.

Brian Keenan & John McCarthy (2000) *Between Extremes*, Black Swan.

Michael Lissack & Johan Roos (2000) *The Next Common Sense: An E-Manager's Guide to Mastering Complexity*, Nicholas Brealey Publishing.

Peter Senge, Richard Ross, Brian Smith, Charlotte Roberts & Art Kleiner (1994) *The Fifth Discipline Fieldbook: Strategies and Tools for Building a Learning Organization*, Nicholas Brealey Publishing.

Gilbert Kaplan was an American millionaire publisher. He had achieved all the key business goals he had ever set himself. He was also a Gustav Mahler enthusiast. His obsession began in 1965, when as a young Wall Street economist he heard Stokowski conduct the Second Symphony. From then on he attended every live performance possible of that symphony, avidly studied every recording, and eventually at the age of 40 conceived the wild idea of conducting the work himself. The experts sniffed. Kaplan's only musical training lay in childhood piano lessons.

When he eventually gave his first public performance people attended out of curiosity and disbelief. They had heard of his obsession but knew what sort of training it took to develop the ability to conduct, in particular to conduct the music of Mahler. As the performance began Kaplan realized that he could not synchronize his conducting with the sound of the orchestra. He was unfamiliar with the acoustics of the hall. The audience were not surprised; after all it was to be expected. The performance was a failure.

Kaplan, however, was undeterred. He believed in his ability eventually to conduct Mahler. He continued to study and was particularly obsessed with Mahler's Resurrection Symphony. He memorized this complex score and traveled to hear the work whenever it was performed. He decided he was ready to give a performance in 1982 and did so with the American Symphony Orchestra. His revealing interpretation confounded the critics and won him worldwide requests to repeat the performance.

Kaplan now devotes his spare time to Mahler research, financing in 1986 a finely documented and superbly produced facsimile of the Resurrection Symphony, whose original score he now owns. He has conducted 33 international performances of the symphony.

14

Write Your Own Lifescript: Beliefs of Excellence

"The problem is not in what we do but what we become."
Oscar Wilde, De Profundis

Our beliefs influence every moment of every day

Our beliefs influence and mold our behavior. They form our lifescript, in the sense that whatever we believe dictates how we respond to the situations and people we meet in our life. If I believe that I will always find a way to succeed no matter what I do, I am more likely to do just that than is someone who believes they can never have what they really want.

Most of our beliefs are formed by the age of seven and are shaped by our parents or the equivalent of parent figures. In most cases we don't realize what our beliefs consist of and yet they influence every moment of every day. And every belief has a structure to it, which we can influence if we choose.

It is a little like carrying round a recording in our heads. If the recording is working for us we can keep it, maybe updating it to refine it from time to time. If, however, the recording is limiting what we think about ourselves, we can take it out and re-record it so we have one that does work for us. It is a basis of NLP that if we understand the structure of what we hold in our thinking, we can change it if we choose to.

If we want to model excellent performance we need to be able to "step into" the beliefs of the person we are modeling in order to influence the way we behave. Equally, to tap into our most resourceful state for a specific context, we need to be able to "step into" the belief that supports us in this (to model ourselves). For example, if I want the confidence to talk with ease at a conference, it helps me to model those times when I fully believe that I do have something of value to share with the conference delegates. In reminding myself of this belief I tap into a resource that I already have but may temporarily have shelved.

Beliefs can be expressed as statements. These are not factual statements but emotionally held opinions that we have reinforced over time. So what are the beliefs that are so vital today? They are as follows:

- ❏ **Each person is unique**. There is a wealth of untapped talent in everyone and we can help to release this talent by the way we relate to people.
- ❏ **Everyone makes the best choice available to them at the time they make it**. By believing this we can learn how to understand, coach high performance, and forgive.
- ❏ **There is no failure, only feedback**. We must be able to take in and learn from changing situations. Consequently we need to be able to learn continuously and this belief is central to our ability to do this.
- ❏ **Behind every behavior is a positive intention**. This belief is fundamental in our being able to take whatever happens to us, no matter how detrimental it might be initially, and turn it into personal learning and growth.
- ❏ **The meaning of the communication is its effect**. We may not be able to control our environment, but what we can do is be aware of the effect we have on it. In holding this belief we take full responsibility for the effect of our communication with others.
- ❏ **There is a solution to every problem**. This belief is characteristically held by people who find new ways of working through or round obstacles and challenges. People recognized as leaders typically hold this belief.
- ❏ **We have within us all the resources we will ever need**. By believing this we can learn how to tap into every resource (skill, attitude, belief) that we will ever need to achieve what we want.

❑ **The person with the most flexibility in thinking and behavior has the greatest influence**. If what we are doing isn't working, then the more choices we have the more likely we are to find a way that does work.

❑ **Mind and body are part of the same system**. And if we listen to our bodies they can tell us what our minds need to know. Hold this belief and learn to listen to the wisdom of your body.

❑ **Knowledge, thought, memory, and imagination are the result of sequences and combinations of ways of filtering and storing information**. If we learn what those sequences and combinations are (the programs), we can influence what is and isn't working for us and do something about it.

Take any compassionate leader. Take any founder of a successful startup. Take anyone who is creating a new business—and you will find a core of these beliefs. Take anyone who is thriving and enjoying life and contributing to the world at large and who rides the waves of change, and you will find that they hold these kinds of beliefs. To hold these or similar beliefs is to be at one with yourself.

To explore the effect of these beliefs we do not have to absolutely believe them initially—we can presuppose them, think about them as if they were true. In this way we can discover what effect they have on our life before we choose to adopt them on a more permanent basis. By presupposing any belief we begin to take on the ways of thinking and behaving that are characteristic of the models of excellence.

To hold these beliefs is to be at one with yourself

HOW BELIEFS ORIGINATE

Jane was a newly appointed manager of a high-class London store. The items for sale consisted of jewelry and expensive leather goods and were displayed in glass cabinets. Closing time was six o'clock. Exactly at that time one of Jane's staff, Robert, would start locking the cabinets whether or not there were customers still in the store. Jane disapproved: She disliked the impression this gave to the customers. She wanted Robert to lock the cabinets, but only after all the customers had left.

She explained to him that it was store policy to lock the cabinets only when customers had left, but it had no effect. The next time it happened she pointed out that senior management disapproved of any locking up in the presence of customers; still no effect. Jane struggled to communicate any authority and sensed a loss of respect on the part of the staff toward her.

In discussion with a friend she realized that what she could have said was, "I want you to keep the cabinets open until all the customers have left." She hadn't previously spoken for herself. She realized that by doing that she could begin to establish her own authority. And she acknowledged that there were many other situations where she could begin to express what she wanted by saying "I want" or "I'd like."

Jane wondered why she hadn't done this before and she came to understand that "I want" was something she very rarely said. She remembered her childhood. Her mother had repeatedly said to her, "I want doesn't get."

This is an example of how beliefs are formed. We accept opinions from influential people in our lives and hold them as facts. They aren't facts at all. They are perceptions formed through our own experience and the views of others.

Beliefs are views about ourselves, others, and the world. These views determine the decisions we take and the way we behave in everyday situations. Our parents or the equivalent of parent figures (and this includes teachers) are the source of many of our beliefs.

Beliefs are views

For example:

- ❏ I want doesn't get.
- ❏ You can achieve whatever you want in this world.
- ❏ You have to work hard to get on in life.
- ❏ You always get what you want and you always will.
- ❏ You'll always land on your feet whatever happens.
- ❏ You're lazy.
- ❏ You'll never get what you want in this world if you don't work for it.
- ❏ You're a grade A student.
- ❏ You're stupid.
- ❏ People can't be trusted.

❏ Children should be seen and not heard.
❏ You've got no respect for anyone's feelings.
❏ You're a liar.
❏ You're the "good" child in the family.
❏ You're a born artist.
❏ You're a lousy mathematician.

You can create your own empowering set of beliefs

The nature of NLP is that you can change your beliefs so that you create your own set of principles to support the way you really want to be. You need not carry around redundant or even destructive belief systems belonging to someone else. You can create your own empowering set of beliefs instead. How many of us carry around baggage that really belongs to someone else? Because our beliefs are principles that we hold entirely within ourselves, they are completely under our influence. We do not have to be limited by patterns of the past; we can write our own lifescript.

Rewrite history

There are several ways to do this. One way is to presuppose that you do hold beliefs that, although new to you, are more in line with the way you want to be. Alternatively, NLP gives you the techniques to rewrite your own history. Because your unconscious mind does not know the difference between what is real and what is imagined, you can imagine the past you would prefer to have had and rewrite your memories. This comes from the belief that knowledge, thought, and memory are the result of sequences and combinations of ways of filtering and storing information. By knowing what sequences and combinations of thought patterns we are using, we change how we represent the memories we hold. We can influence our memories to support us in the way we would like to be now as opposed to the way we happen to be. This is a mental agility that can be learned.

HOW BELIEFS INFLUENCE OUR LIVES

Enabling beliefs

My husband plays squash and he believes he has the potential to win every match he plays. The sequence of events for him is as follows:

Belief
"I have the
potential to win
any match I play"

I prove my belief to
myself

I exercise and keep
fit because there is
a purpose to this

This increases the
chances of winning
and I often do win

I notice when I play a
particularly good shot

I can imagine myself
winning the match. I can
see myself smiling and
shaking hands with my
friends at the end of the
match. I'm saying "well
done, I enjoyed that,"
knowing that I won

I play well

I put my full attention and
energy into the game

I feel confident

If, on the other hand, he believed he did not have much
chance of winning or playing well, the scenario would be like
that below.

Limiting beliefs

Belief
"I don't have
much change of
winning"

I prove my belief to
myself

I don't bother to
exercise because there
isn't much point

I lose the match

I decrease my chances
of winning

I know what will happen.
My friend will play much
better than me and I can
imagine the outcome. I
will feel dejected and
exhausted

I play half-
heartedly

I notice particularly when I
play a bad shot

I feel unmotivated

Self-fulfilling prophecies

Our beliefs act as a self-fulfilling prophecy. We act in a way that proves the validity and value of our beliefs to ourselves. If our beliefs are self-limiting we limit our performance, thus proving the belief to be "true." Over time the beliefs become more and more entrenched as we continue to live them out each day.

However, if we hold empowering beliefs such as the beliefs of excellence outlined below, we act and behave in a way that releases our potential and allows us to express our real self. With NLP we can find the key to generate empowering beliefs for ourselves so that we can learn and grow and achieve the things we really want.

Only recently the winner of the UK national computer game competition said that in order to win he believed that the game was real. Although he knows it is virtual, he believes that in this combat game he can actually die. He said that by believing this he played as if the game were not a game at all but a real-life battle for survival.

THE BELIEFS OF EXCELLENCE

Have you ever wondered how some people achieve success? For example:

❏ How Christopher Columbus held on to his vision of discovering a new route around the world and maintained the courage and tenacity to cross waters that no one had sailed before?
❏ How the Americans managed to break through the limits of what seemed possible to land a man on the moon?
❏ How British hostage in the Lebanon Terry Waite retained his sanity and self-worth when held in solitary confinement bound, blindfolded, and threatened with death?
❏ How previously unheard of entrepreneurial companies such as Yahoo! and Amazon became household names overnight in markets that hadn't existed a year before?
❏ How Richard Branson carved out a share of the airline market for Virgin Airlines in a business already dominated by well-established and powerful organizations?

Many people would have given up after a fraction of the journey. What made these and so many more achievements possible? These people succeeded because they believed they could. Once Roger Bannister had run a mile in under four minutes, within months many other athletes did the same. Once he had broken the barrier, he created a belief in others that it was possible. Once others held the belief, their performance matched what they believed to be possible. Such is the power of what we believe and the influence of those beliefs on other people.

Let's consider what each of the beliefs of excellence means.

This belief is sometimes referred to as "the map is not the territory."

Consider this conversation:

"I really enjoyed the film last night."
"It was rubbish."
"No it wasn't, the photography was beautiful."
"Yes, but the story line was nonexistent."
"That's ridiculous."
"No it isn't!"

EACH PERSON IS UNIQUE

Recognize that? Neither person in this conversation is right or wrong, although they may not appreciate this. However, each has their own way of experiencing life, their own "map of the world." How often does your map of the world bump up against someone else's? And what happens when it does?

Once you accept that everyone has a unique map of the world, you begin to understand and accept difference.

"When I think about other cultures I think about what they represent in terms of human possibilities: a whole set of ways to see and hear and feel about the world that could potentially resonate with my neurology, a place where news of difference is waiting to be discovered."

Judith De Lozier, Turtles All the Way Down

Imagine a world where this understanding and acceptance existed—how different our daily lives would be. How would

Maps of the world

the press survive? What stories would they print? Can you imagine how different the headlines would be?

How often are you party to the following kinds of situations?

Jim was explaining how he saw his future and the sort of obstacles he wanted to overcome. Jane listened to him for a while and then said, "You know, Jim, what you really ought to do is to leave this job and move into sales, you'd be much more suited to that."

"But that isn't really what I want to do, Jane."

"You may not think it is," replied Jane, "but believe me I know it's the right move for you."

Jim sat back and folded his arms. He disagreed.

Diane could not understand why staff were complaining about the new appraisal scheme. She was a member of the human resource development team who were instrumental in its design. The design involved managers rating their team members on a scale of I to 5, 1 being "subject to disciplinary action" and 5 meaning, more or less, "the sun shines out of every orifice." The staff were very unhappy about the form, particularly the rating system. Diane found all these complaints very frustrating and considered the staff to be "difficult."

Perception

Both of these illustrate what can happen when someone doesn't presuppose "each person is unique" to be true and consequently doesn't value others' "maps of the world." This means we all have our unique perception of the world, the way things are, the way people behave, our own experience. And that perception is only a view of those things, an interpretation. It's not an exact representation of reality. Just like a map is only a representation of a territory, highlighting some features, ignoring others, so your personal experience leads you to highlight some features and ignore others.

Accepting this presupposition means that you respect difference.

"Difference is the difference that makes the difference."
Gregory Bateson

The table below compares what it would be like to hold the belief that each person is unique with what it would be like not to do so.

	People who do believe that "each person is unique" is true	People who don't believe that "each person is unique" is true
Have this sort of approach	Cooperative, respectful, and open to difference and feedback	Rigid, inflexible and dogmatic
Hold these sorts of beliefs	Difference is valuable	Their own opinion is right. They know best
Have these capabilities/ limitations	Listening skills, sensitivity to and respect for difference	Determination and single-mindedness
Do and say	Look interested, cooperate, ask questions, are curious about others' experiences and explore differences. Ask for clarification when they get feedback of which they were previously unaware and had not seen in themselves	Speak in terms of what others "should" or "ought" to do. Disagree and interrupt. Dismiss. Do what they have always done. Defend themselves and rationalize away feedback
Feel	Relaxed and curious	Frustrated, irritated, and stressed
Experience	Find new talent, cut new ground	Stagnate

When your colleague argues with you and refuses to see your point of view, *at that moment* it is the best choice available to them. And the way you react to them is your best choice at that time.

If you had learned the most elegant and cooperative ways of achieving what you want, life would be very different. But you didn't. You learned healthy and unhealthy ways of getting what you want. When a child cries and shouts in the middle of the supermarket, that child has learned that is the way to get the attention they want; not the best way, at least not for those around, but the best choice for the child. You do what you do because at some level it works. If what you are doing didn't work you wouldn't do it.

If you run away from potentially painful situations, that is your best learned choice. This does not mean it is the "best"

> EVERYONE MAKES THE BEST CHOICE AVAILABLE TO THEM AT THE TIME

choice overall, but it is the best you can come up with given your experience to date and your emotions and state at the time of making the decision.

However, one thing is for sure:

If you do what you always did you get what you always got.

New choices

Consider for a moment one of your goals. What are you doing now to achieve it? Whatever that is, it is your best choice at this moment. The more choices you have, the more chance you have of getting what you want. If one of your chosen paths doesn't get you what you want, you can choose another and another until you find the one that does, provided you have the flexibility.

Think for a moment about anyone with whom you have felt frustrated within the last month. For example:

❑ The colleague who gave a boring presentation.
❑ The person who dominated the meeting.
❑ A member of your family who made an insensitive comment to you.
❑ The support person who was abrupt with you.
❑ The car driver who cut in front of you.
❑ The salesperson who wouldn't answer your questions.
❑ The receptionist who kept you waiting.

Now step into the belief that "everyone makes the best choice available to them at the time."

Imagine what it would be like if you were to believe that. Now, as you imagine what it is like, how does that affect your feelings toward the people you have listed? Would that colleague really have chosen to give a boring presentation if he had a choice? Would the colleague have dominated the meeting if she had other choices about how to influence you?

This may not be your belief, but you can experience the results of holding it by *presupposing* that it is true for you.

If you don't hold this to be true you might respond to the deliverer of the boring presentation with disdain. By presupposing that this is their best choice, you will be more likely to give them constructive feedback and suggestions for other ways they could present their ideas. It doesn't mean that you have to accept what they are doing in the way they are doing it. It does mean that you are more likely to be in a state where you can influence it.

Choosing responses

The beliefs of excellence give us more resourceful ways of responding to less than ideal situations in ways that are most likely to lead to a win/win outcome. The focus shifts from blame, disdain, and frustration to curiosity, understanding, and concern, particularly in terms of how to enable yourself and others around you to have more choice, so that the best choice for one or a few becomes the best choice for many.

How many people do you know who live their life with regrets? Do you? Knowing what you know now, there may very well be decisions you would change, places you would have gone, people you would have treated differently. But this is you now, with different skills, different knowledge, different experience. At that time the choices you made were the best available to you. Once you can accept this you can let go of regrets; they clutter the places reserved for other more self-fulfilling choices.

Christopher Columbus, John F Kennedy, Terry Waite, Richard Branson, Roger Bannister are all people who persevered to get what they wanted against all odds, people who held the belief that "There is no failure, only feedback." I'm sure if we interviewed Christopher Columbus today he would not say, "Actually, I put it all down to this belief, 'No failure, only feedback'"! However, for him to do what he did this must have been what he believed in order to find the courage and tenacity to carry on with his exploration.

THERE IS NO FAILURE, ONLY FEEDBACK

Experience and acceptance of failure =
defeat and resignation
Experience and review of feedback =
learning and choice

Imagine that you hold this belief to be true. How would it influence how you respond to:

❏ Your acceptance of feedback from others?
❏ Your confidence in giving feedback?

❏ Your self-esteem when presenting ideas?
❏ Your willingness to take risks?

Try it on for size: What would it really be like for you? Imagine the learning potential this can unleash. This is a very powerful belief in the context of self-development. When we truly hold this belief we can learn from everything that happens to us. This belief is taking a new and even greater importance day by day. We live in a world where feedback is ever more available, in real time. The people and companies that are able to take advantage of this are the ones who do believe that there is only learning; there is no failure, only feedback, in many more forms than we have ever before experienced.

BEHIND EVERY BEHAVIOR IS A POSITIVE INTENTION

This belief can be mind-blowing. It means you choose to believe that behind every action there is a positive intention toward you. The key thing to remember here is that it doesn't have to be true. The benefits come from *believing* that it is true. I can choose to believe that if someone behaves aggressively toward me the positive intention behind their behavior is for me to learn a greater independence of state. The person being aggressive does not consciously have this purpose for me; I choose to believe that this is behind their behavior.

By believing this I have choice in how I respond. Without this belief I am more likely to become either nonassertive or even aggressive in response. I might start to lose self-esteem and confidence because of how I am feeling about the way they are with me. People who are able to maintain choices in the way they respond to the behavior of those around them are typically people who hold this belief or something very similar.

Ian and his teenage son had almost come to blows. His son stood in one corner of the kitchen and Ian in the other. They shouted but neither listened to the other. To Ian his son was being a demanding, inconsiderate teenager. To the son his father had a closed mind, was inflexible and completely out of touch. Ian stopped himself from rushing forward and hitting his son and in that moment he gave himself the time to stand back and think about what he was doing. He moved toward his son, put his arms around him and said, "I'll always love you, no matter what you do."

That moment enabled Ian to express what he really felt. That moment would also imprint itself on his son's mind in such a way that when he had a teenage son of his own he had this memory, this role model of how a father can be.

At that point Ian was not consciously thinking, "What is the positive intention behind my son's behavior toward me?" But at a more unconscious level this principle was in operation. It certainly wasn't in his son's mind to think, "How can I be so disagreeable that I cause my dad to give me a role model of parenting for my future?" Far from it! But by acting as if this were the case, Ian turned what might have been a damaging situation into a special one.

Acting "as if"

This is the sort of influence you can have. If you choose to believe that there is a positive intention toward you in the following kinds of circumstances, you can transform the way you respond to the situation. For example:

❏ Your boss criticizes you for your incompetence.
❏ You could choose to believe that the positive intention toward you is to provide you with the opportunity to learn how to stay calm and confident when faced with aggression.

❏ A colleague misunderstands what you tell him or her.
❏ The positive intention is to teach you how to be more flexible in your communication so that you find a way of explaining that they do understand.

❏ Your business takes a dive.
❏ The intention is for you to make a new start and learn how to pick yourself up when things go wrong.

These examples may or may not work for you. It is important to generate your own ideas of what the positive intentions might be, ones that make sense of the behavior for you. This is an opportunity to let your creativity generate some ideas. When you find a positive intention that works for you, you will find the behavior takes on a whole new meaning. More than that, it will free you from giving a compulsive response: It will change your state so that your response is one of choice and not of inappropriate habit.

THE MEANING OF THE COMMUNICATION IS ITS EFFECT

This belief can also be expressed as "the intention behind a communication is not its meaning." The principle operates at many different levels. For example:

❑ Have you ever experienced a moment of frustration when you have carefully explained an idea to someone and they have misunderstood you? Or have you ever given feedback to someone with the intention of helping them to learn and develop, only to find that they felt angry about what you said?

❑ At parents' evenings at school, sometimes I shuddered when a teacher said things like, "This particular class are a difficult group to teach, they aren't good listeners. They've got to learn to pay attention." This kind of comment indicates that the teacher puts the responsibility almost entirely on the pupils and hardly at all on themselves. And if I blame the teacher then I am doing exactly the same thing!

❑ Have you ever appraised someone working for you in a way that devolved all responsibility for their performance from the way you were managing them? How do you think they felt? Have you ever been in the same position? How did you feel?

❑ If you have a team working for you and they are achieving results beyond the norm, that is a measure of your management ability.

❑ If you have a colleague who won't cooperate with you, that is a reflection of your influencing skill.

❑ If you have a child who won't "behave," that is a statement about your ability as a parent.

The other people in these situations have a part too! But you are a part of the system. Something you do is allowing and very likely even encouraging the response you receive.

Responsibility

The power in this way of thinking is that you take responsibility for the responses you receive. If you don't get the response you want at first, you find new ways of communicating until you do. For example, if someone doesn't understand you, you find a way of explaining your thoughts in ways they do understand.

To believe that "the meaning of your communication is its effect" means that:

❏ If you have people working for you who give their all to their work—It is an indication of how you manage them.

❏ If you explain a new concept to a colleague and they don't understand—It is a measure of lack of flexibility in the way you explain.

❏ If you have a warm loving family around you—It is a reflection of how you are.

❏ If you give feedback to a friend and they are offended—It is a result of how you gave the feedback to them.

❏ If people choose you as their main supplier—It is a measure of how you have related to them in the way you conduct business.

Anyone holding this belief does not have problem customers, problem staff, or problem management. Holding this belief means you take responsibility for the reactions you get and take them as feedback on how you are doing. By holding this belief you do not consider others to be a source of problems. You seek to develop your own flexibility so that you find new choices that elicit new responses.

Flexibility

What do you do when you are faced with a problem? Do you give up? Do you persevere until you find a way out? Do you wait for someone else to sort it out?

Imagine what it would be like to believe that you could find a solution to every problem you ever encountered. You would probably spend much less time worrying about how you are going to get on in life. You would have confidence that somewhere, somehow you will find a way to achieve what you want.

That is what it is like to hold this belief. This is the belief of people who make major breakthroughs. This belief is characteristic of people who find new solutions to old problems. They do this because they believe they can. This is the belief at the heart of all creativity.

Edward de Bono explores the consequences of this belief in his books about lateral thinking. There is a solution to every problem and believing this opens the mind to the possibilities, new innovative solutions.

If you hold this belief you trust your instinct in finding a way through problems. What might frustrate you are people who do

THERE IS A SOLUTION TO EVERY PROBLEM

not hold this belief; people who give up when they encounter a difficulty. However, if you truly hold this belief then the chances are that you will find a way to influence them as well.

WE HAVE ALL THE RESOURCES WE WILL EVER NEED WITHIN US ALREADY

The most self-sufficient people recognize that the place to look for resources is within themselves. Most of us have largely untapped reserves of qualities, skills, and attitudes that we have never learned how to use. I have often met people who, if they are aware of some of their untapped skills, keep quiet about them for fear of coming over as arrogant or self-important.

From the day we are born we are experiencing, learning, experimenting, and growing. En route we are developing an immense set of approaches that are unique to our particular circumstances. Even if we only experience a skill briefly, we still have it in our memory banks just waiting to be drawn out and developed when another time is appropriate.

If I am faced with a situation in which I recognize that what I need is confidence to put across what I know with fluency, but what I am experiencing is doubt about my ability, then I can look within myself for resources. If I believe that I have all the resources within, I can search until I find a time in my life or a context in which I had the very resource I want now. Just by asking myself the question "Where do I have this resource (I might name it—self-confidence, or whatever the skill is I need)?" I begin the process of finding and releasing exactly what I want. By now you may realize that if we think about a time (in an associated way) when we had the resources we want, we create the effect of tapping into those resources in the present.

My mother has severe osteoporosis and struggles to walk or move without pain. Her back is now deformed as a result of the decreasing bone density. She often talks about the discomfort in her back and when she does she moves with discomfort and with a tense facial expression. One day she was talking about an Austrian Major that she had met during the war and how whenever she came into a room he would stand to attention. The memory clearly amused her and as she explained how the Major stood to attention, she sprang to her feet and illustrated exactly how he did this. She was smiling and amused by the memory. She was totally unaware of how she moved and overcame all her physical disability in that moment.

At one stage in my career I worked for the training department of International Computers Ltd. We ran a range of skills development courses for customers. At that time I was involved in an influencing skills course in which we taught the delegates choice in the way they expressed themselves verbally. We also taught them how to choose the most effective language to achieve the outcomes they wanted, particularly for meetings.

We returned some highly verbally skilled people to our client companies. Then we started to get complaints from the company sales teams. When a company salesperson was in a meeting with a client who had attended the influencing skills course, the company person was consistently being outmaneuvered by the client in the way they managed the meeting. Needless to say, the company changed its training policy. This course immediately became a key part of the training program for the sales teams!

When Lance Armstrong won the Tour de France in 2001, part of his success was attributed to his high pedaling speed. Most other cyclists turn the pedals more slowly, often using a higher gear. The effect of using a higher pedaling speed Is that the body uses different muscles (low-twitch muscles) to the ones you use if you are pedaling more slowly (high-twitch muscles). Low-twitch muscles can endure for longer than high-twitch muscles and Lance Armstrong has trained in such a way that he can use both. He can also cycle long distances either sitting or standing on the pedals. He can excel on the mountain climbs and yet he is unsurpassed in his time trial speeds. What he has overall is immense flexibility in all aspects of his cycling skills.

THE PERSON WITH THE MOST FLEXIBILITY IN THINKING AND BEHAVIOR HAS THE BEST CHANCE OF SUCCEEDING

The same is true of our mental flexibility. If we have flexibility in our thinking and behavior, we have choice. If one choice doesn't work we can try another until we find one that does.

How does a sports player get flexibility? They train; they exercise the different parts of their body so that they can move freely, so that they can vary their style. Athletes undergo an extensive range of training programs. The most effective exercise is often the simplest but most frequent. By regularly

Exercise your thinking

practicing the skills and techniques explained in this book, you will develop your range of behavior and thinking and consequently your flexibility. You can achieve world-class status as a communicator as a consequence of the way you train your mind.

MIND AND BODY ARE PART OF THE SAME SYSTEM

Anything that occurs in one part of the system will affect the other parts.

Stand up to do the following exercise. Look ahead, stand feet apart, face forward, raise one arm horizontally out in front of you, and gently twist around, keeping your arm horizontal until it is pointing as far behind you as it will go. Keeping your arm fixed in that position, turn round and note what your arm is pointing to. It may be a point on the wall or in the distance that marks how far you have been able to move your arm behind you.

Now look carefully at the scene behind you and decide how far you would like your arm to be able to move beyond the original point. Fix that point in your mind as you turn to face forward again. As you face forward twist again, moving your arm behind you as far as it will go. When you have pushed it as far as it will go, hold it steady, turn round, and see how far you have moved your arm this time.

The power of the mind

Most people find that they have moved their arm further the second time, if not to the point they visualized, then beyond. We know that if you imagine yourself throwing a ball, the muscles of the body that would move if you were actually throwing a ball tense and flex in exactly the same way. Those of you with a vivid imagination probably recoil physically when watching something unpleasant on television or at the cinema. You can reproduce the feelings in yourself that are experienced by someone else. Your body becomes an expression of your thinking. Recent research has shown many connections between what we think and the wellbeing of our bodies.

The point about all these beliefs of excellence is that they don't have to be true. Their power lies in the effect they have when you choose to believe they are true. So what are the implications for you of believing that mind and body are part of the same system?

❏ You are independent, in the sense of believing that you have control and influence over your own experience.

❏ You believe that you can influence your state and health by the way you think.

❏ You are capable of generating whatever state you want in yourself: relaxation, excitement, peace, confidence.

❏ You take care of both your body and your mind and keep them fit.

❏ You create the memories and imaginations that you want to have and you have the ability to do this.

Successful people in any field hold the belief that mind and body are one. They know that by looking after one they are simultaneously looking after the other. As memory and imagination have the same neurological circuits, they potentially have the same impact.

Feldenkrais (named after Moshe Feldenkrais) is a process of awareness through movement. Moshe Feldenkrais helped people who had lost the use of their limbs to find ways to make new neural connections in their brain and in so doing to find ways to relearn movement they thought they had lost. He believed totally that mind and body are one—that by developing new choices in one we automatically create new choices in the other.

This belief is at the heart of all NLP. With NLP we have discovered the details of the way we hold memories and thoughts. We know now that by developing our mastery of the way we represent these thoughts, we can change our experience of the present day.

Remember your first day at secondary school. How do you remember this? What came to mind first? Was it an image, a memory of someone's voice, a feeling? What followed? Another image? Sounds? What are the qualities of the memory? Is it bright, dark, loud, gentle? Your memory and the way you hold that memory are unique to you. That unique representation is what gives the memory its quality.

Without the representation in your mind it is merely a statement, "First day at secondary school." What makes it live as a memory is the way you think about it.

KNOWLEDGE, THOUGHT, MEMORY, AND IMAGINATION ARE THE RESULT OF SEQUENCES AND COMBINATIONS OF WAYS OF FILTERING AND STORING INFORMATION

For me this is an exciting memory, also a slightly scary one. What I have illustrated below is the way I represent that memory and I can, if I choose, change any part of it in the way I think about it. I can turn up the brightness. I can imagine the teacher saying different words. I can change the order of the thoughts.

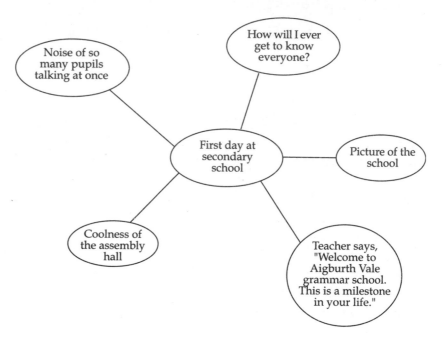

Now imagine tomorrow at work. What does your imagination conjure up for you? Successes? Problems? Satisfaction? Frustrations? Does your imagination create for you a representation of the "tomorrow" that you would like to have? It's all a "con trick" of the mind—so why not "con" yourself positively? You can change these representations so that you have the imagined day that you want to have.

Turn this:

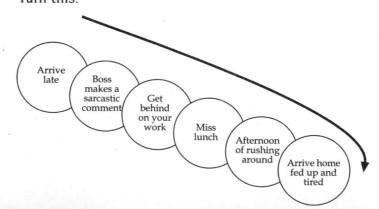

To this:

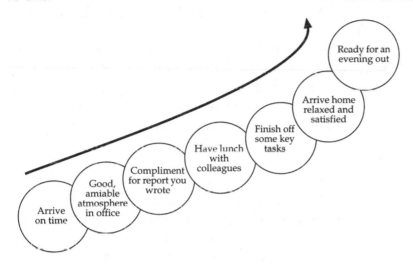

It may not happen exactly like this, but you have increased the chances that it will and you will feel differently in your anticipation of the day than you would if you thought the first way. Managing your thinking process is at the heart of being able to manage yourself. Many of the subsequent sections will address how to do this.

BELIEFS THAT UNDERPIN APPRAISAL

It is valuable to explore the beliefs from which you operate not only as an individual but as an organization. For example, if part of a company appraisal scheme is to review performance against a manager's ability to discipline (as I experienced in one company), there is a belief that discipline will be necessary in the organization. When you see a van or lorry with the inscription "If you have any problems with the way this vehicle is driven please phone...," the belief is there are drivers who will drive badly.

However, beliefs that support appraisal schemes that work—and by that I mean ones that result in motivated staff who are constantly learning and improving their contribution to the business—consist of the following:

❏ **People have all the resources they need to achieve what they want**. Leaders in business who hold this belief are likely to facilitate their staff's development through questioning and coaching rather than by telling them what to do.

❏ **People make the best choice available to them at the time that they make it**. This does not mean that you have to accept the choice they made. However, leaders who do hold this belief will be more understanding in the way they deal with a jobholder who has made a mistake.

❏ **There is no failure, only feedback**. Imagine a company in which all the employees held this belief. It would be an organization with a climate of total honesty, openness, and learning. This is the key to performance improvement.

❏ **The meaning of the communication is its effect**. For communication you could substitute leadership—the meaning of the way you lead your staff is the results they achieve. If your team is performing well, that is a statement about your leadership. Equally, if your team is performing badly, this is also a measure of your ability to lead. The second part of this belief runs: "If what you are doing isn't working, do something different." This is a useful point to bear in mind and act on if your appraisal system isn't achieving what you want it to achieve.

True beliefs

It is valuable to have all the beliefs of excellence. The ones above are those that seem to have the most relevance in a world of change. A company needs to be clear about the beliefs on which it is founded. But there is no value in paying lipservice to this: The beliefs you want as the foundation for your business must be those that are truly held by everyone in the business. One of the most valuable things a top team can do is to explore the actual beliefs held by the management team and decide if these are the ones that support their future vision. If they don't, start challenging them and the people who hold them.

As someone in one of the big financial consultancies said when asked what would happen to the people who did not fully share its newly published values and beliefs, "You are either living them, learning them or leaving."

BELIEFS AT THE HEART OF CUSTOMER SUPPORT

Every organization almost without exception relies on the quality of its customer support. However, sending out a questionnaire and teaching staff to smile as they greet customers will not go far unless customer support and care form an integral part of everything you do. Does the concept of delighting your customers run through your entire operation or is it only surface deep?

Customer support is an integral part of you and your organization if you hold beliefs that support your thinking about your customer. A specific set of beliefs that support caring and delighting your customers are as follows:

- ❏ **The response you get is a measure of the service you provide**.
- ❏ **Whatever your customer says and does to you has a benefit to your business**. This is true if you accept there is a potential benefit to you in any situation.
- ❏ **There is no failure, only feedback**. Knowing and acting on feedback will keep you in touch with your customers and ensure that your business meets and even anticipates their needs.
- ❏ **Each person is unique**. By understanding and relating to that uniqueness you will earn your customers' respect.
- ❏ Whatever your customers' circumstances, by believing that **there is a solution to every problem** you will find new and creative solutions with which to move forward together.

By holding beliefs such as these, you will learn how to deal with your customers appropriately.

BELIEFS THAT SUPPORT NEGOTIATION

Skilled negotiators, those who are able to resolve conflict and bring situations to a solution that has the commitment of all parties involved, believe the following:

- ❏ It is desirable and possible for all parties to meet their needs in negotiation.

❏ The other parties have ideas and views that can benefit everyone.

❏ I have a positive intention toward the other parties and whatever they say or do has a benefit for me if I choose to open my mind to what that might be.

❏ We all have a common goal even if we don't yet know what it is.

❏ There is a win/win outcome in most scenarios if we are willing to learn, to forgive, and to move on.

SHORTCUT TO STEPPING INTO A BELIEF OF EXCELLENCE

Imagine trying on a new outfit of clothes. You can have them for as long as you want, so that you can discover how they feel, whether they look the way you want them to look, what reactions you get from people around you, and whether they fit. If you don't like them you can return them and wear your original clothes, or you might keep one or two items and wear them with some of your existing clothes. Or you can keep them and make them a part of your wardrobe.

Beliefs are like this. You can presuppose that they are true; you can "try them on." If they work then it is likely that they will become a belief. If not you can put them to one side. To help you do this use the following shortcut.

1 Think of a situation (A) where you would like more choice and where you believe that taking on one of the beliefs of excellence would make the difference you want. Pick the belief of excellence that you think would be the most appropriate here.

2 Identify another situation (B) when you did hold this belief or one that was very similar.

3 Associate into this time (B) and anchor the feeling of holding this belief that was working positively for you.

4 Repeat the process until you experience what it is like to hold this belief.

5 As you hold this belief, re-experience situation (A) doing the following as you do so:

❏ Being aware of where you are and how you are experiencing this environment.

❏ Knowing what you are saying and doing that demonstrates that you are holding this new belief.

❏ Realizing what skills and qualities you are bringing to this situation.

❏ Knowing what is important to you and how you are fulfilling those needs, both for you and for anyone else involved in the situation.

❏ Appreciating how what you are doing and the way you are feeling fit for you personally.

❏ Discovering how you are influencing bigger systems of which you are a part, both right now and at other times.

6 Reflect on what your experience has been of holding this belief as you re-experienced the situation.

7 How do you feel about the situation now and how you might approach it in the future?

8 How do you feel about this belief and how it can work for you (assuming that it can)?

9 Repeat the process for two other situations that you know will occur in the coming week.

10 Decide what you will specifically commit to doing or believing in the future.

SUMMARY

Winning is not about facts and figures—it is about belief. If we believe we can't, we won't. If we believe we can, we just might.

The pilot who landed a plane that had an engine failure and saved the lives of the majority of his passengers in doing so said, "It was belief that kept the plane in the air. I believed against all the odds that I could get the plane safely on the ground."

Beliefs are emotionally held thoughts about ourselves, others, and situations. They are not based on fact but on our perception of events at the time they were formed. In studying figures of excellence we find certain core beliefs underpinning their ability to excel and achieve. These are the beliefs of excellence.

We can step into (presuppose) these beliefs and experience the consequences of holding them to be true. By trying them out and finding the ones that work for us, we can, over time, turn them into beliefs for ourselves.

THOUGHT PROVOKERS

1 Identify someone to whom you do not relate to as well as you would like:
   ❏ In your family.
   ❏ In your work.
   ❏ In your social circle.
   For each of them list what you believe about them. Think of an occasion when you communicated with them and it was not the way you would really like it to have been.

   Now think of someone in each of these groups with whom you have a good/excellent relationship. Identify one of the beliefs you hold about them. Imagine holding the belief that you have about the family member with whom you have a good relationship for the family member with whom you would like to improve your relationship. Imagine having an interaction operating from that belief. What are you seeing, hearing, and feeling? How are they responding to you? If they are not yet responding in the way you would like, re-experience the belief of excellence until you have it more firmly or strongly in your mind.

   Repeat the process. Now repeat the whole process for the person in your work and then the person in your social circle.

2 Think of a goal that you want for yourself but have not yet achieved and you are not sure why not. What beliefs do you hold about:
   ❏ Your ability to achieve this goal.
   ❏ Your right to achieve this goal?
   What beliefs might be limiting you in the achievement of this goal? What beliefs might you hold instead of the limiting ones?

3 Which of the beliefs of excellence do you already hold?

4 Which beliefs of excellence would you like to hold?

5 Which one belief of excellence would make the biggest positive difference to your life if you held it? What do you imagine would be the effect of holding this belief for you?

REFERENCES

Edward de Bono (1990) *Lateral Thinking*, Penguin.
John Grinder & Judith DeLozier (1996) *Turtles All the Way Down: Prerequisites to Personal Genius*, Metamorphous Press.

Once upon a time there was a young prince who believed in all things but three. He did not believe in princesses, or in islands, or in God. His father, the king, told him that such things did not exist. There were no princesses or islands in his father's domain, and no sign of God. The young prince believed his father.

One day, the prince ran away from his palace to the next country. There, to his astonishment, from every coast he saw islands, and on these islands, strange and troubling creatures whom he dared not name. As he was searching for a boat, a man in full evening dress approached him along the shore.

"Are those real islands?" asked the young prince.

"Of course they are real islands," said the man in evening dress.

"And those strange and troubling creatures?"

"They are all genuine and authentic princesses."

"Then God must also exist!" cried the prince.

"I am God," replied the man in full evening dress, with a bow. The young prince returned home as quickly as he could.

"So you are back," said his father, the king.

"I have seen islands, I have seen princesses, I have seen God," said the prince reproachfully.

The king was unmoved.

"Neither real islands, nor real princesses, nor a real God, exist."

"I saw them!"

"Tell me how God was dressed."

"God was in full evening dress."

"Were the sleeves of his coat rolled back?"

The prince remembered that they had been. The king smiled. "That is the uniform of a magician. You have been deceived."

At this the prince returned to the next land, and went to the same shore, where once again he came upon the man in full evening dress. "My father, the king, has told me who you are," said the young prince indignantly. "You deceived me last time, but not again. Now I know that those are not real islands and real princesses, because you are a magician."

The man on the shore smiled. "It is you who are deceived, my boy. In your father's kingdom there are many islands and many princesses. But you are under your father's spell, so you cannot see them."

The prince returned pensively home and when he saw his father he looked him in the eyes. "Father, is it true that you are not a real king, but only a magician?"

The King smiled and rolled back his sleeves. "Yes my son, I am only a magician."

"I must know the real truth, the truth beyond magic."

"There is no truth beyond magic," said the king.

The prince was full of sadness. He said, "I will kill myself."

The king, by magic, caused death to appear. Death stood in the door and beckoned to the real prince. The prince shuddered. He remembered the beautiful but unreal islands and the unreal but beautiful princesses.

"Very well," he said. "I can bear it."

"You see, my son," said the king, "you too now begin to be a magician."

The Magus, © *John Fowles, Jonathan Cape, 1977. Reprinted with permission.*

Achieve What You Really Want: Well-Formed Outcomes

"Imagination and faith are the same thing, giving substance to our hopes and reality to the unseen."

John V Taylor

D o you have a vision for yourself that is so compelling it influences the way you live moment by moment, day by day? If so, you are one of the small percentage of people who do. Statistics suggest that only 6 percent of the population thinks strategically, and this includes the ability to set and hold compelling goals. Yet thinking in this way is available to all of us. Some people inherit this influential way of thinking from their parents or parent figures. Some people learn through adversity what makes the difference and subsequently learn how to think like this for themselves.

Surprisingly, most company training schemes do not teach the real difference that makes the difference with respect to goals, even though they might spend millions of pounds on objective-setting programs and appraisal schemes. Why is this? As we frequently find when we use NLP to model what makes a difference, the key pieces are so often either taken for granted or so subtle that they are omitted from the training.

Many training programs concentrate on formats such as SMART goals (specific, measurable, achievable, realistic, and timebound). Do you really think that the high achievers in life, the people who act as the inspiration to the rest of us, sit down and wonder if their goals are realistic? The high achievers act out of passion and a love for what they do.

High achievers act out of a passion and a love for what they do

The difference lies in our ability to be prepared to pay the price, which often means letting everything go so we can achieve what we really want. The things we believe we cannot live without are often the very same things that we need to let go of if we are to realize our deepest desires.

Compelling goals

People who achieve what they want in life have compelling goals. There is a pattern to the structure of their thinking around their goals of which they are usually unaware. By modeling and continuing to model high achievers in all fields, we have uncovered the structure of their thinking. By trying on the elements of this structure we can explore how they work for each of us and how they fit with the thinking we already do. We may even find we confirm that what we are doing is right on track in supporting us to achieve our own success.

Ellen MacArthur is a 24-year-old British sailor who took part in the Single Handed Round the World Yacht Race at the beginning of 2001. I was tempted to describe her as the person who won the race, but in fact she came second to a French competitor. However, many people do believe that she won the race, such was the influence she had with the way she took part. Not only did she potentially sacrifice her place in the race by diverting her course to rescue another sailor in distress, she also made major repairs to her damaged boat in high seas and treacherous weather. She stood by her values and principles no matter what the circumstances to achieve a position in this race that no other woman of her age had achieved before.

Although British, MacArthur attracted the passionate support of many other nations, especially the French who gave her a bigger homecoming than even their own competitor. As her boat approached the finishing point on the French coastline, her parents, who were watching her progress, commented tellingly that most likely what she would be wanting right now was not to get off the boat to all the recognition but to turn around and do the whole trip again, such was her love of sailing. And indeed, when interviewed on her boat at the finish Ellen said that the happiest time was the welcome she was experiencing at that very moment and the saddest would be the next minute when she had to step off her boat on to the quayside.

Ellen MacArthur is the epitome of all that constitutes successful outcome thinking. The joy of what we see in her is that we each have our equivalent achievable success. What we will explore in this chapter is what success can mean for each of us individually and how we can think and act in a way that makes that success possible, not only in the future but also the present.

"All men dream: but not equally. Those who dream by night in the dusty recesses of their minds wake in the day to find that it was vanity; but the dreamers of the day are dangerous men, for they may act their dreams with open eyes, to make it possible."

T E Lawrence

PROBLEM THINKING

Let's consider some contrasting examples, ones that are all too familiar, to me at least.

Kevin was constantly searching for success. He'd had eight different jobs in five years. Each had failed to meet his expectations. Every time he'd fallen out with his manager or the market conditions for each business had not been "quite right." "Customers just aren't coming through the door," he stated frequently. Lack of success certainly wasn't due to lack of effort. Kevin tried very hard. He was constantly busy; he rarely had time to spare for anything else. He regularly talked about it being "a tough world out there" and yet each new challenge resulted in the same familiar disappointment. He talked about not wanting to make the same mistakes again, particularly in terms of his choice of business and manager, but somehow he always did.

Jim worked for a large organization. He had fulfilled his particular ambitions by continuing in the family tradition of engineering. Although he had developed quickly within the organization, he somehow felt that the job he had wasn't quite what he wanted to do, but he wasn't really sure what that was. He felt as though he was constantly searching for what his future might be. Initiative and ambition, particularly in younger managers, were generally frowned on, although Jim's own manager had been supportive toward him. His family, however, were pleased with what they considered to be his success. In their terms he had done well.

These two examples illustrate some very common thinking patterns that often lead to disillusionment and perceived failure to achieve the "real" outcomes. In the UK especially this is the kind of thinking that is unwittingly often encouraged and even taught. But it is not the thinking of satisfaction and fulfillment. And it is certainly not the thinking that is required in the entrepreneurial business culture in which we live today.

"What do I really want?"

Ask yourself the question: "What do I really want?"

❑ Today?
❑ Tomorrow?
❑ This year?
❑ Next year?
❑ In the next five years?
❑ In my career?
❑ In my life?

This is not about what you must, should, or ought to do. Nor is it about what you don't want to do or what you will try to do. Those kinds of thoughts tend to be the legacy of the goals that others want for you rather than those outcomes you truly want for yourself. Either that or they arise out of your fears of what you don't want to lose. Outcome thinking is to do with what *you* really *do* want. That might seem selfish, but we cannot make others' goals come true for them, although we do influence others by what we achieve for ourselves.

We cannot make others' goals come true for them

Thinking about what you don't want is *problem thinking*. What is happening when you are thinking this way is that what you are imagining in your mind is how things are today—that is, what you want to change—even though you might be saying how you want to change it. This leads to an *away from* motivation, in that you are motivated away from what you don't want. For example, you might change jobs to get away from what you don't like about your current one. You might leave your partner because you are not happy with your relationship, or you might go away on holiday to get a break from the stress you are feeling in what you are doing. This kind of goal might be expressed like this:

- ❑ I want to lose weight.
- ❑ I don't want to have another argument with him.
- ❑ I want to give up smoking.
- ❑ I want more spare time.
- ❑ I want less stress in my work.
- ❑ I must clear my desk.
- ❑ I should go to that meeting.

The language in all of these indicates that what the person is thinking about is how things are at the present, even though they want to change them.

OUTCOME THINKING

Goals expressed in *outcome thinking* mode indicate that the person is imagining what they do really want as if they have stepped forward in time and have got it. The motivation generated by this way of thinking is *towards*, in that the owner of the outcomes is motivated towards what they do really want. For example, they might change jobs because they are so attracted to a new job opportunity. They might exercise because they want to be really fit, and they might go on holiday to a particular location because it is a country they have always wanted to experience.

Outcomes expressed in this way are as follows:

- ❑ I want to be really fit.
- ❑ I want to achieve agreement about how we go forward.
- ❑ I want to be in good health.
- ❑ I want to have balance in my life.

❏ I want to be really relaxed.
❏ I want to have a really attractive, orderly office.
❏ I want to make a key contribution to that meeting.

"What do I really want instead of that?"

If you find you are thinking in a problem-centered way, the question to ask yourself to switch to outcome thinking is, "What do I really want instead of that?"

By modeling people who are achieving what they want in life we have uncovered "conditions for success." Below is an example of someone whose thinking *does* adhere to these conditions:

Jill works for a large organization and is clear that although the organization is slow and bureaucratic in its style, she wants to stay and make a difference. She wants to be a key player in the management of change toward a culture that is more open, supportive, and honest than at present. She recognizes that her level of influence in her current role is limited and has mapped out the future roles she wants that would increase her influence to introduce the changes she believes to be important. She knows that if she waits for others to make this happen she might wait forever.

One thing that strikes you about Jill when you meet her is that she wants passionately to achieve this future. Her whole presence is captivating as she talks about what is important to her. She talks positively of what she wants and she is always respectful of other people's views and opinions. People are attracted to her.

What precisely is the difference in the way Jill thinks about her outcomes and the way Kevin and Jim think about theirs? Jill certainly seems to be on track to achieve her outcome *and* is enjoying the journey toward it.

How is it that some people are satisfied, highly motivated, and consistently achieving the sort of success they want? What exactly is the difference? Let's explore this in a way that will enable you both to set compelling outcomes for yourself and support others to do the same.

KNOW WHAT YOU WANT

"Until one is committed, there is hesitancy, the chance to draw back, always ineffectiveness. Concerning all acts of initiative and creation, there is one fact, one elementary truth, the ignorance of

which kills countless ideas and splendid plans. That the moment that one definitely commits oneself then providence moves too. All sorts of things to help one that would never otherwise have occurred manifest themselves. A whole stream of events issue from the decision, raising in one's favour all manner of unforeseen incidents and meetings and material assistances that no man could have dreamed would have come his way."

W H Murray

Consider this statement: "Don't think about kangaroos!" Can you not do that? I doubt it. Your unconscious mind cannot recognize negatives. When you tell yourself not to worry or not to make a mistake, you are actually programming yourself to do just that. However, if you program yourself to think about being calm or getting things right, you are dramatically Increasing the chances that this is how you will be.

"Don't think about kangaroos"

Often people have expressed concern to me about the programming aspect of NLP, or what they believe the programming aspect to mean. They say it sounds like a brainwashing technique. The truth is that we are brainwashing ourselves all day long by what we choose to think about and more especially *how* we choose to think about it. What we get with NLP is the recognition and awareness to program ourselves in a way that will not only work for us but for others too.

My husband used to manage a team of software developers who had been very successful in winning business with their contribution to the sales pitches for new systems. In 2000 they were taken over by a bigger company and my husband reported to a new director. The bigger company asked the development team to pitch for the software business for some of their existing accounts that they had been at risk of losing. Normally this team's style had been relaxed and confident and this was how they approached the new challenges, until the director instructed them "On no account lose this business." He followed this up with "You just can't afford to go wrong here." After several days of these problem statements the tension in the team began to mount and they found themselves feeling unusually stressed by the prospect of the presentations. They did not get the business.

Program yourself

Top sports people have usually mastered this self-programming technique: They have either taught themselves how to do it or have been coached into this positive way of thinking. They know that if they start worrying about hitting the ball out of court or off the green, that is what they are programming themselves to do. Even if the bulk of their thinking is positive, they know that a fleeting negative thought can make the difference between winning the point and losing it. They have modeled themselves on excellence.

How often have you said to yourself "I mustn't do that" only to find yourself doing it? Just this morning my husband said he wanted to be sure that no one dropped his new kitchen knife as it has a fragile ceramic blade. He was indirectly telling the rest of our household to take care if we used it. But those weren't the words he used. Within an hour of saying this he had dropped the knife! What you think influences how you feel and how you communicate.

What we think influences what we feel and what we communicate

Two teams had been given the job of identifying ways in which their business could pull itself out of recession and achieve new business objectives that had been set. The teams had been asked to develop their ideas and come back on a specific date to present their conclusions. They returned with new proposals as agreed.

One team looked dejected. They presented their ideas: how to cut costs, reduce overheads, and rationalize the workforce. They felt this was the way forward. An air of gloom hung around them. The rest of the room was silent.

The second team presented their ideas. They looked delighted. This team was made up of people from the manufacturing side of the business. Previously they had looked at ways of improving quality and reducing wastage. This time they had decided to take a different stance. They had thought about the future they really wanted: the number of plants they would like to build, the amount of research they wanted to do, and the people they wanted to employ. They were fired up with their ideas and their passion for the future. They had decided it was time to turn the company around. It should be they who were telling the salesforce how much business they needed to support this program, instead of them responding to whatever the salesforce sold, as had been the case in the past.

The difference in the enthusiasm and sheer energy of these two teams was dramatic. One had thought about what they had to cut back and lose and the other about what they really wanted. It is almost inevitable that if you think about what you don't want you become disheartened. You will develop the feelings and responses that are triggered by being in an environment of circumstances and people and events that you don't like. It is no surprise that if you think about what you really want, if you imagine what it is like to have what you really want, then you will be committed, you will be motivated, and you will be influential because your enthusiasm will be infectious. This is one of the reasons visionary leaders are compelling.

I recently worked with a group of trainers and was with them as they met the groups they were going to train. One of the trainers, who had been nervous but excited and looking forward to the challenge, entered the room with their prospective delegates. This trainer believed that the delegates could really gain from the training program and was positive about everyone's potential to change. The group greeted this trainer with warmth and acceptance.

Yet another trainer entered the room when I was with another of the groups. This second trainer had doubts about the abilities of the members of the group, particularly their ability to change. He also had a tendency to talk in problem-centered language: "I won't let the group get out of control," "I'm not worried about how the group will react." When this trainer entered the room the atmosphere seemed to change from fun to confrontation. The group asked challenging questions and wanted proof of how the program would help them personally.

A team of researchers set out to quantify the relationship between the speaking styles of US Presidents and the inspiration felt by citizens. They measured charisma and greatness, charisma being the emotional bond between leaders and followers, and greatness measuring perceptions of actual achievements. Then they studied the inaugural addresses and key speeches of US Presidents. Examples were taken from speeches by John F Kennedy and Jimmy Carter.

Visionary leaders

John F Kennedy, a clearly charismatic President, used phrases like "Together let us explore the stars, conquer the desert, eradicate disease, tap the ocean depths, and encourage the arts and commerce." Jimmy Carter's 1977 address, in contrast, included "Let our recent mistakes bring a resurgent commitment to the basic principles of our nation, for we know that if we despise our own government, we have no future." The differences are striking. John F Kennedy's speech is an example of communication based on outcome thinking, whereas Jimmy Carter's is almost entirely problem centered. And the hypnotic language patterns (see Chapter 7) in both evoke very different unconscious responses. Compare "let us explore the stars, tap the ocean depths" with "despise our own government, we have no future." It is in the words.

It is in the words

KEEP IT UNDER YOUR CONTROL

Some things lend themselves to outcome thinking and some things very definitely do not. There is good news and bad news. The bad news is that goals that include the following are not achievable with this way of thinking:

❏ To be number one.
❏ To win the race.
❏ To cut the legs from under your competitors.
❏ To be managing director of this company.
❏ To achieve the profit target.
❏ To make my children happy.

That might surprise you, as it is very likely that some of your goals do fall into some of these categories. The point is that some goals are indeed outside of our control, or they are not ecological for other people. You will see the significance of these goals as I go through the other conditions for well-formed outcomes in this chapter. The only part of the world for which we can set outcomes and hope to achieve them is in the kind of person we want to be.

However, the kinds of outcome that you can expect to achieve with this way of thinking include:

❏ To be an example of a caring, entrepreneurial leader.
❏ To achieve my personal best in whatever field I choose.
❏ To work in a way that is supportive of others.
❏ To achieve a role in life that is a position of leading others

in a high-tech business.
- ❏ To create a climate of learning and fun in all or most of my interactions with others.
- ❏ To be a caring, understanding, and guiding parent.

One of the top salespeople in a telecommunications company has targets to achieve and does quite naturally want to achieve them. However, when he considers his existing and potential customers, what he thinks about is not how much he is going to make out of each of them but rather how he can make their time with him valuable and enjoyable. To do this he thinks about his state and how he wants to be when he is with them. He puts his attention on what is within his control, his way of being in the world. He achieves all his financial targets with remarkable consistency.

In the example at the beginning of this chapter, one of the reasons Kevin did not achieve his goals was that those goals depended on others and on external circumstances. When he didn't achieve what he wanted it was because his manager or the business climate or his customers weren't quite right. He had not asked himself how he could be different whatever the external circumstances. He wanted others to be different. A useful question here is to ask yourself, "What kind of person do I want to become?"

Where is your attention in relation to your outcomes? On yourself or on others? Do your outcomes depend on someone else being there or responding in a certain way? If so, they are not self-maintained. In a story in *Waiting for the Mountain to Move*, Charles Handy describes a traveler who, journeying around the world, came to a road and across this road was a mountain blocking the way. The traveler sat down and waited for the mountain to move. If your outcomes are not self-maintained then you too will be waiting for the mountain to move.

Waiting for the mountain to move

When Lance Armstrong recovered from cancer and was considering entering the Tour De France, his goal was not to win the Tour, it was to cycle competitively. He won. When David Hemery took part in the final of the Mexico Olympics as potentially the slowest candidate, his goal was not to win the race but to do his personal best. He won.

KNOW WHEN YOU'VE GOT THERE

What will it be like to have what you really want? If you can imagine it then it is virtually yours. The more you step into this imagined future, the more you are programming yourself to get there. Think again about one of the outcomes you really want for yourself. Imagine yourself having achieved what you really want.

❑ **What does it look like?** What do you see? What is around you? Is there anyone else in the picture? Look around, take in the details.

❑ **What does it sound like?** What do you hear? What are you saying to yourself? What are others saying? What sounds are there?

❑ **What does it feel like?** Physically what does it feel like? What can you touch and what sort of feeling is that? What textures do you experience?

❑ **What does it taste like?** What sort of taste do you get in your mouth? What is that like?

❑ **What does it smell like?** What is the aroma of achieving what you really want?

❑ **What does it feel like?** Emotionally? What are the emotions that you feel in achieving what you really want? What is the quality of those emotions and where do you feel them?

Act as if it is true

Your unconscious mind does not differentiate between what is imagined and what is real. The more vividly you imagine yourself achieving what you want, the more your unconscious mind believes it already has it and will program you to act as if you do. And of course, the more you act as if you have it, the more likely you are to get it!

Once you have established your outcome in all your senses in this way, it begins to take on a momentum of its own. This ability to step into your outcome is characteristic of NLP. The difference comes from being able to imagine yourself (associate) into the future that you want. Although planning to get there is important, the steps in the plan will almost begin to present themselves to you automatically because you will begin to recognize opportunities when they occur.

Watch a player take a goal kick in rugby. If you are lucky, the camera will show how the player prepares his thinking. I have just watched Johnny Wilkinson playing for England against France in the Six Nations Rugby Union Cup. The camera zoomed in on his face as he prepared the kick. He looked at the ball and then tracked the trajectory that he wanted the ball to take up and through the goal posts. He repeated this three times, then very quickly, almost without looking this final time, kicked the ball. Every goal he kicked, he converted.

Sometimes people say to me, "Won't I get disappointed if I imagine what I really want and then I don't get it?" I have found that those people who consistently achieve what they really want, often against the odds, also hold a belief that whatever happens is learning. In this way they are happy with the journey toward the goals as much if not more than arriving at the destination. This outcome way of thinking is a way of influencing the way we journey through life.

Whatever happens is learning

It is likely that you will want your outcome in some situations but not others. For example, if you want a feeling of certainty and self-confidence, this could be very appropriate when giving a presentation or planning your future, but inappropriate in a situation where you had some partly formed ideas and wanted your colleagues to develop their own thinking about these ideas.

So ensure that you put your outcome into context. Where, when, and with whom do you want your outcome?

If your outcome does depend on someone or something else, sometimes this can be the painful part. Can you let go of that need to have someone or something else change? Once you can, then in a strange way you increase the chances that you can have what you really want.

PUT IT IN CONTEXT

Can you let go of the need to have someone or something else change?

Outcomes that are sustainable over time are ones that are not only a win for the person setting them but also a win for the key others in their life. These key others might be family members and partners. They might be colleagues and other employees. They might increasingly be suppliers and competitors. If the outcome is a win for the bigger system,

CHECK THAT IT IS A WIN/WIN

then that bigger system will support you. If the outcome is a loss for the bigger system, then those significant others will either consciously or inadvertently block its achievement.

Business has been locked into a win/lose mentality for some time now. One of the most cut-throat markets has been the travel industry. Each company has fought with the others to the point where they have all lost business. There has been an annual battle for the release of the next year's holiday brochures, with each travel organization attempting to release its brochure ahead of the rest. This competition has come to the point where the brochures are released so far ahead of the holiday periods to which they refer that they are almost irrelevant.

The more forward-looking organizations are finding ways to help their competitors succeed by promoting them, providing links to them through their website, and finding ways to collaborate so that together they promote the market to which they both belong.

IS IT WORTH WHAT IT TAKES?

What will it take to achieve what you want?

❑ Risk?
❑ Feelings of discomfort?
❑ Giving up something you have now?
❑ Pain and sadness?

Is having the outcome worth what it takes? You may decide it is not, in which case you can give it up or decide to go for a part or a variation of the outcome. If you decide the outcome is worth what it takes, you are making a decision to commit and to proceed to the next step.

When I was thinking about leaving my full-time job at International Computers Ltd, I was apprehensive, even scared, of leaving the team of people behind that I had worked with for the previous five years. I was afraid also of losing what I believed to be the security of a large corporate organization. However, I did also want to run my own business, so to do this I had to decide if I was prepared to let go of those things I felt I must have. It wasn't an easy decision or an easy time. I remember having many panicky moments when I wondered if I was doing the right thing.

However, I decided eventually that what I wanted outweighed what I was afraid of losing. Ironically, many of my colleagues also eventually left and became independent consultants and I had more of their company subsequently than I would ever have imagined possible. And I have come to realize that nothing and nowhere is truly secure. Security is all in the mind. Looking back, I am delighted that I made the decision I did and even if I could go back I would make exactly the same decision again.

WHAT DOES YOUR PRESENT STATE DO FOR YOU?

Even though you have your outcome, your present state satisfies a need in you. If it didn't, you wouldn't maintain it. Think carefully about how your present state serves you. It may seem odd but, for example, someone who wants to be fit and healthy may find that being unhealthy gets them sympathy and attention. Equally, someone who is nonassertive but who wants to be assertive may find that being nonassertive is a way of avoiding risk and responsibility.

It is important to consider these needs and either how you will challenge them or meet them in different ways in the future to leave you free to achieve your outcome. Once you have identified what it is that you get out of your present state, you explore how you might satisfy that need but in a different way through your outcome.

UNDERSTAND YOUR HIGHER PURPOSE

Understanding your higher purpose puts your outcome into context and opens up options for ways you might achieve it. If, for example, your goal is to be healthy and fit, the higher purpose of this might be to be the kind of person who can play and join in with what your children are doing. If your outcome is to reach agreement in the meeting, it might be so you are able to negotiate collaboration for a future way of working together. And if your outcome is to run your own business, it may be that your outcome is to create a balance between your work and your personal life. Knowing your higher purpose keeps your outcomes in perspective and ensures that you stay on track with what is important about what you achieve.

Another way of thinking about your higher purpose is to consider what you will be giving other people by achieving what you really want. We all have an influence in the bigger systems to which we belong—the question is what positive influence you want to have. Another way of thinking about it is to consider what added value you will bring to those bigger systems by achieving what you want.

ENSURE YOUR OUTCOMES FIT WITH WHO YOU ARE AND WHAT YOU WANT TO BE

Peter had achieved great success in developing a professional presentation style on a training course. When the group commented on how impressed his team back at work would be with his new skills, he responded, "You must be joking. I'd stand out like a sore thumb if I used this style back at work."

Having these skills did not fit with the person Peter considered himself to be at work. There was little likelihood that he would ever use them.

Check out your outcomes with the kind of person you are or want to be. If they don't fit, forget them—find ones that do. Only by doing this will you ensure that every part of you is rooting for your success.

Ultimately, all goals are about how you are developing as a person. You might get so locked into thinking about shorter-term outcomes that you lose sight of what it is all about for you personally. Keep in mind the kind of person you are and the kind of person you want to become. In this way you will make sure that what you achieve is a fit for you as a person.

"Whatever you can do or dream you can do, begin it. Boldness has genius and power and magic in it. Begin it now!"

Goethe

TAKE ACTION

What action steps will you take? What steps are realistic for you? I see so many action plans on company appraisal forms that have grand statements such as:

❏ Improve managerial effectiveness.
❏ Develop better communication.
❏ Build an effective team.

This sort of statement is "pie in the sky." Vague statements like these are expressions of intent and tend to stay just that, intentions. To really test your commitment to your outcome, be as specific as you can about what your next steps will be.

When I set myself an outcome of buying a home in Wiltshire, it seemed like a major decision. It was frightening when I thought of all it entailed for me at that time. My action steps were very small. Each one felt safe at the time I took it. My plan was:

1 *Find out what sort of magazines/brochures would have details of the kind of house I wanted. (I didn't even buy the magazines at this stage.)*
2 *Register with the sort of estate agents who had details of this type of property. At this stage I made it clear I didn't want to view any properties.*
3 *Drive through areas where I thought I might want to live.*
4 *Visit one or two chosen properties, but on the clear understanding that I was not ready to buy.*

It was a year from the time I started this process to the time I found a house I wanted to buy. Each step was a realistic one for me at that time. The result was I found a cottage with which my family and I fell in love.

Small steps to success

It helps to set a time frame for each of your action steps. Give yourself a date by which you will have achieved each one. It may not always be necessary to know them all in advance, but set out the first one or two. This way you will have started your journey toward your outcome.

ORGANIZATIONAL OUTCOMES

The characteristics of well-formed outcomes work in just the same way for organizations as for individuals.

Problem-centered organizations are moving away from what they don't want. They are more likely to react to the competition and in so doing to become dependent on what the competition does next. They are driven by market trends and are directly affected by the economic climate. They step into a "fire-fighting," crisis-based way of working. Their goals are set in reaction to others. They have difficulty planning and then sticking to any plans that they do manage to set. Their actions are determined by what other companies do next. Organizations functioning solely in this way cannot maintain

Problem-centered organizations are more likely to be reactive

success for long. The climate inside a company of this style is typically one of tension and worry.

When Unipart managed a turnaround of its business against all market predictions, it did a number of things. One was to change the way that it ran meetings. Managers recognized that the emphasis in their meetings previously had been on problems, even though they were nominally called progress meetings. They acknowledged that they did not consider or imagine what they really wanted from their meetings or their projects prior to considering how to get there. So they began every meeting with a discussion of what they did really want—an outcome.

Outcome-oriented organizations set market trends

Outcome-oriented organizations, on the other hand, have a clear vision of where they are heading. This is an expression of what the employees in the company really want. Because of this there is a high level of motivation and commitment to the future. Staff enjoy their work. The vision is an inspiration both to those who work within the company and to those with whom they come into contact, their customers, and their suppliers. This style of company sets market trends. It influences its customers to move forward with it to their vision of the future. Outcome-oriented companies are innovative and influential. They do take account of market trends, the economic climate, and competitors, but they do this in the context of having a clear, compelling outcome and business plan.

Lentern Aircraft, discussed in Chapter 13, is a family business making components for aircraft. The family spirit extended to everyone in the business and the members of the board especially had a strong rapport with each other. They decided to invest in their development as leaders and underwent several teambuilding exercises that strengthened rapport even further. They then took time out to imagine the outcomes for the business. Collectively they imagined what future they wanted for the business so that they could see, hear, physically feel, smell, taste, and emotionally feel what that was like. They did this individually and then shared their thoughts.

The measure of their rapport was that what they had each imagined individually was either identical to or complemented what others had imagined. Nothing they imagined conflicted with the outcomes of anyone else on the board. They each visualized the extent of the business, the culture they wanted, how the business looked, including its international premises, how they perceived themselves, the role they were fulfilling and the feeling of achievement.

If our attention is centered on problems, problems are what we get. Even if we focus our attention on the reduction of problems, we are still paying attention to the problems. In contrast, if we have imagined what we really do want and concentrate on how we will recognize when we have it, we influence the likelihood that this is what we get.

What you measure is what you get

Consider the following potential measures of customer satisfaction:

Reduction or absence of complaints

Number of problems solved

Reduction in time taken to deal with customer calls

Extent to which you can keep customers off your back

Amount of resource allocated to your customer

Number of system crashes

Amount of downtime

Amount of praise received for a job well done

Number of thank-yous for the service you give

Voluntary feedback on the benefits resulting from using your service or product

Amount of repeat business

Evidence of improvement in customers' work processes

Amount of smiling and fun

Amount of business generated from visits to your website

The column on the left contains some traditional ways of measuring customer satisfaction. They are typically problem based. If your customer satisfaction measures are expressed in terms of what you don't want, that is where you will put your attention and that is exactly what you will get. If you measure complaints, this presupposes this is what you expect and, sure enough, that is what you will get.

What we appreciate appreciates

I returned from a very enjoyable cycling holiday to find a "customer care" questionnaire waiting for me. In it I was asked to say not "What was my opinion of the overnight accommodation?" but "What problems did I experience with the accommodation?" What did I do? I immediately began to search in my memory for problems that might have existed. Through their questionnaire the company was directing me to remember and search for the unsatisfactory elements of my holiday.

One travel company I know has a whole floor of staff to deal with customer complaints. I saw no equivalent floor to deal with customer compliments!

SHORTCUT TO ACHIEVING WHAT YOU REALLY WANT

1   Think of something you really want—not something you don't want or want less of or feel you should have.

2   Is it within your control? (To be the next Prime Minister is not, to have your partner behave differently is not. To be an example of professionalism is, to work with the people you enjoy is, to take part competitively is.) Find the part of the outcome that is within your control.

3   Imagine yourself having achieved what you really want. Let your unconscious do this for you—allow yourself to dream. Using your unconscious is a key part of the process. Be aware of what you are seeing, hearing, feeling physically, smelling, tasting, and feeling emotionally. Be sure to do this "from your own shoes."

4   In which contexts are you imagining yourself with this outcome? In which ones do you want to have this?

5   Imagine how this can be or is a real benefit to the significant people in your life. It is vital that it is win/win. If there is anything you need to do in your thinking to make it win/win, do that.

6   What sort of cost will have to pay to achieve this? Are you willing to pay this price? If not, let go of the outcome and put your energies into something else.

7   What does maintaining your present state do for you (assuming you could have achieved this outcome before)? How might you build in the benefits of the present state into the achievement of the desired state?

8   How does achieving this outcome contribute to a higher goal for you or an overall purpose that you have in your life?

9 In what way does achieving this outcome fit with who you are and who you are becoming?
10 What specifically are you going to do that demonstrates your commitment to achieving this outcome? When specifically will you do that? Be very precise here about your action plan. It need only be the first step, but it does need to be precise.

SUMMARY

By following the steps to setting a well-formed outcome you are modeling the way successful people think about outcomes. By imagining yourself achieving what you want in all senses, you are programming yourself to get what you want. Your mind cannot distinguish between what is imagined and what is real, so you are managing your imagination to work for you in a way that makes your dreams become your reality.

Outcome thinking is a very powerful approach to achieving what you want. The elements of outcome thinking are drawn from people in all walks of life who consistently achieve what they want in a way that is compatible both with those around them and with their environment. Ironically, although outcome thinking appears to be all about the future, it is as much if not more to do with how we live in the present. Outcome thinking is how we can influence our journey to that destination. And outcome thinking can be about how we move toward our life goals or with how we make ourselves understood in a two-minute conversation. It is about the long term and the short term, the future and the present.

You may have read this chapter and thought to yourself, "Yes, that makes sense." Nevertheless, we can know the principles and still not apply them. I recommend that if you have not done so already you experience outcome thinking, either by taking yourself through the process or by experiencing training or coaching that supports you to do so. All of this theory is common sense—it is the extent to which we apply that common sense that makes the difference.

Your mind does not distinguish between what is imagined and what is real

THOUGHT PROVOKERS

1 Are the following towards or away from?
   a I really want a job that involves working with other people.
   b The company I work for currently is very bureaucratic. I want somewhere else to work.
   c I have a clear vision of myself working abroad.
2 You ask another department to agree a level of service with you. When you have explained what you need, they say they will try to meet your requirements. How confident would you be that they would deliver?
3 What was the basis of your decision to take your existing job? Were you moving towards your ideal or away from something you didn't like? And your previous job?
4 Imagine yourself doing the type of work you would really like to do. What can you see/hear/feel?
5 Think of examples of action plans you have set yourself in the past. What is characteristic of the action plans that you have carried out compared with the ones you haven't?
6 How do you decide how to spend your holidays? How well does the reality match up to your expectations?
7 How often do you finish up with the things you don't want compared with the things you do?
8 Think about what you would really like to achieve by the end of this week. Pay attention to what is in your mind. Is it what you do want or are you imagining the problems of the things you don't want?
9 If you have lost sight of what it is that you want for yourself, start small and identify what you want for yourself by the end of today, for example, or by the end of the next meeting you have.

REFERENCES

Sue Knight, *Personal Selling Skills*, Sue Knight Books & Talks.
Sue Knight (1999) NLP *Solutions: How to Model What Works in Business to Make it Work for You*, Nicholas Brealey Publishing.

Once upon a time there was a couple who had achieved many of their ambitions in life, yet there was one main goal outstanding: They wanted to swim to Japan.

They reflected on this goal for a long time and one day they set off. They were not used to swimming so they found it difficult. They were aware of how heavy their limbs felt. They ached with the constant effort, especially when the strong current was against them. Gradually, however, their bodies got used to swimming and they developed a style that became effortless and rhythmical.

They began to notice the water around them, for example how it changed color as the days went by. In the early morning it would be clear and blue and in certain lights it sparkled emerald green. As the sun set it developed the rich warm colors of the evening sky. And they became aware of the creatures in the water, the small silver fish that swam with them in the day, the dark shadows that skimmed by them in the deep. They became aware of how the sound of the waves changed as the water lapped their ears and they felt the subtle changes of the weather as breezes turned into winds and died down again. They learned how to find food in the water, how to nourish themselves, and how to use their bodies effortlessly. They developed a refined sense of smell so that they could detect changes in the environment by the scent carried to them on the breeze.

They swam for days and weeks with no sight of land. One day they saw the dark profile of land on the horizon. They swam on and they recognized the shoreline of Japan. As they approached they became quiet and eventually they looked at each other and they knew. At that moment they turned back to the sea and swam on.

Part III
Lead with NLP

W e can lead others only when we lead ourselves. Lead with NLP is the last part of this book for that very reason. It is tempting to want to have a go with these skills on other people, but that is not the way they work—they work only because you are applying them to yourself. Make it a goal to be such an attractive example of what you have done with NLP for yourself that others want some of the same. That is the measure of success.

Develop a climate of trust: Rapport

One of the most important skills discovered in people who are models of excellence is their ability to influence and bring about change in ways that are far-reaching and sustainable over time. There is one common element in all their approaches: their ability to build immediate rapport with the people with whom they are working. I believe this is one of the most important skills in business. Without rapport few management systems will work. If you think you can get by with technical skills alone you are wrong. You need cooperation, commitment, and respect to stand a chance of succeeding in anything you do. In Chapter 16, Develop a Climate of Trust: Rapport, I show you how to build and maintain rapport with the people with whom you come into contact through whatever medium you choose.

Negotiate your way through life: Perceptual positions

All elements of NLP are complementary. Each adds another piece to the jigsaw of excellence. A more recent development in NLP thinking is experiencing situations from different perspectives in order to find a win/win, explained in Chapter 17, Negotiate Your Way Through Life: Perceptual Positions. This approach complements outcome thinking and is a way of taking a balanced approach to situations and outcomes. Those who are most able to negotiate conflicts in work and life have the ability to appreciate situations from different perspectives. Some NLP techniques involve paying attention to the details of thinking and behavior; perceptual positions thinking provides a powerful shortcut to achieving the same results.

Chapter 18, Resolving Conflict: Parts Integration, covers a topic that has long been a part of the preliminary training I offer in NLP. It would be good to think that conflict will not exist if you put all the other principles into practice, but that would be unrealistic. Conflict also plays an important role in our lives: Through it we can learn, heal, and grow in ways that don't occur in other contexts. This chapter shows how to learn to resolve conflicts in your life by resolving the conflict within to resolve the conflict without.

Resolving conflict: Parts integration

Giving and receiving feedback is becoming so important that it warrants a chapter to itself, Chapter 19. NLP is about how we elicit feedback from our minds, our language, our behavior, and the ways we use these together to achieve outstanding performance. And it is about constantly testing to see how our discoveries work and continue to work. Nothing is static. We depend on feedback to maintain excellence. This is an important chapter: I encourage you to read and reread it, but above all to do it.

Giving and receiving feedback

Closely linked to our ability to give and receive feedback is our ability to coach ourselves and others. Chapter 20, High Performance Coaching, is in a nutshell what all of this book is about. We need to know how to coach ourselves and others if we want to grow our potential as individuals, as teams, and as organizations. And we need to know these skills if we want to grow our relationships, our marriages, our families, and our communities. Coaching is about learning and learning is about life. I have found NLP-based coaching to be life giving. I wish the same for you.

High performance coaching

16
Develop a Climate of Trust: Rapport

"I am only through communication with the other."

Karl Jaspers

*I*f you do not believe in the importance of rapport, then you may as well shut up shop now. Autocracies are dead. Hierarchies are crumbling. The only place for command-and-conquer management is in a museum. Relationships and influence are the only way to build the networks you need to succeed. And not only do you need rapport to build your business, you need it to succeed in life.

Rapport creates a climate of trust and understanding

Rapport is the ability to connect with others in a way that creates a climate of trust and understanding. It is also the ability to appreciate one another's point of view (not always to agree with it), to be on the same wavelength, and to understand and accept one another's feelings. Rapport is essential for any form of communication to take place—unless, of course, you don't want to make progress!

I guarantee that most of your customers choose you because of the level of rapport you have with them. And more significantly, the customers you keep when things go awry are the ones with whom you have this kind of relationship. You are more likely to buy from, agree with, support and stay with someone to whom you feel connected than you are when this isn't the case.

You can build rapport face to face, over the phone, via email, through text messages, through letters, or just in your imagination. And you can build rapport over time, shortly after you have met, instantly on meeting, or in advance of even making someone's acquaintance. No matter what the circumstances or who the people are with whom you want to build rapport, it is without doubt the quality of the rapport that makes the difference.

Near to our home in France is a restaurant, which was owned by an English couple when we moved into the area. We had sworn to ourselves that we would not become part of the English community in this part of France but rather part of the French community as far as they would allow us. So we avoided this restaurant—after all, why go an English restaurant when we could do that back in England? However, one day we called there just for a drink and the way we were greeted was such that we felt our resolve not to return soften. We could not avoid feeling welcome and well cared for, even though the service was not over-attentive. We decided there and then to return, such was the subtle influence of the relationship that was built in those few moments.

We learned subsequently that the owners' approach had won the hearts of the local French people who also frequented the bar and the restaurant. We became regular customers. Imagine our disappointment, then, to discover that this couple decided to sell the restaurant, which was now a thriving business throughout the year. The new owner took over in 2001. He inherited an immense amount of goodwill and regular trade—within six months he had lost it all. Nothing much had changed about the restaurant itself and the food was still good. However, this owner did not relate to the French customers and gave no impression of any rapport building. This once flourishing restaurant is now closed most nights of the week and is rumored to be up for sale again.

The skills involved in building and maintaining rapport were some of the earliest to be discovered with NLP and they have become essential to the networking economy. The people who were chosen as models of excellence, particularly in situations of influence or change, demonstrated that rapport is one of the most important factors needed for change to take place.

"The new economy has three distinguishing characteristics. It is global. It favors intangible things—ideas, information, and relationships. And it is intensely inter-linked. These three attributes produce an new type of market place and society, one that is rooted in ubiquitous electronic networks."

Kevin Kelly, New Rules for the New Economy

The skill of rapport goes well beyond body language

If you think building rapport is just about matching people's behavior then think again. The skill of building and maintaining rapport goes well beyond the level of body language. Rapport involves not only relating to people face to face but also remotely by appealing to their style of communication and their expectations.

One of my clients received this email:

Jane
Have been looking further at the issue of your company's fees—which as you know, we are very concerned about. Your day rates not only equal those of the parent company but my investigations among my contacts have shown that they have increased exponentially since 1999. I attach a comparison of your fees today compared with those charged in a previous proposal that you did for us a year earlier. Can you please justify to me:
1 Why you feel you can charge the same rates as the parent company?
2 Why there has been such a movement upwards in fees over the last two years please?
I feel very concerned about this. Thanks.
Wendy Smith

My client emailed back as follows:

Wendy
I have discussed the issues that you have raised with our parent company and internally with our fee discussions regarding company X. Please find attached a detailed explanation on both of the points that you have mentioned which I hope will serve to clarify our position on rates and illustrate that our rate increases are actually quite different to those you have indicated. Once you have had a chance to read this through I think it might be

sensible for us to speak or even meet up to discuss the next
stage.
I look forward to hearing from you.
Regards
Jane

To which, not surprisingly once you understand the principles
of rapport, she received the following reply:

Thanks for the email which read with interest; however I still feel
that my questions are not fully answered ... May I suggest that I
meet with you at your office to clarify the matter of the fee rates
so that I can be reassured that the fees do fit for the work that
you are proposing.
Wendy

How would you have replied? Could you have found a way of
replying that would have avoided the need for a meeting? We
will come back to this email at the end of the chapter and what
Jane did eventually send after we had a session on rapport
building.

It is as important to know what rapport is *not* as it is to know
what it is. Many people think rapport is chatting about the
weather, the family, and the like. It may be, but only if that is
what the people you are talking to are doing the same. If not,
then to chat about these things might achieve completely the
opposite effect of rapport. If you are with someone who is
aggressive, then although you may not want to be literally
aggressive, you would certainly want to match the strength of
their style in some way. There are some clues later in this
chapter as to how to do this.

> Many people think rapport is chatting about the weather!

Rapport is not about passing the time of day. Rapport is
about joining people where they are in their style so that you
connect with them in a way that supports all future
communication. Rapport may be as much about being hard in
your approach to someone as it is about being soft. And
rapport is *not* about accepting what anyone says or does. In
fact, by creating an environment of rapport you create the
climate to discuss and influence those things that do present
problems between you and others.

> Rapport is about connecting

HOW TO BUILD AND MAINTAIN RAPPORT

Think of someone with whom you feel you do have good rapport. What is true about your contact with them that isn't true for others? If you are in the company of other people, look around you. What would you say is your level of rapport with the people you see? Have you checked this out? What do you think your colleagues would say about the quality of rapport you have with them?

Consider some of the written communication you have with others. Who do you find it easy to communicate with? What is it about their style that you like? And whose communication do you find challenging? What is it about them and the way they communicate that you have found harder to relate to? If you are tempted to gloss over this question take care—you might be missing the very thing that will make the biggest difference for you in your life.

People like people who are like themselves

Pay attention to the physical mannerisms of the people around you. People in rapport typically adopt the same posture, move and gesture in similar ways, laugh together, adopt the same style and rhythm in movement and speech. They "match" each other. This happens naturally when two or more people are in rapport. They almost certainly aren't consciously aware of it happening. The result is that their thinking and feelings will be similar. How is your behavior similar to that of those around you now? Or not? Have you ever had that uncanny experience of having someone say exactly what you were thinking, or finding that you know exactly what someone else is feeling? When you adopt the same body language as someone else you create the likelihood that you are engaging the same thinking and feeling circuits. So even if you are not thinking the same thing you are very likely going to be thinking and feeling in the same way.

One of the core beliefs consistently held by people chosen as models of excellence in much of the research in NLP is that:

Mind and body are part of the same system. What occurs in one part will affect all the other parts.

By modeling people who have deep levels of rapport we discover that they adopt the same or a similar style of:

❏ Posture.
❏ Movement and gestures.
❏ Breathing levels.
❏ Voice tone and quality.
❏ Language content: visual/auditory/feelings, and key words.

They also hold similar or in some cases identical:

❏ Beliefs.
❏ Values.
❏ Sense of identity.
❏ Purpose in work and life

When people demonstrate a similarity in any of these, we say that they are matching that characteristic.

Bill was a software developer who headed up a technical team. He dealt with many other departments in the company and frequently accompanied members of the sales team in meetings with clients. Technically he was highly skilled, but he didn't feel at ease in the company of others. He had attended many training courses on the techniques of running effective meetings, making presentations, and communicating confidently, but he still didn't enjoy most situations that involved talking to other people, especially if it meant meeting people for the first time. He found these initial meetings extremely stressful.

Consequently, the clients in these meetings tended to direct their conversations away from Bill. Occasionally he met with someone with whom he seemed to "click" straight away, but this wasn't often. The emphasis in his role was changing. As his department grew he was expected to represent it more often, not only in sales meetings but in internal meetings with senior managers.

Rapport is essential for any meaningful communication to take place. You need rapport to be able to conduct a productive conversation, to engage someone's attention with a message, to run an effective meeting, or to expect others to follow your lead and want to buy into your sense of direction. Without rapport, very little communication of value will occur.

"Just because you are making a noise in my direction don't think you are communicating."

David Gordon

Building rapport

So what happens when this connection doesn't naturally occur? This is when your skill of rapport building is most needed. The real test is whether you can build rapport when it is not returned in kind by the people with whom you are dealing. Let's explore the characteristics of people who do this.

Skillful communicators build rapport by:

❑ Seeking to connect with everyone with whom they come into contact in a way that demonstrates respect for difference. They respect the beliefs, values, and styles of others even though they may be different to their own.
❑ Being aware of the degree to which they are similar (or not) in any of the following—recognizing that significant dissimilarity probably indicates lack of rapport:
  ◆ **Posture**—Position of the body/position of the legs and feet/weight distribution; position of the arms/hands/fingers; shoulder tension or relaxation; inclination of the head.
  ◆ **Expression**—Direction of the look; movement of the gaze.
  ◆ **Breathing**—Rate of breathing; position of the breathing, in the chest/abdomen or low stomach.
  ◆ **Movement**—Signature rhythm (overall tempo of movement), fast/steady/slow/still.
  ◆ **Voice**—Pace/volume/pitch/tone/type of words, intonation.
  ◆ **Language**—Visual/auditory/feelings patterns.

The more you can subtly get into the style of the person with whom you are communicating, the more you will begin to understand what their motives, attitudes, values, beliefs, and feelings must be for them to be doing and saying what they are doing and saying.

And in the language of written communication:

- ❏ Words used.
- ❏ Senses preferred.
- ❏ Values highlighted.
- ❏ Chunk size.
- ❏ Sequence of the communication, e.g., big picture first, details later.
- ❏ Problem or desired state orientation.
- ❏ Use of time during and between communication.
- ❏ Passive or active language.
- ❏ Use of metaphor or precision language.

This can be a long list to attempt to work on at one time. Some of these may come naturally to you. Choose one of the less natural ones and practice that until you can do it automatically. Choose occasions to practice matching when you are an observer and do not have to engage in conversation. Using your written communication with someone is a good place to start as you have time to analyze what they are saying and how they are saying it. You also then have the time to match your response to take into account their preferences.

Be prepared, however. One of my friends who sat silently matching the behavior of a manager who was engaged in conversation with a colleague was taken by surprise when the manager turned to my friend and said, "I'd really like to know what you think." It's interesting what happens when you actively demonstrate rapport, silent or otherwise!

Silent rapport

RAPPORT AS A FORM OF INFLUENCE

Rapport is influence. When you are communicating with someone else you are part of a system. The higher the level of rapport that exists between you, the greater the influence you have on each other.

This usually doesn't require much conscious attention. When you have rapport you know it, you feel at ease in the other person's company, conversation flows, and equally silence is comfortable. What occurs is like a dance: As one moves the other

Rapport is influence

follows. It is impossible to tell who leads and who follows. Conversation flows as you understand the meaning and intention of what the other person says. You appreciate and respect each other's feelings. It does not mean that you necessarily agree with everything the other person is saying, but you understand what they say and why they say it.

Pacing

Pacing is the next step. It is about respecting the state, style, or feelings of others. For example, if someone is feeling concerned, to pace them is to show understanding for that concern. If someone is having fun, to pace that would be to enter into that fun with them.

When you match and pace, you create an environment in which you can lead. This constitutes influence.

Examples of how and when you might want to use rapport to lead and influence:

❑ In a discussion or interview with someone who is nervous or hesitant, to help them to relax and open up.
❑ When you want to attract potential customers to your company, either by face-to-face contact or remotely.
❑ When you want to introduce new ways of working to an individual or department that has become fixed in their thinking.
❑ When someone is angry, to help them calm down.
❑ When someone is worried and tense, to help them relax.
❑ When you want to teach a new concept, by relating to what people know already.

Match/pace/lead

Match, pace, and lead mirrors the martial arts philosophy of going with the direction of the movement and using the energy of your partner to take them where you want them to be.

Below are some examples of matching, pacing, and leading in conversation.

❑ I can picture the new system that we want to develop.
❑ So when you see this system and imagine what it looks like, what are you saying to yourself?

❑ I feel uncertain about the customer presentation this afternoon.

❏ I can understand that you feel uncertain. How would you like to feel?

❏ My colleagues told me that they really valued the ideas I put forward at the meeting.

❏ I can understand that—I value the ideas that you put forward too. What did you feel about them?

I recently received a text message from one of my children in the following style:

Can you ring me wen u get bak I need 2 ask u a favour about nxt wk – Ta!

It would be inappropriate to send an eloquent, enriched language message back! It would be much more on the same wavelength to say

Will do c u soon I hope 2 – Luv S

However, what about an email like this, which I received through my web page not so long ago?

Also a little story for your info-tainment.
A few weeks ago, I started a new role and during my lunch was strolling thru a mall (as you do) and there was a bookseller selling remainder books. Well, as I moved around the table ambling thru the various biogs, Ancient Greek tombs, and associated vegetarian cookbooks what should catch my ear but somebody talking about your book—NLP at Work. A fairly lively debate ensued between the woman thinking of purchasing your book and the bookseller justifying why he was selling it. Anyways to cut a long story to a small duplex, the woman put the book down and as I leant over to pick it up, she picked up the vegetarian book I was (past tense) planning to buy and said "I'll have this one, it's bound to be more useful—can't cook nuffin with NLP." So what am I to do—she's taken my book and here I am holding your baby— so to speak—well I took it home, read it and give it a good.
So you say why are you telling me all this...? Well a week or so later I'm in this same mall and here I am positioned in front

of this same bookseller and he says to me "You know that book you bought last week, well I've got 8 more copies—do you want to buy them—ha ha ha." So I did and I think it was his biggest pattern interrupt all day.

When I got home I thought what am I doing with nine (9) copies of the same book and then it came to me. "I'll give them to my friends the next time they ask—hey what's all this NLP stuff about." So I guess you can cook somethin' with NLP ... after all.

A very different style of response is appropriate here. The sender is a storyteller and uses a lot of dialog, some in the form of internal questioning dialog, and auditory style language as well as metaphor throughout. To respect that style would be to write in a similar way. (And I had a lot of fun thinking about my answer!) If you are curious about my answer, take a look at "Ask Sue Knight" on www.sueknight.co.uk.

Systems that fit

The same principles apply on a bigger scale. For example, it is crucial to ensure that new systems match the style and culture of a company. The concept of match, pace, lead works at every level, not only between individuals but when introducing any new element to a system. It is important that any system you introduce fits with what you already have.

"Match–pace–lead" works at every level

For example, I've sometimes seen small, informal organizations attempt to "bolt on" more formal appraisal systems that belong to a much larger, more bureaucratic organization. One of the simplest and most effective appraisal systems asked only four questions: What are your goals? How well did you do? What skills would help you develop further? What actions shall we commit to? This was successful because the style matched the informality and openness of the company in which it was introduced.

Similarly, it is important to ensure that rapport exists between the managers and the jobholders. To continue with appraisal, for a jobholder to accept feedback from his or her manager and vice versa there needs to be rapport. With rapport the appraisal will find its own style and form. Appraisal is about learning and development; it is a vehicle that provides the stimulus for continuous improvement.

MATCHING AND PACING VALUES IN NEGOTIATION

Achieving a state of rapport is the most important outcome at the beginning of a negotiation. From then on it is important to ensure that you maintain that rapport throughout. Without rapport you have no negotiation. If at any time you lose rapport, rebuild it, and only continue on to anything else of import when you have restored it. When you have rapport the structure of the negotiation suggests itself. The process of what is happening determines the content.

Genuine commitment to a solution will only exist if it is built on the values of each of the parties involved. Values are the principles by which we live and are core to who we are as a people. A partnership, a relationship, a team, and a company unite typically because they share common values. People are attracted to you because of the values you communicate.

It is not enough just to *think* about the values of the other party. Respecting and pacing values is a way of building a deep level of rapport. Without this, any other attempts to match and pace are superficial and temporary. Identifying and pacing values is therefore crucial to skilled negotiation. There are different ways to do this. For example, if someone holds the value of security, they will look for a solution to the negotiation that satisfies this value, but they will also want the negotiation to be conducted in a way that respects their need for security. They may, for example, want the points to be presented in a nonthreatening way. If someone's value is fun, it is possible that they will want their representation of fun to be present both in the way the ideas are put to them and in the solution.

Your partner in a negotiation will be evaluating you and the way you present yourself, the venue of the negotiation, and the ideas you discuss, among many other things. They evaluate these things against their own values. If they judge a person by their ability to listen, they will be judging you by the way they recognize this. And even more significantly, they will have a unique way of knowing how each of their values has been met. They know this by a set of rules and standards that constitute their evidence of fulfillment.

Communicators who are considered to be excellent in their ability to achieve understanding and influence are people who

Building on values

Each person is unique

can match, pace, and lead the other person's values. They identify what conditions have to be true for those values to be satisfied. They operate from the belief that *each person is unique*.

Learning the unique indications that have to be present for someone to feel that their values are respected and fulfilled is one of the most sophisticated skills you can develop to negotiate your way through life. The evidence of fulfillment for each of the following values could be (they will be different and unique for everyone):

Value	Evidence of fulfillment
Openness	A willingness to express feelings. Someone who is prepared to state their views before others state theirs. Someone who talks about what is happening in their personal life as well as in their business life.
Security	An acceptance of solutions to problems that have been tried and tested and shown to work in other situations. The ability to express ideas without having them ignored or dismissed.
Creativity	Agreements and ideas that haven't been applied before. People who can think laterally and who can provide a new way of thinking about existing situations.
Listening	Someone who doesn't interrupt, who is curious about what is being said and who asks clarification questions. Someone who leans forward and maintains eye contact for the majority of the time someone else is speaking.

To find out values—watch and listen

To find out someone's values, watch and listen. Pay attention to what excites them and what changes their state to one of interest and curiosity. What do they pay attention to? If they are constantly looking at their watch and want to get on with discussions straight away, you may find that attention to time and to the way time is used is important to them. The more you develop your sensory acuity, your awareness to notice even the smallest of changes in the person with whom you are dealing, the more you will begin to be able to determine when their state changes. Eventually you will be able to "calibrate" these different patterns of behavior to the different states so that you know what outward signs symbolize the different states for your partner.

One of the surest ways of knowing that you have touched on someone's values will be a skin color change. If you make a proposal that meets the values and evidence of fulfillment for the other person, they are very likely to blush. By matching and pacing your partner's values and their evidence of fulfillment you are building a deep level of rapport. Understanding your own values is a way of beginning to understand those of others.

Calibration

WHOLE BODY LISTENING

Business people who listen with care and skill are still in the minority. The people who have this ability are usually those who generate immense respect and influence. And we usually find that rapport is a major component of their ability to listen. When you listen with rapport you are listening with your whole body. Not only do you hear what the other person is saying, you also gain insights as to what they are thinking and feeling. You are influencing the interaction with your nonverbal behavior more often than anything that you do. Tom Peters In A *Passion for Excellence* says, "Listening is the highest form of courtesy." Whole body listening can be the trigger that influences someone to gain insight, to find their own solutions, and to generate commitment to those solutions.

Contrast the difference between someone whose attention is internal, on themselves, and someone who is listening with their whole body, illustrated overleaf.

People whose attention is internal

They think of their own thoughts, make evaluations and judgments. They worry about and concentrate on what just happened, what was just said, or even what might happen next.

Their intention is toward themselves.

Their gaze may be defocused or moving around.

Their body posture is often quite still, even though there may be varied eye movements.

Their language is like to be "I" and "me" centered. They make statements and often express beliefs as facts.

People who are listening with their whole body

They are in a state of curiosity. Their attention is entirely on the other person.

Their intention is toward the other person.

Their gaze is on the other person, looking away occasionally to process what the other person is saying.

They match the other person's posture.

Their language is "you" centered and they use key words and language patterns that match the person they are speaking to. They predominantly ask open questions.

Whole body listening means being able to give all of your attention to someone else. It is the ability to keep your attention external to yourself rather than thinking through your own thoughts. Some textbooks on listening advise you to make eye contact. You can probably remember those situations when, although someone was looking at you, you knew that their mind and spirit were somewhere else entirely! Eye contact alone is no proof of listening. NLP provides the techniques to enable you to listen with your whole body. Rapport is a demonstration of whole body listening.

Detecting the clues

Everything someone says and does will give you some information about their values. They will tell you some explicitly and some may be unknown to them, but they are there. You only have to look and listen.

"I want to talk to you about doing some design work for us. We've worked with one company for a long time now, but they seem to be getting behind the times with their ideas. We've got less time to spend on this than we had in the past, so we want a company who is going to take the initiative to find out what they need to give us what we want. We don't have a lot of time and I'd appreciate you telling me whether you genuinely can work in this way with us."

Let's say that the values of the speaker in the passage above are:

❑ Effective use of time.
❑ Openness and honesty.
❑ Up-to-date ideas.
❑ Initiative.

The depth of the rapport you build will depend on your ability to match these values in what you say and what you do. If you start to ramble in the way you respond and if you wait to be asked the next question, you probably won't be very successful.

If, on the other hand, you answer concisely and openly, telling the other person frankly what you can and cannot do, and if you take the lead in asking questions, then you will probably make good progress. This will only ring true, however, if they are values that you also hold.

At one of our open evenings I was talking to a manager of a computer call center. He was explaining the problems they had been having with their computer system. He also explained that when he raised these problems with the software suppliers they poured people on to the site. I also happen to know the software suppliers and I know that when they did that they believed they were satisfying the customer's needs. They didn't have a surplus of staff, so it was a big decision to put so much resource into one place. How sad, then, that it wasn't what the customer wanted! They had made a judgment about what to do based on their own values and evidence of fulfillment for customer satisfaction, not those of the client.

What was in fact important to the customer was personal one-to-one reassurance, not only that the current bugs in the system would be fixed but explanations of what the supplier was doing to prevent any similar bugs appearing in the system in the future.

Everyone has their own way of satisfying their needs, their evidence of fulfillment. It is crucial to know your customers' evidence of fulfilment and to find ways of meeting this if you want to succeed in business.

"What would have to be true for you...?"

Ask your customers the most important question of all: "What would have to be true for you to want me to be your main supplier for the future?" Then sit back and listen. You will learn some of the most valuable information for meeting your customers' needs that you will ever need to know.

THAT EMAIL

Have you come to any conclusions about what didn't work and what might work with the email at the beginning of this chapter?

My client realized that her response to the original email had been predominantly auditory when her client's email was visual and feelings. In particular, the client was saying (covertly) that her feelings were not being acknowledged and that was true—in the communication they weren't.

The consequence of this was that Jane replied matching not only the sensory preferences but also the sequence in which she used them, so that they matched the sequence her client had used in her email. They did subsequently have a meeting in which Jane addressed and explored Wendy's feelings. Previously she had assumed that because Wendy was in the purchasing department it would be inappropriate to bring feelings into their communication (despite all the clues in the emails). The consequence was that both parties said they had the most productive meeting they had ever had and they reached full agreement on fees and a way forward.

SHORTCUT TO BUILDING RAPPORT

Before any contact with the other person:

1 Choose the person with whom you would like to enhance the rapport you have or expect to have.
2 Imagine yourself having the kind of rapport with them that you would really like to have.
3 Imagine yourself being connected to them in a way that fully respects who they are.

During contact with them (whether that is face to face or remotely):

4 Pay attention to how they communicate as much if not more than to what they communicate.
5 What is significant about their:
   ❑ Behavior?
   ❑ Language?
   ❑ Body language?
   Pick one of the above to concentrate on.
6 Match the element you have chosen.
7 By being similar to this person, what do you detect as being important to them? (For example time, silence, integrity, immediacy, innovation, decisiveness, action, strategic thinking, acknowledgment of feelings, sense preference (visual/auditory/feelings), etc.
8 How are you/can you respect this aspect that is important to them?
9 Monitor how the connection between you strengthens.
10 What else can you do to build the rapport even further?

After the interaction:

11 How would you evaluate the strength of the connection between you?
12 What made a difference?
13 What else could you have done/could you do in future interactions?

SUMMARY

Rapport has become a vital skill on which to pin the success of your business. Through your ability to build rapport you can help other people feel at ease in your company—they choose to be with you because you make it easy for them to be so. People relate to you and the services you offer because they feel you are sympathetic to their needs. Even if you are not technically perfect, the rapport you have with the people with whom you live and work determines the lasting nature of the relationship. By building rapport you build trust and understanding.

THOUGHT PROVOKERS

1   The next time you are in the company of others, pay attention to the elements we have covered in this chapter. Notice their posture and their movements. Listen to their voices and the words they use. Identify which people seem to be most in rapport with each other. What similarities are there in these elements?

2   Seek out the company of two people you know who have excellent rapport with each other. What do you see and hear them doing and saying that are similar?

3   Choose one element per day, e.g., head movement, voice tone, body position, etc. Pay attention to that element for each person you meet.

4   Ask a friend to engage in conversation with you. Notice each time your attention changes from external to internal.

5   Choose two pieces of written or typed communication that you have sent recently. To what extent did you consider what was important to the other person when you sent them? If you had paid more attention to their values and their style of communicating, how might you now change this communication?

6   How would you rate the attention you pay to the rapport you have with:
   ❏ Your boss?
   ❏ Your key client?
   ❏ A significant member of your team?
   ❏ With each of your children (if you have any)? If it differs, what is that you do differently with each?
   ❏ Your life partner?
   ❏ Your parents?
   ❏ Your suppliers?
   ❏ Three people you came into contact with when you last left your home?
   ❏ Three people you expect to meet up with when you next leave your place of work?

REFERENCES

Kevin Kelly (1999) *New Rules for the New Economy: 10 Ways the Network Economy Is Changing Everything*, Fourth Estate.

Tom Peters & Nancy Austin (1986) *A Passion for Excellence: The Leadership Difference*, HarperCollins.

Many years ago in the hills of Patagonia there was a village. Its inhabitants were starving. They lived in fear of a dragon that they had seen in their fields and they would not go to harvest their crops.

One day a traveler came to the village and asked for food. They explained that there was none because they were afraid of the dragon. The traveler was brave and offered to slay the dragon. When he arrived at the fields he couldn't see a dragon, only a large watermelon. So he returned to the village and said, "You have nothing to fear; there is no dragon, only a large watermelon." The villagers were angry at his refusal to understand their fear and hacked the traveler to pieces.

Some weeks later another traveler came to the village. Again, when he asked for food he was told about the dragon. He too was brave and offered to kill the dragon. The villagers were relieved and delighted. When he arrived at the fields he also saw the giant watermelon and returned to the village to tell the villagers that they were mistaken about the dragon—they need have no fear of a giant watermelon. They hacked him to pieces.

More time passed and the villagers were becoming desperate. One day a third traveler appeared. He could see how desperate they were and asked what the problem was. They told him and he promised he would slay the dragon so that they could go to the fields to harvest their crops. When he got to the field he too saw the giant watermelon. He reflected for a moment, then he drew his sword, leaped into the field, and hacked the watermelon to pieces. He returned to the villagers and told them he had killed their dragon. They were overjoyed. The traveler stayed in the village for many months, long enough to teach the villagers the difference between dragons and watermelons.

17

Negotiate Your Way Through Life: Perceptual Positions

"If you wish to be fully alive you must develop a sense of perspective. Life is infinitely greater than this trifle your heart is attached to and which you have given the power to so upset you."

Anthony de Mello

H ave you ever wondered how it is that some people seem to be able to navigate their way through life achieving most of what they want and somehow supporting the people with whom they come into contact to do the same? Maybe you are one of those people? I believe we can all do this to some extent, but there are some people who seem to be able to do it consistently. They seem to have some magic formula that enables them to transform just about every situation into one that has benefits for all involved. If you are one of these people then it is unlikely that you know exactly how you do this. If you are not, my guess is that you would like to know exactly how to do this. The good news is that this is a skill that can be learned and refined whatever your ability right now.

We can learn how to:

Finding the magic formula

❏ Express what we really want in ways that bring others along with us.

❏ Increasingly tap into what is important to us and express it in ways so that others will listen.

❏ Deal with people who we feel are regularly trying to block our path.

❏ Negotiate a win/win in situations that might otherwise be blocked or compromised.

❏ Empathise with others and yet not take on the burden of all their emotions.

❏ Stand back from situations and take learning from every one of them.

❏ Deal with situations as they arise, manage them in a way that is in everyone's best interest, and move on.

❏ Let go of resentment, anger, frustration, and guilt.

❏ Increasingly move through work and life as a learning journey that becomes increasingly enriching with every step we take.

It really is quite simple and of course common sense—once we know *how*. This chapter presents some of the work done by John Grinder and Judith DeLozier to provide shortcuts to powerful techniques such as these. This is an example of what is sometimes referred to as New Code NLP. The strategy that John and Judith developed is a way of learning to take different perceptual positions on a situation in order to find a balance in how we go forward to a solution. Because of this, the strategy for negotiation is often called perceptual positions. After all, the perceptual positions we take in our heads and in our physiology are all we have to work with in this life.

TAKING A BALANCED APPROACH

When John Grinder and Judith Delozier modeled people who were skilled at negotiating a way forward that was a win for themselves and also a win for the person or people with whom they were negotiating, they found that these people were able to experience a situation from many different perspectives and that it was this mental agility that enabled them to gain the insights that provided the breakthrough. What are these different perspectives and how can we take ourselves through them in a way that gives us the breakthroughs we want in our personal and business lives?

There are three primary positions (you can take many more if you choose, but we will concentrate on three).

OWN SHOES (1ST POSITION)

By putting ourselves in 1st position we are able to fully appreciate what is important to us personally. To do this we need to be able to see, hear, and feel the situation from our own perspective (in our own shoes). In this position we think in terms of what is important to "me," what do "I" really want. We speak using language such as "I feel," "I want," "I hear," "I see." We tap into the truth of our own perspective on the situation. This is a way of thinking that allows us to know what we really want. We can see and hear the other person (or people) and we experience them from our "map of the world."

THEIR SHOES (2ND POSITION)

By putting ourselves in 2nd position we are able to understand where the other person is coming from and what has to be true for them to be doing or saying what they are. It is quite different to "put yourself" in the other person's shoes as opposed to "thinking" about what it must be like to be in their shoes. By putting ourselves in the other person's shoes we experience the situation as if we are them. We are able to imagine how it is to look out of their eyes and hear out of their ears and be in their body, such that we see, hear, and feel the situation as if we are them. Of course we can never absolutely do this, but it is amazing just how uncannily close we can get when we are skilled in this way of thinking.

When you are fully in the other person's shoes and have their perspective on the situation, you are able to understand their map of the world. No matter how bizarre someone's behavior might have seemed from your own perspective, in their shoes it is normal and perfectly understandable. To put ourselves fully into the shoes of another person allows us to tap into the emotions behind what they are doing and saying. This is often a position of amazing insight about what is really going on for the other person in a situation.

This is the ability to stand back from a situation and experience it as if you are a detached observer. In your mind you are able to see and hear yourself and the other person as if you were a fly on the wall. You are unlikely to have emotions in this situation as you dissociate from what is going on. You may have concern, but not the emotions that you would have in either 1st or 2nd position.

This is a position of analysis and learning—in fact, it is the only place in which it is appropriate to do analysis. It is in this position that you can stand back and be aware of the dynamic that is going on between 1st and 2nd positions. You can be aware of how inextricably linked you and the other person are in the dynamic of what is happening. This is the position in which you can get the bigger picture, the systems view of what is going on. It is here that you can gain insights about what learning the other person is unconsciously offering you. Here is where you can identify how you can change to make a difference (and it is only you who can change!).

To fully experience what it is like to be in each of these positions, work through the shortcuts at the end of the chapter.

OBSERVER (3RD POSITION)

The ability to stand back

WHERE AND WHEN CAN WE USE THIS APPROACH?

The glib answer is to say everywhere and at all times. However, there is often a belief that these approaches work in face-to-face situations and nowhere else. This is far from the truth. This way of thinking can certainly benefit us face to face (and we can learn to do this in real time while we are in conversation, in advance as a form of preparation, or afterwards to review what has happened), but it is just as relevant for remote communication. For example, we can apply this thinking to ensure that we phrase our emails in a way that creates the effect that we really want.

I received an email recently that just said:

Jones
See you on Monday.
Brian

I can learn to put myself in others' shoes

Computer games use different perceptual positions

We can help others to appreciate situations

At first I thought it was for someone else. Then I thought my colleague had dreamt up a nickname for me, Jones. Eventually I realized he was answering a question I had asked him in an email several days earlier (for the surname of a mutual contact). In Brian's shoes he read my question and, treating it like a regular conversation – answered the question and closed the message. However, if he had put himself in my shoes he might have realized that a lot of emails had flowed through the ether between the time I had sent him this question and getting his answer, and the original question was not at the forefront of my thinking.

I cannot make him put himself in my shoes, but I can learn to put myself in his shoes in order to think about how I can learn from this and save myself time in the future.

Perceptual positions thinking works in our design of anything that involves other people. It is interesting how computer games have developed in their use of these different positions. And what is also interesting is the preference people have for the different positions in their choice of game. For example, there are first person games (usually first person shootouts) in which you are associated into the shoes of the key player. Consequently you are likely to experience the emotions of being that player. And there are "command and conquer" games where you take a third position and manage many players or situations from an overseeing position.

The closest to second position would be RPG (role playing games) in which you advise and instruct one of the players in the game but from an overseeing position, so it is a mix of second and third position thinking. If you play or know people who play computer games they probably have a preference for which kind of game (depending on the position they adopt) is their favorite.

We can help others to appreciate situations and services by taking them through any one or all of the perceptual positions. For example, the author of the following article is helping us appreciate some of the design features of a website by putting us in the shoes of the web page user.

"Browsing the shops one day, imagine you walk into a department store called, say, Inter-Net Universal Superstores. There's no proper signposting and you can't find an information

desk or any staff. You look for your favourite magazine but can only find hundreds of magazines, newspapers and paperback books, all mixed up. You try to find a loaf of bread but again, there are no signs. And when you do eventually stumble across the bread shelves, most of them are empty.

You think you'll try the clothing department—but where is it? You turn the corner and trip over a trolley dumped in a darkened corner. You come across a big sign, 'Grand Sale Next Week = 50% off,' but then you check the dates and realise 'next week' has long passed. By now you've had enough. You want to tell the manager how annoyed you are—but no one knows where he is...

It's hard to imagine any shop quite that bad, yet cyberspace is spattered with sites that are the Internet equivalent of our fictitious Store From Hell, many of them put there by people who ought to know better."

@demon newsletter

This insight into how we present ourselves to our audience comes from the ability of the author to put themselves into the shoes of the people on the receiving end of what we do. This skill is essential in developing our ability to judge how what we are doing and saying is being received. Skillful negotiators in all contexts and all media instinctively use all three positions as a way of taking a balanced approach to a situation.

IMBALANCED POSITIONS

An imbalanced use of any of the positions has implications for your ability to make progress.

Aggression

James often had to attend meetings as part of his work. He usually prepared for these meetings by carefully thinking through his proposals. He often had ideas for ways the department could handle new projects. He couldn't normally see why he wouldn't get the go-ahead from his manager. He felt that his manager's style was to stall and throw out objections. James usually felt extremely frustrated by the response he received. As far as he was concerned, his manager was being stubborn. Sometimes his frustration reached such a level that he wondered if it was worth staying with the department.

Excessive use of 1st position leads to lack of understanding of others

Excessive use of 1st position can lead to a lack of understanding and subsequent dismissal of other people's feelings and ideas. You might push for the achievement of your outcomes but at the expense of others. So, although you may achieve what you want, your achievement is likely to be short lived and may backfire in some way. You may feel overcome by your emotions.

Nonassertion

Diane was considered by her team to be caring and compassionate. She became concerned if any of her team experienced problems and would endeavor to help them solve those problems through discussion. However, whenever she did this she found herself experiencing the feelings of the person she was counseling. Not only did she experience these feelings during the discussion, but she found they stayed with her, often for the rest of the day and sometimes longer. She began to avoid getting into such discussions for fear of the burden of emotions she might subsequently carry.

Excessive use of 2nd position leads to loss of self-esteem

Excessive use of 2nd position can lead to a loss of self-esteem if you identify with other people's needs and feelings at the expense of your own. Essentially you would be giving others priority over yourself. It is possible that by overly identifying with the other person you stop yourself achieving and even thinking about what you really want. You may find yourself taking on other people's feelings and being unable to shake them off. Over time the weight of others' emotions can be mentally and emotionally fatiguing if carried in this way.

Detachment

David was a member of a project team engaged on a high-profile task for the company. The project team was working to a tight schedule and sometimes tempers flared and discussions would become heated. David, however, seemed untouched by this emotion. Physically and emotionally he seemed to distance himself. This often irritated the other team members, who felt that he didn't care about the success of the project.

Excessive use of 3rd position creates an image of being unemotional

Excessive use of 3rd position can give an image of being detached and unemotional. You would be likely to be objective and analytical without the capacity to experience the emotion of the situation.

The ability to use all three positions in a balanced way leads to cooperative, assertive behavior and increased choice and understanding.

WHEN SHOULD YOU USE EACH POSITION?

1ST POSITION

1st position is a good one to adopt when you want to stand up for yourself, see things from your perspective, hear things for yourself, get in touch with your own feelings, or when initially setting outcomes for yourself. It is a position from which to ask yourself the question, "What do I really want?" It is also an appropriate position in which to do an ecology check for any outcomes you set yourself, i.e., does this outcome fit with who I am/want to be? Developing your ability to experience 1st position can be a way of moving from nonassertive to assertive behavior.

2ND POSITION

When you can't understand another person's behavior, 2nd position is a way of getting behind their behavior and into their experience and feelings. Once you understand or seek to understand (because there will be times when you cannot absolutely check out that you are right), this will communicate itself to the other person and will often give them a feeling of reassurance that you do understand their position. More especially, it will give you greater understanding and therefore choice about how to deal with the situation taking into account how the other person is affected by it.

3RD POSITION

This position can be valuable when you want to stand back, take stock, and think objectively about a situation. It can be particularly valuable when you don't want the emotions attached to either being in or thinking about a situation. People who are able to handle aggression from others in a controlled and unemotional way often do this from 3rd position so that they are not, for example, experiencing the feelings of anger, frustration, or hurt that they might be feeling if they were in 1st position.

Andy Wilman was making a documentary about the skills of the fastest people on the planet. He interviewed racing driver Michael Schumacher and Ferrari Technical Director Ross Brawn and in an article in the Daily Telegraph *analyzed Schumacher's ability to detach in a way that gives him an edge on all other drivers racing today.*

"Calmness is another Schumacher asset. Pure wind in the hair speed doesn't blow his frock up. 'When I'm racing my heart rate is very low,' he says. 'Probably lower than yours is sitting here right now.' Such detachment from speed goes hand in glove with another factor vital to every member of the speed elite: the ability to carry out several functions all at once. He can function as an F1 driver and on top of that he can think about the race that is going on around him. You know he'll come on the radio and tell us to keep an eye on the weather because there are dark clouds forming on one side of the circuit. 'I have worked with other drivers and they just about cope with the driving [said Ross Brawn]. There's no spare capacity. When Rubens Barrichello first came to us I suppose I was expecting to have the same sort of discussions on the radio that I have with Michael, but for the first few races he struggled. Every time I spoke to him he lost half a second a lap. Since then he has raised his game.'"

IN BLOCKED SITUATIONS

If you want still further choices in a situation when there is conflict or blocks to making progress, then step into the presupposition "Behind every behavior is a positive intention toward you." This is one of the beliefs of excellence explained in Chapter 14.

As with all the beliefs, this does not have to be true. You only have to think and act as if it were true. Some creativity helps here in your thinking about what the positive benefit might be. What is the potential benefit in the situation for you? How can you turn the situation into an opportunity even though it may not have initially presented itself to you in this way? For example, if you are faced with someone who is asking you awkward questions, they may be doing that to test the validity of your ideas so they can decide whether or not they want to back them. That is a reason for them to ask questions for themselves. However, a benefit for you may be that they are providing you (unconsciously) with the opportunity of learning how to deal with awkward questions and thereby improving your skills as a presenter and negotiator.

In the scenario involving James earlier in this section, his ability to adopt different perceptual positions and to consider the positive intention behind his manager's behaviour will affect his response to the situation.

James was experiencing the situation with his manager from a dominant 1st position. When James did eventually step into 2nd position, i.e., he put himself into his manager's shoes, he experienced a strong feeling of insecurity and perceived the ideas being presented to him by James as a threat to his position. James (in 1st position) had never realized this possibility and was shocked to appreciate how his manager might be feeling. When James considered the situation objectively from 3rd position, he realised that the more the James in 1st position pushed and initiated new ideas, the more his manager resisted and blocked him. By continuing to do more of the same he was intensifying the response he received.

And the benefit to James of his manager's behavior? (Remember, this does not have to be true. He only has to act as if it were.) It could be that.

❏ He wants James to learn how to show real empathy toward someone else.
❏ He is helping James to learn how to approach solutions at a slower pace than previously.
❏ He wants James to prioritize and think through his ideas so that he only puts over the ones that are of the highest importance to everyone.
❏ He wants James to develop 2nd position thinking!

When James re-evaluated the situation, having experienced it in 1st, 2nd, and 3rd positions, he decided to take a different approach to the next meeting. He took more of a back seat initially and supported the ideas his manager put forward. He waited until his manager asked him for an idea before volunteering any, and explained what support he would need for the idea to work. He invited his manager to develop the idea further. He regularly checked out how he thought his manager might be feeling as he did this.

Over time he gained more and more of his manager's support. Eventually he was able to put forward his ideas without waiting to be asked and he and his manager worked together more cohesively as a team than they had ever done before. When James's manager was appointed to the position of director of special projects, he invited James to join him in the new department as senior project manager.

ORGANIZATIONAL IMPLICATIONS

We can also detect preferences in thinking in company cultures.

IMPLICATIONS OF COMPANIES OPERATING PRIMARILY FROM ONE POSITION

❏ **1st position** There may be a fire-fighting, crisis management style. The company may jump to conclusions about what the solutions to problems might be without checking that they are the solutions in, say, their customers' minds. They are more likely to be problem oriented rather than solution oriented because they don't stand back, take stock, and consider situations objectively. Many high-tech companies have operated this way sometimes as a result of lacking the softer, people understanding skills.

❏ **2nd position** The company may "go overboard" to do what the customer wants without seeking to influence the solution or the outcome. They would typically make unrealistic promises just to keep the customer happy in the short term. Even though they may "jump" to the customer's requests, they invariably lose customer respect.

❏ **3rd position** This company stays emotionally detached. This is characteristic of some large, bureaucratic organizations where there is no "personal touch." Correspondence will be written in the third person, rarely signed by identifiable individuals. It is difficult to attach accountability to anyone in particular. Organizations such as this often handle buyouts ineffectively, with the buyout seen purely as a business acquisition with little or no attention paid to the emotions of the people involved.

The ideal is a company that takes all perceptual positions. It doesn't guarantee success, but it puts it head and shoulders above most other organizations.

CHARACTERISTICS OF A COMPANY THAT TAKES ALL PERCEPTUAL POSITIONS

- ❏ **1st position** It has a clear mission statement expressing the vision and mission of the business in a way that provides direction for all its employees. Shareholders in the business participate in the development of the business mission. It has agreed, published values that are upheld and lived out by everyone in the company. Employees' goals and roles tie in totally with the business strategy and are understood by everyone.
- ❏ **2nd position** Employees spend time with their customers (internal and external), finding out their true requirements and collecting regular feedback about how they are doing. They listen to what their customers have to say. The company does whatever it can to ensure the success of its customers no matter what that takes, and does this not only with customers but also with suppliers. The enlightened company takes a systems view of commerce and looks for ways to work with organizations that might once have been their competitors.
- ❏ **3rd position** Individuals and teams take time to stand back, take stock, and review how they are doing. They pay attention to process as well as content. They learn from experience and in so doing ensure they are on a track of continuous improvement. They see the impact of their behavior on others in the system and equally the effect of others' behavior and actions on themselves. They take the strategic overview.

TAKING A BALANCED POSITION ON ASSERTION

Assertion is the ability to stand up for your needs and desires in a way that takes account of other people's needs and desires. This is a process of cooperation that leads to the increased likelihood of a win/win outcome. We know from the principles of outcome thinking, explained in Chapter 15, that dovetailing outcomes in this way increases the chances that you

Achieving win/win

will achieve what you want. So assertion is about balance, balance between yourself and others.

Many books and training on assertion teach phrases to use and body language to adopt. They teach behavioral solutions. NLP research has shown that for meaningful and lasting change to occur, it is important to understand the implications for identity, beliefs, values, capabilities, and environment as well as behavior. For example, it is pointless teaching someone to behave assertively if they believe that aggression is the way to get on in business. The logical levels of change model, explained in Chapter 13, offers insight about the different levels that need to be addressed.

Managing the thinking process

Our awareness of the subtleties in our thinking can transform our ability to act assertively. If you are thinking how difficult it will be to negotiate a good deal with your customer, it is unlikely that you will handle the situation confidently. Your thinking influences the outcome.

Dawn's colleagues considered that she behaved aggressively in many everyday situations. Typically, she would promote her own ideas and plans without consulting others. She felt her own ideas were generally more appropriate and worthwhile compared with the ideas of her colleagues. She often got frustrated with others but was generally unconcerned.

When Dawn explored the patterns of her thinking about these situations, she realized she was outside herself (dissociated). However, it was as though she was somewhere on the ceiling looking down on the situation. She also noticed that she was much closer to herself in her imagination than she was to others. Although she could see the others and she could see them moving their lips as if they were speaking, she couldn't hear any words.

Dawn experimented with her thinking. First of all she changed her position in her thinking so that she was at eye level with the people in her remembered situation. She also made herself equidistant from herself and the other people. She then associated into her picture of herself so that she could see the situation as if from her own eyes, hear it from her own ears, and experience the feelings of being there. Eventually as

Dawn brought this balance into her thinking, she began to notice that she brought a greater balance into the way she handled situations.

Pauline had felt very stressed for several months. She was concerned about her son, whom she believed was sometimes being bullied at school. She was also concerned about her mother, who had been ill for some time. She herself had recently taken on a lot more responsibility at work. The result of this was that she was constantly feeling tired and depressed.

When Pauline described how she thought about these situations she invariably saw the situation either as if she were in the other person's shoes, or sometimes if she was dissociated she would be close to the other person. Even in this dissociated state she experienced feelings and discovered that the feelings were not her own but those of the other person. There was no place in her thinking where she was free of emotion and, not surprisingly, she felt unable to think about these situations objectively. She was weighed down with everyone's feelings most of the time.

Pauline discovered that by stepping out of 2nd position and giving back the feelings to the rightful owner, she began to feel more relaxed (more like herself again). She positioned herself so she was equidistant from herself and the other person in her thinking; she effectively started to take a more balanced view of the situation. She began to be able to handle situations more objectively.

Giving back feelings

Your thinking patterns are the template for your experience. If your thinking about a situation is out of balance, then you will probably find yourself giving one part of the situation or one person a greater priority than others. Typically, nonassertive behavior results from giving others a higher priority than you give yourself. Aggressive behavior results from giving yourself a higher priority than those around you. Excessive use of 1st position thinking can result in aggressive behavior. Excessive use of 2nd position thinking can lead to nonassertive behavior.

Similarly, the balance, or lack of it, in your thinking about the situation will influence your level of assertion. If you imagine other people as larger than life with booming voices and yourself as small with a quiet, squeaky voice, it is not surprising to find yourself responding nonassertively.

However, the difference in using NLP techniques to achieve assertion compared with more traditional approaches is that by changing your thinking process you will find your own words and phrases. You will discover your own assertive nonverbal behavior. NLP gives you the space to discover your own solutions and styles that fit with who you are and who you want to be. It assumes you already have all the resources you need to achieve what you want. NLP is a process that enables you to draw on these resources when and where you want them.

SHORTCUT TO PERCEPTUAL POSITIONS

1 Put yourself in your shoes and identify:
   ❏ What you are seeing.
   ❏ What you are hearing.
   ❏ What you are feeling physically and emotionally.
2 Break state.
3 Put yourself in the shoes of the other person and identify:
   ❏ What they are seeing (as if you are them).
   ❏ What they are hearing.
   ❏ What they are feeling.
4 Break state.
5 Put yourself in the shoes of an outsider so that you can see yourself and the other person from a distance and ask yourself:
   ❏ What are you seeing and hearing?
   ❏ How are these two people (you and the other) maintaining a perfect system by being the way they are being and doing what they are doing?
   ❏ What is it that the more the you out there does, the more the other person out there does?
   ❏ What is the positive intention behind what is happening for you (the you out there)? (You could also ask this question as "What is the learning intended for you in this situation?")
6 Go back into your own shoes with this balanced thinking about the situation. How does that feel? How might you now go forward in this situation?

SUMMARY

By developing our ability to experience situations from different perceptual positions we gain a balanced approach in thinking, not only about outcomes but also about any other situation. In situations where you feel there is little or no understanding or progress, perceptual positions can provide a way of developing understanding and creating new choices. This is a very powerful technique for finding congruent solutions that are likely to transform your experience of the whole situation. Putting yourself in your client's shoes transforms your ability to present yourself and your business in a way that fits for them. It doesn't matter whether that client is someone you know well or someone you have never met, and may never meet, someone who lives on the other side of the world.

Perceptual positions are an elegant and powerful way of creating choice and understanding in situations that might otherwise be blocked. The ability to take on different positions is a way of stepping beyond the limitations of everyday behavior and appreciating the different maps of the world from which we all operate. It is a way of understanding situations from others' perspectives. It is also a way of removing yourself from the emotions of a situation when you need to be able to think in a more detached and objective way about what is going on. And it is a way of getting in touch with your own feelings and desires.

The balanced use of these positions, either as an individual or as a company, gives you flexibility and an increased chance of achieving a win/win outcome to which all parties are committed.

THOUGHT PROVOKERS

1 What could be the positive intention toward you of the following behaviors:
   a Your manager refuses to let you take on the extra responsibility you have requested.
   b A colleague appears not to listen to what you have to say.
   c The senior management team in your company reorganizes the structure of the company just as you were beginning to feel settled and secure.

    d   The company you have applied to for a job turns you down.

    e   A colleague in another department fails to respond to your requests for the information you need.

2. From which position (1st, 2nd, or 3rd) do you think each of these people is operating:

    a   Peter was explaining to his team what he wanted from them. When the team members didn't understand he became frustrated and started to explain again in more detail. He felt that although he had put forward ideas that would undoubtedly benefit them in the long term, they were being unreasonable by not appreciating what he meant. He found the whole process depressing and decided to continue with it anyway without consultation, as he knew they would appreciate it in the end.

    b   Jenny was a member of a project team. The success of the project was crucial for the company and the team frequently worked late and intensely to achieve the deadlines. Often the discussion in these late night sessions would become quite heated. Jenny stayed calm and couldn't always understand why the other members of the team got so upset. Sometimes they would get frustrated with her and accuse her of not caring about the project. She knew that she did, however, and was often able to help reconcile different points of view within the team.

    c   Diane was considered to be a caring manager. She always took account of the feelings of her team. She was cautious about change, however, particularly changes that would upset anyone. She was always available to counsel friends and colleagues, but found that she would take on their feelings and often ended the day feeling upset and depressed, even though she knew that she had helped her colleagues by listening to them.

3   From what perspective do you operate primarily with:

    ❑   The person closest to you?

    ❑   Your colleagues?

    ❑   Your boss?

    ❑   The different members of your family?

4   If you have a website, imagine yourself in the shoes of someone viewing it for the first time. How do you do? How does your experience compare with the Store from Hell described in this chapter? (Hopefully not at all!)

5 Read through the three most recent emails you sent. From which position did you write them? How might you write them differently now?

6 Read *English Passengers* by Matthew Kneale.

REFERENCES

Robert Dilts, *Encyclopedia of Systemic* NLP *and* NLP *New Coding*, www.nlpuniversitypress.com.

John Grinder & Judith DeLozier (1996) *Turtles All the Way Down: Prerequisites to Personal Genius*, Metamorphous Press.

A father and his son owned a farm. They did not have many animals, but they did own a horse. One day the horse ran away.

"How terrible, what bad luck," said the neighbors.

"Good luck, bad luck, who knows?" replied the farmer.

Several weeks later the horse returned, bringing with him four wild mares.

"What marvelous luck," said the neighbors.

"Good luck, bad luck, who knows?" said the farmer.

The son began to learn to ride the wild horses, but one day he was thrown and broke his leg.

"What bad luck," said the neighbors.

"Good luck, bad luck, who knows?" replied the farmer.

The next week the army came to the village to take all the young men to war. The farmer's son was still disabled with his broken leg, so he was spared. Good luck, bad luck, who knows?

18

Resolving Conflict: Parts Integration

"The point of our crises and calamities is not to frighten us or beat us into submission but to encourage us to change, to allow us to heal and grow."

Kathleen Norris

Sadly, it is too easy to name the countries in which conflict has broken out since I first wrote NLP *at Work*. I have been sickened by news and pictures from Bosnia, the former Yugoslavia, Indonesia, Israel, and now Afghanistan, among too many others to name here. And the conflict continues closer to my home, where the UK still struggles to find a lasting recipe for peace in Northern Ireland. Homing in even more, violence has flared on several occasions in the capitals of several UK cities, and in 2001 we witnessed the tragedy of the attack on the World Trade Center in New York.

In the work I do in many commercial organizations, the issues are not so much to do with the changing environment but with the battles that smolder between departments. On the home front, who among us has not experienced a situation where our personal relations have gone through a difficult patch? Conflict exists at every level. It seems to be a symptom of our times. But does it need to be and how can we personally influence this strife-torn world that we live in and make a positive difference?

Conflict exists at every level

Some of the most innovative business thinkers advocate personal coherence as being the only way to navigate the choppy waters of global enterprise. It does indeed make common sense to seek to achieve personal harmony in order to deal with the external world. However much we might want to do this, we need to know *how* to achieve this state. The format proposed in this chapter addresses that question.

One of the principles I have emphasized throughout this book is that we can only influence by our example. It is within ourselves that we need to look for a way forward and by changing ourselves we influence those systems of which we are a part. This is so easy to say and yet I know of no one who fully achieves this in practice, and I know of many who would subscribe to the principle of what I am saying and still continue doing what they are doing in exactly the same way as before. It takes discipline and skill to resolve the conflict within ourselves. Maybe this chapter will give you the push you need to take a next step in creating and finding an inner peace.

ON THE ONE HAND... ON THE OTHER HAND...

More often than not it is the symptoms of inner conflict that grab our attention and energy. Rightly so, as the symptoms are one of the ways our body has of telling us that something is amiss and we need to stop and take stock of how we are. Our body has a wisdom beyond the capacity of our conscious mind and we need to learn how to listen to what it is seeking to tell us. If we don't listen, the chances are that the physical symptoms will increase in volume and intensity until we do.

Which of the following have you experienced?

❏ Moments when you know that you are acting in a way that is not being true to what you say is important in life.
❏ Times when what you are doing is at odds with what you are saying.
❏ Decisions when a part of you wants to act and move forward and a part of you—say, a concern or a fear—is holding you back.
❏ A feeling of going round in circles when what you want to do is move ahead in a straight line toward your goals.

❏ An ill-at-ease feeling with a goal you have set yourself or one you have accepted from someone else.
❏ Times when the right hand just does not seem to know what the left hand is doing.
❏ Phases of life when you feel that how you are living and working is not being true to the way you really want to be.

The following were incidents when either I or one of my colleagues was being given signals by our bodies to which we needed to pay attention:

❏ A headache when faced with someone who seemed determined to oppose everything that was suggested.
❏ A recurrent illness that seems to be triggered by stress.
❏ An earache when someone close was constantly complaining about the relationship with them.
❏ A frozen shoulder at a time when others' needs were taking precedence over their own.
❏ Sickness when faced with unwelcome change.

And there are subtler bodily signals that indicate a lack of coherence:

❏ An asymmetrical posture.
❏ Indicating an issue on one hand in conflict with an issue on the other hand (the hands used literally to illustrate this).
❏ A stammer when talking about a particular issue.
❏ A difficulty of vision when unable to focus on a future goal.

I am sure you can add many other examples of conflict within yourself that you may be experiencing or have experienced in the past. We live in a world where the pace of change and the pressures to which we can succumb can lead easily to stress and frustration.

WHY BOTHER?

Why is it important to find a way to resolve these forms of stress? Most of us want some form of peace in our lives.

However, there are many other reasons for wanting to resolve our inner conflicts. When we have any form of inner conflict the results are:

❏ We operate at less than our true potential so we reduce our effectiveness in whatever work or play we are engaged in.
❏ We use energy to manage the conflict within and so we have less energy and ability to concentrate on what is happening around us; we are less able to listen fully to others.
❏ If we have a goal then we shut down the filters that are able to recognize the opportunities in line with that goal, and so hamper our progress toward it.
❏ The stress or whatever symptom we experience starts to become a habitual feeling—we get comfortable with that and it becomes more difficult to get out of the rut.
❏ Other people start to shut us out—we get excluded from work opportunities, we are avoided, and we are not consulted on issues that matter.

In contrast:

❏ When we are in a state where we are at harmony with ourselves and are without conflict, we are in a state when we have potentially our maximum influence on the people and the world around us.
❏ The state of alignment or coherence is the only state in which we can manage ourselves through the complexities and ever-changing circumstances of life.

LISTENING TO THE WISDOM OF YOUR BODY

By resolving conflict within we influence the conflict we experience around us. There were several clues in the list of types of conflict you may have experienced. For example, "Decisions when a part of you wants to act and move forward and a part of you—say a concern or a fear—is holding you back." I refer to 'parts' of ourselves and this is a useful and powerful way of thinking about this. We are not literally in parts, but by considering the differing desires in this way we can act as arbitrator to our own emotions.

A way to think about this conflict is to imagine that we do have parts, each one with its own identity and characteristics. Imagine that you have an inner team and each part is a player in that team. If the parts are communicating with each other and in harmony, then we have a state of coherence; you are in rapport with yourself. If some of the parts are at odds with each other and not communicating effectively, then you have incongruence and the accompanying stress.

For example, have you ever felt that a part of you felt obliged to do what you had been asked to do, but another part felt that you were violating what is important to you? And then again, have you ever felt that everything about you was saying "yes" to a conclusion you had reached and a plan you had set yourself and that the motivation to carry out that plan was unstoppable? These are examples of what it is like to be without coherence and what it can be like to have it.

Managing the inner team

These parts often communicate with us through physical symptoms. For instance, you might get a sharp pain above the eyes whenever you think about a particular decision. The part that is giving you the pain might be the part that lacks the courage to say "yes" to the decision you are considering. By learning to communicate with these inner parts, we learn what they want to tell us; we learn to listen to the wisdom of our own body. By listening to these parts we are learning to listen to our unconscious mind. And by learning how to coach these parts to communicate and work together in harmony, we increasingly create a state of coherence within ourselves.

SHORTCUT TO "PULLING YOURSELF TOGETHER"

You must have heard the advice (often given somewhat aggressively) to "pull yourself together." The outcome of the advice, if not the style with which it is given, is sound. To resolve conflict we do need to pull ourselves together, as we do to achieve a state of rapport and resourcefulness. The question is how. By modeling those people who are skilled at resolving their inner and consequently their outer conflict, we find that they have a structure for pulling themselves together. These are the steps to follow:

1 Identify the parts that are in conflict with each other. For example, the part that wants to say yes to an offer you have been made and the part that wants to wait, the "yes" part and the "waiting" part.

2 Take some time to acknowledge these parts in turn. This is the opposite of what many people feel like doing with parts that have been causing conflict. The temptation can be to ignore or delete or get angry with them. The key here is to realize that all parts are working on our behalf and that they do it in their own way, even though we might not at first appreciate that. So thank each part in turn for communicating with you. Listen and sense *how* each part communicates with you. Some parts might give you an image or a sound, or they might cause a particular sensation. You may notice nothing at first but thank the parts nevertheless. It is amazing what cooperation you can get from something or someone to whom you show genuine appreciation.

3 In this step you are going to detach yourself (dissociate) from the emotions of the parts to consider how they can cooperate with each other. Hold your hands out in front of you and use your instinct to decide which part you want to put on your right hand and which part you want to put on your left hand. Imagine that those parts of yourself are actually in your outspread hands. Hold them out and take a look at both.

4 Decide which part you wish to communicate with first. Now consider that part and describe its characteristics and qualities. For example, it might be a part of you that is aggressive and talks to you in terms of what you must do, using language like "Get on with it" and "What are you waiting for?" Each part symbolizes some aspect of your life. Explore what each represents for you.

5 Every part is working on your behalf, even if you have not known consciously how it is doing this. Ask this part what it wants for you; what outcome is it seeking to achieve that is positive for you? Be aware of whatever comes to mind—that is how your unconscious mind communicates with you. Appreciate what answer you get in whatever way you get it.

6 Now repeat steps 4 and 5 with the part that you have on the other hand.

7   Considering each part in turn, ask yourself what quality or attribute this part has to give the other. For example, identify what gift the first part has that would enhance the other part if it were to accept it. You may need to explore with the receiving part in what way it would like this gift in order for it to accept it.

8   Imagine this exchange of gifts. If at first this does not happen, ask each part in what way or what form the other part could give this gift in a way that the receiving part can accept. Now imagine the exchange of gifts.

9   Typically at this point if the previous two steps have been successful there will be an automatic drawing together of hands. This physical bringing together is an indication that you are integrating the two parts in your thinking. If this does not happen automatically, you can suggest it by considering how these two parts might integrate with each other and exist together in cooperation and bring your hands together as you do so. If necessary, go back and repeat steps 7 and 8 until this step is successful.

10 Now imagine how these parts together are a part of who you are, and in so doing bring both hands together to the heart of your chest. How has this enhanced who you are and how you can go forward into your future?

In effect, what you are doing is encouraging different parts of yourself to work in harmony. So often when parts are in conflict our tendency can be to think that we have to go one way *or* the other, when in fact it is by exploring how we can have one *and* the other together that we get the breakthrough in our thinking. The effect of this integration is to create a state of rapport with yourself so that you are being fully who you are and who you can be.

If you are witnessing conflict in other people, you first need to go through this process so that you have resolved the conflict that you experience within. If, for example, I see two friends in conflict with each other, there is nothing I can do to resolve their conflict. However, I can resolve the conflict between the parts of myself that are symbolized by these friends. Interestingly, when I have found the resolution within myself, my external experience will change too, as will my way of dealing with that external experience. Our experience of people around is reflected by our perceptions of them inside ourselves. To change what we experience externally we must change our attitudes and perceptions within. To achieve a change in my circumstances, I first of all need to be able to imagine that change having taken place in the way I want it to.

For the process outlined above to become second nature (so that you are using it unconsciously and in real time, for example while you are in a conversation with someone), it helps to work through it "offline" first of all. Do this with a situation that you have experienced in the past or one that you anticipate may happen in the future. It is rehearsal and practice that make this an unconscious skill.

SUMMARY

The structure for resolving conflict outlined above is a way of continuously learning and growing in positive and constructive ways from what might be a negative and uncomfortable experience. With this kind of structure we can manage our thinking no matter what the circumstances. Subsequently we find that we are influencing the environments of which we are a part.

THOUGHT PROVOKERS

1   What parts of yourself do you recognize might be in conflict with each other today?

2   What conflict do you experience between people outside of yourself? How do the people outside of you symbolize parts of yourself?

3   Remember a time when you experienced conflict and you found a way to resolve it within yourself. How did you do that?

4   What physical symptoms do you recognize as signals from your unconscious to you? How well do you listen and act on what your unconscious is telling you?

One day a fisherman was lying on a beautiful beach, with his fishing pole propped up in the sand and his solitary line cast out into the sparkling blue surf. He was enjoying the warmth of the afternoon sun and the prospect of catching a fish.

About that time, a businessman came walking down the beach, trying to relieve some of the stress of his work day. He noticed the fisherman sitting on the beach and decided to find out why he was fishing instead of working harder to make a living for himself and his family. "You aren't going to catch many fish that way," said the businessman to the fisherman. "You should be working rather than lying on the beach!"

The fisherman looked up at the businessman, smiled and replied, "And what will my reward be?"

"Well, you can get bigger nets and catch more fish!" was the businessman's answer.

"And then what will my reward be?" asked the fisherman, still smiling.

The businessman replied, "You will make money and you'll be able to buy a boat, which will then result in larger catches of fish."

"And then what will my reward be?" asked the fisherman again.

The businessman was beginning to get a little irritated with the fisherman's questions. "You can buy a bigger boat, and hire some people to work for you." he said.

"And then what will my reward be?" repeated the fisherman.

The businessman was getting angry. "Don't you understand? You can build up a fleet of fishing boats, sail all over the world, and let all your employees catch fish for you!"

Once again the fisherman asked, "And then what will my reward be?"

The businessman was red with rage and shouted at the fisherman, "Don't you understand that you can become so rich that you will never have to work for your living again! You can spend all the rest of your days sitting on this beach, looking at the sunset. You won't have a care in the world!"

The fisherman, still smiling, looked up and said, "And what do you think I'm doing right now?"

19

Giving and Receiving Feedback

"We pardon as long as we love."

Duc de la Rochefoucauld

Today I am working in a remote part of France. All of my work contacts are at least 500 miles away and yet I can interact with each of them in seconds. The systems we use are designed increasingly to give us instant feedback on how we are doing. As I type this page any spelling mistake is immediately underlined and any grammatical error highlighted. Yesterday afternoon I entered the chatroom on my website and was able to share and receive thoughts instantaneously with delegates on my programs. On my bike I have a "flight deck" computer that gives me immediate feedback on my cadence, my current speed, my average speed, and much more. The feedback systems to which we have access grow in number and sophistication every day.

Gone are the days when we were given a month to prepare for our appraisal system so we could hear how we are doing. Although this fast becoming archaic management system still exists, we are nevertheless bombarded with instantaneous feedback on our performance in every sphere of our lives. It is by learning to love and thrive on feedback that we can excel in the spontaneity of today's business climate.

Yet in my experience of working with many different people and organizations, there are very few who have this ability.

Living in a world of feedback

Most of us have well-developed mechanisms for doing just the opposite, for keeping feedback at bay. If I were to choose one skill in this book that would put you head and shoulders above most people (not just in business but in life), it is the ability to receive feedback. Receiving feedback is a fundamental precursor to being able (and having the right) to give it.

Receiving feedback is a precursor to giving it

The head of the creative department in a marketing organization wanted to develop the creative team so that they would be open to giving each other feedback and subsequently be increasingly open to feedback from their clients, both within the business and externally. He called a team meeting and told them beforehand that he wanted feedback from them.

In the team meeting he invited them to prepare individually to give him feedback and gave them time to do this. He asked them to think of something they would like him to do more of, something they would like him to less of or differently, and something with which they were happy. He then invited them to give him the feedback and he modeled all the principles of how to accept what they were saying with openness and learning. He demonstrated how to live out the beliefs that underpin effective feedback. He was open, accepting, and curious about what they had to say. He was not in any way defensive or attacking.

The team members also became more and more open and at the end of the meeting they commented on how valuable they had found that time with him. Each subsequently volunteered that they would like to go through a similar process for themselves. This team has become a model of excellence for the rest of the company.

Feedback on performance is the main contribution I make to the individuals and companies with whom I work. No matter whether I am coaching one to one or at an initial meeting with a client, or whether I am working with the board or the key leaders within that company, feedback is what I believe makes the biggest difference to their performance. If they were consistently and skillfully to give each other feedback, my role with them would be redundant; indeed, this is my ultimate aim, for them to do this for themselves without the need for anyone external to the business. I aim to encourage and train people, especially those at the head of the organization, to receive feedback constructively and openly. And then to learn how to give it in a way that strengthens the team and the relationships within it and subsequently encourages improved performance of both the individuals and the business.

There are many books and business models that talk of continuous learning and development, learning organizations, appraisal systems, double loop learning, and much much more. If we are to be able to achieve any of these then we must first be able to receive and give feedback. Once we can do this we will be contributing to business in a way that offers learning from all people and all circumstances.

FEEDBACK AND MODELING

The ability to give and receive feedback is essential to the process of modeling. When we model someone (let's say someone other than ourselves for the moment) we are studying the structure both of what they do and how they do it. To do this without contaminating that structure, we need to be able to accept what they do in *exactly* the way they do it right now.

On one of my NLP training sessions we invited someone we considered to be a model of excellence for leadership to be modeled by the delegates on the program. He was someone who had led a program of immense change in a manufacturing company that had to close half its production sites. This meant he had to find a way to cut the workforce at one plant by 2,000 people. What was special about this man was that he had done this in a way that gained the support and respect of the employees involved. He had managed an immense cutback and had done so with compassion and support for everyone involved. However, he also realized that there were aspects of this whole process that he could have handled differently if he had to do it again (which he sincerely prayed would never have to happen). During the modeling process one of the delegates started to offer some thoughts along the lines of "What if you had done it this way?" and "Had you thought that maybe you might have or still could...?"

The ability to give and receive feedback is essential in modeling

This totally defeats the objective of modeling, which, in the first instance, is to elicit the structure of the subject's experience. It is not to change that structure or to advise or coach the subject to change, just to unpack the structure of how they do what they do. But to do this we have to be able to accept (receive) unconditionally what the other person does. And to determine if what we have elicited fits with the subject's experience of how they do what they do, we need to be able to give feedback completely nonjudgmentally.

We need to be an "empty vessel"

That might sound straightforward, but doing so requires immense skill. It requires that we be totally objective in how we do this—that we accept what others do without influencing it with our own thoughts about what is right and wrong. We need to be an "empty vessel" in which we can learn what is new to us. We need to be able to recognize and, more than that, accept difference.

BELIEFS THAT SUPPORT FEEDBACK

Our beliefs influence our capacity for feedback. A belief that is fundamental to our ability to give and receive feedback constructively is *there is no failure only feedback*, or to put it in other words, *there is only learning*. If you truly believe this, the ability to learn from feedback will be second nature to you. It will be fundamental to your existence as a learner in this world.

There is only learning

There are other beliefs that support our ability to give and receive feedback. The first is that *everyone's perception is their truth*. We only have perception and each person's perception is unique to them. It may be similar to that of other people; it may be significantly different. That does not make it right or wrong, it just makes it true for them. By accepting a perception from someone else we are accepting that part of ourselves as they experience it. We are also contributing to the self-esteem of the giver of the feedback in acknowledging their map of the world. If we do not accept their feedback, we do not accept that part of who they are and therefore we are not fully accepting them as a person.

I was listening to a manager receiving feedback from one of his team. Each time he heard a piece of feedback he either said "That's right" if it aligned with what he believed about himself, or he said nothing if it did not. His response indicated that he did not accept that everyone's perception is their truth and he was not at that time open to learning from other people's perceptions. Gradually his team stopped giving him feedback. He became distanced from what he needed to know in order to run the business.

The second belief is that *what we recognize in others is true about ourselves.* An extension of this is that the characteristics in others that touch us emotionally are a pointer toward those things being characteristics that we don't want or like to accept in ourselves.

My husband gets frustrated when he is behind a driver that he considers to be dawdling on the road. Just this week he found himself behind several drivers who were proceeding very slowly and holding him up. He commented in exasperation that he would never do that. Later that day he was getting some money from a cash machine and as I approached I noticed there was a lady behind him also waiting to use the machine. He had been totally unaware of this person and had been dawdling in using the machine and getting information about his account. When I pointed out that someone had been waiting for some time, he was horrified to feel he had been holding them up in a similar way to how he had been held up by other drivers.

I certainly don't always want to own the traits I see in other people. I am like my husband in the above example in that I prefer to dissociate myself from the characteristics I don't like in others. Yet I do know that it is typically those traits that are my "blind spot" and this is where some of the most powerful learning lies for me. If we can recognize a trait in others, then we have that structure in our thinking. This does not mean that we would behave in exactly the same way (my husband was dawdling by the cash machine rather than dawdling in the car), but whatever structure we have in our thinking we have the capability of enacting in some way. How many of us, although condemning of violence in the world around us, are capable of the same or worse in our thinking? It is a small step between thinking something and doing it.

This is an essential foundation of NLP—it is the structure we hold within that influences our perception and our feelings toward what we experience outside of ourselves.

I am rarely annoyed by delegates on my programs. One of the things I believe I have learned with NLP is that difference is valuable and a source of learning. However, I did have one delegate who was the exception for me. I began to notice how distracting she could be by dropping her papers, coughing, sneezing, or in some way making a noise that disrupted the session. What was interesting was that she seemed to do this at the same point in every session—about five minutes after the start. I found I started to expect this disruption and became tense as the first few minutes elapsed. Then on one occasion at the same point in the session she got up and walked across the room in front of me to get herself a cup of coffee. In doing so she rattled the cups, seeming to have no awareness of the effect of what she was doing on the rest of the room and on me. She walked back across the room with her cup of coffee and sat down. I said nothing, but I felt frustrated and annoyed that she had done this.

At the end of the session I told one of my colleagues how I felt. He asked me what it was about her behavior that had bothered me so much (he had been more or less unaware of what had happened). I replied that it was her focus on what she wanted for herself and her insensitivity to the effect of that on others around her that bothered me so much. And my colleague then said, "And how is that true about you, Sue?" I was quite shocked at first to think that I was like the delegate. Then I realized that I did have similar attributes: a tendency to go for what I wanted and to do so without sensitivity to those around me. I was really amazed how what I saw in her was what I didn't like in myself. Eventually I became quite amused, wondering what aspect of myself she might mirror back to me at the beginning of the next session. And she didn't do anything distracting ever again!

What is important in the context of giving feedback is that if that delegate had been disruptive again and I had chosen to give her feedback, I would have been doing so from a position of identification with her. If I had given feedback to her prior to recognizing how we were alike, I would have done so in a "holier than thou" way, which would most certainly have sounded patronising and not been accepted by her. By identifying with the person to whom we choose to give feedback, we create a connection that increases the likelihood that we will give the feedback in a way that will be accepted.

We recognize attributes in others because we have the structure of those attributes within ourselves. Those traits in others (good and bad) that affect us emotionally are those very same traits in which we have an imbalance in some way. For example, we might be frustrated by what we see as aggression in someone else because we need more of that within ourselves (not to be aggressive but to be more assertive). And it is our frustration with our previous inability to develop this aspect of ourselves that we project on to this other person who is mirroring our imbalance back to us. It may equally be that we have too much of what we see in the other. This was the case with the delegate in my example. I had too much focus and too little sensitivity in some contexts of my life, for example when I set myself a business goal.

To hold this belief—that I recognize in others what I am capable of myself—is to have access to one of the best personal development tools available. It means that whenever we experience something in someone else that we either admire or that bothers us in some way, we have the key to releasing the equivalent potential within ourselves. Our acceptance of this feedback enables us to recognize the traits to which we might otherwise have been blind.

To fully hold this belief is to let go of frustration and anger with others and to realize that there is only one place to look for the answers to our dissatisfactions—within ourselves. Once we change the perception within ourselves, it is amazing how suddenly the world around us, including those people who may have pushed the most sensitive of buttons, seem to change. Energy directed negatively toward others is wasted, life-draining energy. Energy directed inward to accept our own inadequacies and our strengths is life giving, not only to ourselves but to the people with whom we come into contact.

We recognize attributes in others that are true about us

We have the key to releasing the potential within ourselves

The sense of recognition of what is similar creates an unspoken connection. This allows for an openness of feedback that might not otherwise be possible. From this belief flows the skill of giving and receiving feedback outlined below.

RECEIVING FEEDBACK

"Feedback isn't absolute truth but it is truth for the person who is delivering it."

Gene Early

I put the skill of receiving feedback first as I have found that to give it we need first of all to be able to receive it. Your ability to receive feedback is central to continuous learning and growth, as well as being key to healthy, sustainable relationships, both in business and in life.

What can you do to model excellence in the way you receive feedback?

❑ Get yourself into a resourceful state for receiving the feedback. Anchor a state that has worked well for you in this way in the past. The state could be one of learning, for example, or one of openness, self-confidence, humility, or curiosity.

❑ Remind yourself of the beliefs above.

❑ Respond in a way that presupposes acceptance, saying things like "In what ways do I do this?" "What effect does this have on you?" (Use present tense language.)

❑ Always anticipate feedback and always invite it when appropriate so that feedback is in constant supply to you.

Every employee in Cisco Systems has an open feedback form online to everyone else in the company. Anyone can add feedback to this form whenever they choose so that each has a continuous supply of current feedback from anyone in the company.

❑ If the feedback is personally challenging and you find it potentially uncomfortable to take it on board, then dissociate for a moment, step back as if you are an observer of yourself. Having dissociated, check out what further personal resources you need to be able to accept the feedback and then give those resources to yourself before stepping back into your own shoes (associating) in order to accept the feedback for real. If you have not done this before, it helps to do it in your imagination "offline" with feedback that you either anticipate getting and you feel might be challenging, or that was offered to you and you found difficult to accept at the time. The more you do this the more you are able to do it "online" whenever you need more resources to accept what is being offered.

❑ Take full responsibility for building and maintaining rapport with the giver of the feedback even (and especially) if the giver is not taking any responsibility for this themselves.

❑ Seek fully to understand the feedback by questioning (precision questions, Chapter 6, work wonderfully in this situation). For example, ask, "In what way do I do that?" "What is it that I do that gives you that impression?" "Give me examples of how I do this?" These would all be questions that would demonstrate your willingness to accept the giver's perception and learn from it. (What they don't do is rationalize, explain, defend, or attack in any way whatsoever.)

❑ If the feedback indicates that you have upset, annoyed, or caused any negative emotions in the giver of the feedback, apologise for that even though you may have been unaware of that effect at that time. In this way you are taking responsibility for the effects you have on others.

❑ Check out what it is that you can do instead. Ask, "What do I have to do for you to know that I do… (whatever the giver is saying you don't do)?"

❑ Imagine yourself having taken on board the feedback and now behaving in way that demonstrates you have done so. Do this in a way that fits not only for the giver but also with the other key people in that context.

Seek to understand the feedback

The effect of accepting feedback in this way is to encourage the giver to want to give more feedback in the future. You are thus making a significant contribution to creating a climate of learning, whether in a business or a personal relationship.

"Man is part of a chain of connecting humanity within a greater universe. Feedback is a behavioural manifestation of beliefs and values about the importance of interconnectedness between people. By practising and developing feedback I nurture and develop the connections between us and release myself to become who I truly am. 'I' becomes 'we/us'. By connecting with you, I release myself from my own internal prison."

Brian Keenan

GIVING FEEDBACK

The bonus of modeling is that as a result of the process we have feedback to use for our own development and feedback to give to the person or people we have modeled. However, just having the feedback is not a sufficient qualification for giving it. A number of other factors need to be present before and during the process of offering and delivering the feedback. By giving feedback we can also verify that what we believe we have detected is also recognized by our subject.

Below are some steps that help ensure that the feedback we have to give is received in a way that enhances learning for both the giver and the receiver:

❏ Check that you are in rapport with the person to whom you propose giving the feedback. If you are not, do whatever it takes to get that rapport before you even start the process.
❏ Ask yourself, "How is this feedback as true about me as it is for the person to whom I am offering it?" In this way you will create a connectedness in your thinking and in the way you offer the feedback.
❏ Imagine how by accepting the feedback both you and the other person can improve. Create this as a well-formed outcome in your thinking.
❏ Frame the feedback first to say how it has come about or what area of performance it relates to, so that you warm up the receiver to what you are going to say next.
❏ If the other person does not immediately accept the feedback, find another way to give it so they can understand what you are offering them. Their ability to

receive the feedback is a measure of your ability to give it.

❏ Maintain direct eye contact and imagine the receiver of the feedback both accepting and using the feedback constructively as you do so.

❏ Recognize that the response you get from others is coming from the part with which you are choosing to engage. If you do not understand what I am telling you, it is the "nonunderstanding" part with which I am choosing to engage.

❏ Be an example at all times of the response you want from others.

❏ Ask the receiver of the feedback to tell you what they are going to do with what you have given them. Sometimes it helps to ask this before you give the feedback, e.g., "If I give you this feedback what will you do with it?" (This is useful if you know that the person has a habit of shrugging off or avoiding feedback.)

The ultimate measure of your skill in giving feedback is that as a result of the process both you and the person or people to whom you have given the feedback learn from it and deepen your connection with each other.

"Today we give each other feedback and we learn from it. What we used to give each other was abuse!"

Delegate on an in-company course

1 Choose someone to whom you would like to give feedback.

2 Think of the feedback that you would like to give them and the win/win outcome that you want to achieve by giving them this feedback.

3 Imagine the context in which you would like to give the feedback that will be most conducive to its being accepted.

4 Think about how this feedback is as pertinent to you as it is to them.

5 Think of what resources you need to be able to give this feedback constructively.

6 Imagine how you can ensure that you are in very strong rapport with the other person before you give the feedback.

7 Imagine giving the feedback and imagine the other person receiving it in the way that you would like them to.

SHORTCUT TO DEVELOPING YOUR ABILITY TO GIVE FEEDBACK

8 Step back so that you can see yourself and the other person in this process. Are there any other resources that you need to make the giving of the feedback any more constructive? Imagine yourself in that scenario with those resources, giving the feedback in the way you want to.

9 Imagine both you and the receiver of the feedback learning from the feedback in such a way that you strengthen your relationship in the future.

10 What have you learned from this whole process?

SUMMARY

The opportunities for feedback surround us in every medium in which we choose to work. We can learn and grow continuously if we choose, provided that we have the beliefs and skills to give and receive feedback. Feedback is how we can know if what we are doing is working. What could be more important than that?

THOUGHT PROVOKERS

1 Identify someone who is significant to you in:
   ❏ Your personal life.
   ❏ Your work.
   ❏ Your community.
   Decide on a time and a way in which you can ask each for feedback on the extent to which you support them in the way they want you to.

2 Identify someone with whom you have some difficulties. Think of a way in which you can ask them for feedback on what you could do that would make a positive difference between you.

3 Identify someone in your work or your life generally that you wish would be different in some way. Ask yourself how you are not being what you want them to be and how you can be an example of what you do want them to be.

4 Who is your most important customer? When did you last ask for feedback from them? How might you ask for feedback now? How might you set up a feedback system for your most important customers if you don't have one in place right now?

5 How could you reproduce a similar system to the one in Cisco Systems whereby you are getting continuous, real-time feedback?

REFERENCES

Brian Keenan (1993) An Evil Cradling, Vintage.
Peter M. Senge (1993) The Fifth Discipline: The Art and Practice of the Learning Organization, Random House.

At the age of fifteen, in the middle of my junior year, I quit Exeter, one of the most highly regarded preparatory schools in the nation. As I look back on that turning point in my life, I am amazed at the grace that gave me the courage to do it. Not only was I dropping out of a prestigious prep school against my parents' wishes, but I was walking away from a golden WASP track that had all been laid out for me. Hardly aware that it was what I was doing, I was taking my first giant step out of my entire culture. That culture of "the establishment" was what one was supposed to aspire to, and I was throwing it away. And where was I to go? I was forging into the total unknown. I was so terrified I thought I should seek the advice of some of Exeter's faculty before finalising such a dreadful decision. But which of the faculty?

The first candidate who came to mind was my advisor. He had barely spoken to me for two and a half years, but he was reputedly kindly. A second obvious candidate was the crusty old dean of the school, known to be beloved to tens of thousands of alumni. But I thought that three was a good round number, and the third choice was more difficult. I finally hit upon Mr. Lynch, my Maths teacher, a somewhat younger man. I chose him not because we had any relationship or because he seemed to be a particularly warm sort of person—indeed, I found him a rather cold, mathematical kind of fish—but because he had a reputation for being the faculty genius. He'd been involved with some kind of high-level mathematics with the Manhattan Project, and I thought I should check out what I was considering with a "genius."

I went first to my kindly advisor. He let me talk for about two minutes and then gently broke in. "It's true that you're underachieving here at Exeter, Scotty, but not so seriously that you won't be able to graduate. It would be preferable for you to graduate from a superior school like Exeter with lesser grades than from a lesser school with better grades. It would also look bad on your record for you to switch horses in midstream. Besides, I'm sure your parents would be quite upset, so why don't you just go along and do the best you can?"

Next I went to the crusty old dean. He let me speak for thirty seconds. "Exeter is the best school in the world," he harrumphed. "Damn fool thing that you're thinking of doing. Now you just pull yourself up by the bootstraps, young man!"

Feeling worse and worse, I went to see Mr. Lynch. He let me talk myself out. It took about five minutes. Then he said he didn't yet understand, and asked if I would just talk some more about Exeter, about my family, about God (he actually gave me permission to talk about God!)—about anything that came into my head. So I rambled on for another ten minutes in all, which was pretty good for a depressed, inarticulate fifteen-year-old. When I was done, he inquired whether I would mind if he asked me some questions. Thriving on this adult attention, I replied, "Of course not," and he queried me about many different things for the next half-hour.

Finally, after forty-five minutes in all, this supposedly cold fish sat back in his chair with a pained expression on his face and said, "I'm sorry. I can't help you. I don't have any advice to give you. You know," he continued, "it's impossible for one person to ever completely put himself in another person's shoes. But insofar as I can put myself in your shoes—and I'm glad I'm not there—I don't know what I would do if I were you. So, you see, I don't know how to advise you. I'm sorry that I've been unable to help."

It is just possible that that man saved my life, and that I'm able to be sitting here writing this today because of Mr Lynch. For when I entered his office that morning over forty years ago, I was close to suicidal, and when I left I felt as if a thousand pounds had been taken off my back. Because if a "genius" didn't know what to do, then it was all right for me not to know what to do. And if I was considering a move that seemed so insane in the world's terms and a genius couldn't tell me that it was clearly, obviously demented, well then maybe, just maybe, it was something God was calling me to.

So it was that man, who didn't have any answers or quick formulas, who didn't know what I should do and was willing to be empty, who was the one who provided the help I needed. It was that man who listened to me, who gave me his time, who tried to put himself in my shoes, who extended himself and sacrificed himself for me, who loved me. And it was that man who healed me. It was an extraordinary act of civility.

Reproduced with permission from M Scott Peck (1997) The Road Less Traveled: A New Psychology of Love, Traditional Values and Spiritual Growth, *Simon & Schuster.*

20
High Performance Coaching

"If you are unable to make progress it is just that you do not yet have sufficient awareness."

David Hemery

Most people are familiar with coaching in a sporting context. There are football coaches, tennis coaches, skiing coaches—there aren't too many sports that don't have some aspect of coaching associated with them. And what about personal fitness coaches/trainers? It seems that more and more people have someone to support or push them to a state of fitness. Only recently one of my colleagues, with the support of a personal coach, trained to run the London Marathon and went from never having run before to completing the marathon in five hours after just eight weeks of training. And more recently you may have seen the term life coaching. It is as if there is an awakening to the value of developing oneself to achieve a state of physical and mental fitness.

In my work I have experienced a boom in the demand for personal coaching. Leaders in business are not content to rest on their laurels but want to concentrate on how they can achieve greater personal effectiveness. And those leaders also want to learn how to coach their staff to do the same. It is as if we have explored all the external possibilities for gaining a competitive edge, which are becoming more and more unreliable, and people are now beginning to look within themselves for new answers.

David had changed companies three times in the past two years. In each company where he was employed he was always one of the top salespeople. However, he felt frustrated as his goal was to lead a team rather than to work as an independent salesman for the rest of his career. He had been given a few opportunities to prove himself and most recently had been put in charge of a team in his company. Nevertheless, each time he assumed such a role he started having problems in his relationships with some of the key people. The result was usually that he got so frustrated that people didn't cooperate in the way he expected them to that he eventually left and found another sales position. He did this until he worked his way once more to a leadership role. The pattern kept repeating itself.

This is a familiar trend in many companies and there are many similar examples of people who have ambitions they seem destined not to realize. What is the typical solution? Usually it is to let the person go. Some companies might invest first in some management training, believing that there are techniques of people management that can be learnt to resolve the issue. Some companies might invest time in personal appraisal, where David would be given advice as to how best to deal with the person with whom he was having problems. Some companies might just shake their heads and say, "You always lose a good salesman when you try to make a manager out of him." So where does NLP coaching come in?

THE AIM OF NLP-BASED COACHING

The aim of NLP-based coaching is to support people to realize their true potential. It is based on the premise that most of the limitations to our true potential are not represented by other people but by unhealthy strategies that we have learnt and that are entirely within ourselves. NLP is sometimes referred to as "the study of the structure of subjective experience." In David's case this means that there is a structure to how David is creating this repeated experience. The fact that it is repeated is a clue. His problems lie not in the other people (he re-experiences the same problems no matter who the people are) but in himself.

The study of the structure of subjective experience

Your patterns

What patterns do you have in your life that repeat? Do you for example:

❑ Find that you frequently lose key people in your team?
❑ Invariably end up in conflict with your management and finish up leaving the company?
❑ Often find yourself in disagreement and frustrated with people in authority?
❑ Find it hard to stay in long-term relationships?
❑ Find that you prefer to distance yourself from anyone who gets too close?
❑ Somehow seem to miss achieving your important goals just as you are on the brink of success?
❑ Find that most work is difficult and hard?
❑ Feel that you are often hard done by?
❑ Experience life as being not fair?
❑ Find that the people in whom you pin your hopes always seem to let you down?

On the other hand, are you one of those people who:

❑ Seem easily and almost effortlessly to achieve what you want consistently?
❑ Are frequently surprised by just what a good hand life seems to have dealt you?
❑ Find that you seem to attract good people to support and work with you?
❑ Are surprised by the opportunities that come your way and feel you have been very lucky?

The significance of all of these, good or bad, is that they are learned patterns that we impose on the world no matter what the quality of the external circumstances. NLP-based coaching is about discovering those patterns and either coaching ourselves or others to make choices that do lead us to achieve what we really want and realize that true potential. In essence, the purpose of NLP-based coaching is as follows:

❑ To discover our own and/or others' patterns (strategies), especially those of our outstanding talents, so that we can reproduce them or transfer them to other contexts. For example, if you have an outstanding strategy for connecting with people socially but find it challenging to do the same when you are in a business meeting with new contacts, you can learn how to transfer the strategy that works socially into the business context by using NLP.

❏ To discover the strategies that are leading us to get results we no longer want in our lives. By finding out how we are doing what we are doing we can reprogram ourselves or coach others to reprogram themselves to make new choices. For example, if you lack sensitivity in a sales situation to the signals the other person is giving you and subsequently inadvertently sabotage good sales opportunities, you can discover what you are doing and learn a new strategy that works for you in getting you the results you do want.

❏ To learn how to self-coach yourself through problem issues in your work and life and support others to do the same.

❏ To support yourself and others to develop the self-confidence and self-esteem to recognize that you already have all the strategies you could ever want in your life. With NLP coaching you can learn how to build this confidence and tap into these strategies when you choose.

❏ To enable you to find your own unique brand of excellence so you achieve the success that only you can. In other words, with NLP you can learn how to differentiate yourself with the natural talents you have already.

❏ To learn how to manage yourself to achieve what you want by influencing yourself from within or coaching others to do the same.

❏ To develop the ability to learn from every circumstance in your life and coach others to achieve that same level of empowerment.

NLP AND OTHER KINDS OF COACHING

If David were to come to me for coaching, I could concentrate on what is going wrong in the current situation between him and one of the key people in his team. I could explore with him what he is doing wrong as a leader and what he could do instead. However, if I were to do this, it might help him fix the problem for a while but it would not resolve the underlying pattern.

I could go back to the source of the pattern. It is possible, for example, that David experienced such difficulties as a child with his father or father figure equivalent that he was unable to cope emotionally. When children experience overwhelming emotional situations that they cannot deal with in a productive way, they shut them out. Either that or they dissociate from the experience or distort it in some way so that they are able to make sense of something that is beyond comprehension for them. I could take any of these approaches, but with NLP what we are interested in is how we make sense of our experience in the present. David has a structure that he brings to each of the situations he experiences. Changing his place of work or the people with whom he works will not ultimately make a difference. What is important is that David learns how to change the structure of his thinking and behavior that leads him to replay a pattern of the past.

NLP-based coaching is about the process and not about content. When we find a way to develop the process of what we are doing, we influence all of the situations of the same kind.

When we teach a man how to fish we feed him for life.

So in essence what we are doing when we coach using NLP is making the person being coached aware of the process they are living out. Just becoming aware that this process is a choice we are making in the present is an influence in itself. And standing back and reviewing the structure of that experience and deciding which bits we want to keep and which develop is life changing. This is how with NLP we can learn to remove the self-learned barriers and the obstacles to realizing our greater potential.

> We are interested in how we make sense of our experience in the present

---

CREATING A PLATFORM FOR CHANGE

An intruder recently broke into my mother's house in Liverpool. He stole jewelry and money. She is 90 years old and the shock of the experience disturbed her more than the loss of any possessions. Just last week the police asked my mother if she would be willing to help in an identification parade. She is an invalid and any activity is very painful and upsetting for her. However, she has very strong principles and wants to help to prevent similar crimes being carried out in the future. I could tell that she was emotionally upset when she called me to ask my advice. "Do you think I should help with this identity parade?" was her question. A part of me wanted her to say "No" to prevent her having to go through the emotions of the experience, but my instinct was to say "Yes, I believe that is the right thing to do." That is what I said and she thanked me for my answer.

If any business colleague were to ask me a question with the same format, "Do you think I should...," and if my outcome were to support them to find their self-esteem and confidence, then my principle is to say "Yes." By saying yes I am confirming the perception they have already formed within themselves. I am confirming that their map of the world is valid. By saying yes I am presupposing that they do have all the resources they need within themselves already. And by saying yes I am acting in a way that is more likely to boost their independence and self-esteem and confidence than if I were to offer a solution of my own.

The main role of a coach is to support others to realize their true potential. I also believe that the fastest and most effective way to do this is to help them to find the resources they already have within themselves. In the context of coaching it is often more appropriate to find ways to boost self-esteem and confidence than it is to get the "right" solution. I have certainly had some of my most powerful learning experiences through the mistakes I have made. Coaching requires us to be prepared to give others the space to make their own mistakes and realize their own successes. They can only do this if we encourage them to do things their way and learn from doing so.

Ironically, although my mother has been very shaken by her experience with the intruder, it has also given her momentum to ensure that justice is done. In a way, by supporting the identity parade she feels she is making a more significant contribution to society than she has done for years. Who am I to seek to take that away from her to protect my own fears?

> The role of a coach is to help others realize their true potential

When we coach others we need to be very clear about whose emotions we are dealing with.

To develop someone's confidence in themselves and therefore in their ability to draw on their own resources, I want to reward and confirm any opportunity when they are indicating that this is what they are doing. So if someone has the structure of the answer in their question, then my role as a coach is to reinforce that.

The question presupposes the answer

Examples of questions in which the answer presupposed is "Yes":

❑ Do you think I should take the job I have been offered in this new company?
❑ Do you think I can find the confidence to do this?
❑ Should I really reconsider that decision?
❑ Am I being very direct in the way I am saying this?

This last question invites direct feedback—"Yes." And yet I have witnessed many coaches seeking to reassure in response to a question like this, rather than confirming the truth that the questioners already know within themselves—and of course giving and receiving feedback, which is the subject of Chapter 19.

FINDING OUR INNER RESOURCES

In Chapter 11 I introduced the TOTE (Test→Operate→ Test→Exit). This is a flowchart for mapping the strategies we use to get ourselves from our present state to a future desired state.

On my bike I have a mini computer that can track the speed, the average speed, the distance covered, the top speed, and more. One of the measures is cadence or pedaling speed, the rate at which I am turning the pedals. Learning to manage cadence is one of the ways in which skilled cyclists develop their racing ability. The faster they can turn the pedals, the more efficiently they can use their energy. I aim for a cadence of 90 so as I cycle I watch the feedback on how I am doing. If the cadence drops below that then I change my pedaling speed. If I am unable to increase my speed then I change down to a lower gear until I reach my target cadence once more. When neither of these strategies works I explore my inner state to find ways in which I can tolerate a greater level of discomfort to increase my pedaling power.

This process mirrors the elements of the TOTE. My desired state is a cadence of 90. By watching the bike computer I TEST to see that it stays at that rate. If the feedback I am getting indicates that I have dropped cadence speed, then I OPERATE by pedaling faster. If that works (the present state matches the desired state) when I TEST by reading the monitor, then I temporarily EXIT. If by OPERATING in that way I do not achieve the desired state, then I carry out another OPERATION by changing gear and TEST again. The more OPERATIONS I can carry out, the more likely I am to achieve my desired state and therefore EXIT the TOTE. And so it is that the person with the most flexibility in the way they can think and behave is the person most likely to achieve their outcomes.

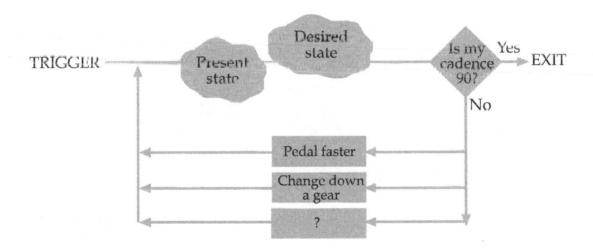

Once we understand how this works for ourselves we can use the same process to coach other people.

The belief that "We have all the resources we ever need" is key to the TOTE process. The question is: How do we find them?

Suppose that you are about to make an important business presentation and you fear you will be unable to handle interaction in the presentation because you are so nervous.

Your present state is one of nervousness and your desired state is one of ease, especially ease with your ability to deal with questions.

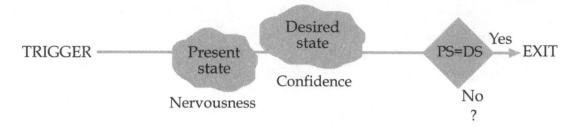

Your present state most certainly does not yet match your desired state. What steps can you take yourself through?

1 Identify what you believe you need in order to achieve the desired state. What you identify is an emotional state of confidence. The question is how to get it.

2 On the premise that you have this resource already, the question to ask yourself is: Where in my experience (no matter how fleeting) did I have the kind of confidence I want right now? You can find a situation in your experience even it if is months or years old.

3 Step back into that time (associate) so you relive it, especially that confidence. To do this it helps to imagine what you were seeing then, what you were hearing and feeling physically, and to do this from your own shoes so that you now re-experience what you were feeling emotionally—that state of confidence.

4 Once you have this, anchor it with a touch, a word, or an image and bring the state of confidence back to you in the present as you prepare your thinking for the presentation.

5 Now test again. Does your present state match your desired state? If yes, you have what you want; if no, ask yourself what else you need to realize your desired state.

6 This time you realize that what you need is to build rapport with some of the people who will be at the presentation.

7 Explore and plan ways in which you might do this. You can either imagine yourself doing this to test if that is all you need, or you can do it in reality and go through the TOTE again.

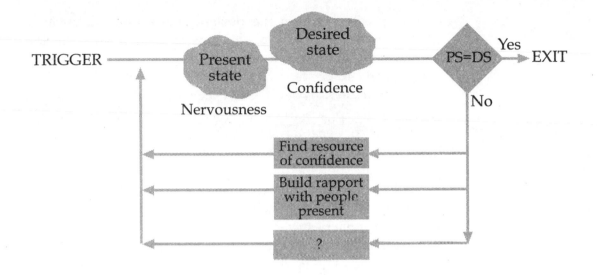

Whatever resource you need, the belief is that somewhere you have it. Examples of emotional resources that we have somewhere in our experience include:

❏ Courage.
❏ Peace of mind.
❏ Enthusiasm.
❏ Motivation.
❏ Determination.
❏ Fun.

We each have our representation for each of these kinds of big chunk words. What matters is that we know what we need and we know where in our experience we can find it.

RECOGNIZING A STATE OF HIGH POTENTIAL

It is not just knowing what our desired state is—we also need to recognize when we have it. The value of feedback is that it enables us to regulate what we are doing and how we are doing it. If we know the characteristics of the state we want, we have a means of measuring when we have got there. Objective, factual feedback is a potent influence for change. If we know what characterizes what we want and we know what we have got (and it is not yet the desired state), then we create a tension between the two. This tension is what we might call motivation and it has a momentum of its own that seeks to close the gap between what we have and what we want.

One of the ways of using this knowledge is in the domain of coaching. For each of us our most influential state is congruence. Congruence is a state of total rapport with oneself when all aspects of who we are and what we are doing are in alignment. Sportspeople often call this state the flow zone. It comes as a result of much training and discipline and is the culmination of everything when the sportsperson can achieve their personal best with effortless ease.

In Chapter 13 I introduced the logical levels of change model. The same model is a way of thinking about the degree of congruence we have within ourselves.

Think (just briefly) of a time when you felt uncomfortable with what you were doing and how you were doing it. It might have been a time when you felt emotionally uncomfortable and ill at ease with how you were handling a situation. You might have felt that you were violating something you consider to be important or compromising some deeply held beliefs or values. You will have felt in conflict with yourself and possibly you were having an inner dialog with yourself to that effect, to the point where you were unable to give the kind of attention you would truly have liked to give to the people or the situation.

Stand outside of yourself and look and listen to how you were being at that time. What do you notice about your nonverbal behavior? What is characteristic in how you sound? Can you specify your behavior at that time such that you would recognize if you were to be in the same state again?

Think of a time (which might be right now) when you felt that what you were doing and how you were doing it were just right for you—a time when your natural abilities just flowed and everything you wanted to achieve seemed to come together and you felt that your body and mind were saying "Yes" to how you were as a person.

Stand outside of yourself and look and listen to how you were being at that time. What is characteristic of you now? If you were to tell someone else, how they could recognize you in this state? What would you tell them?

One of the roles of a coach is to give this kind of feedback to the person they are coaching. This involves watching and listening to the person you are coaching to such a degree that you can tell when they are in a state of congruence and when they are not. If someone has come to you because they have been in a problem state for some time, you might only get a fleeting glimpse of their congruent state. However, you need to be sufficiently vigilant to catch it when it happens.

Here is an example of what you might see:

❏ Tension in the facial muscles.   In the incongruent state
❏ Pale complexion.
❏ Glazed, fixed expression.
❏ Asymmetrical body posture.
❏ Reference to problem people by pointing to them in the air outside of themselves.
❏ Use of the words "must," "try," and "should."
❏ Emphasis on a problem state characterized by vocabulary such as "don't want," "not," and "never."

❏ Relaxed facial muscles.   In the congruent state
❏ Flushed complexion.
❏ Active eye movements.
❏ Symmetrical body posture.
❏ Consistent gesturing to within themselves.
❏ Use of words such as "want to," "can," and "really like."
❏ Nodding of the head.
❏ Pauses in the conversation.
❏ Use of active language.

This will not be the same for everyone. It is your role as a coach to be able to tell the difference and give precise feedback on the characteristics of each. This is liberating information; once someone has this information they have choice. They can choose whether they stay in a stuck problem state or whether they choose the congruent state (typically a state of self-fulfillment).

THE LADDER TO SUCCESS

What prompts a desire or a need for coaching is usually a state of incongruence. Maybe we feel we are working in a way that contradicts what we feel is really important. Or maybe we are contemplating a decision that means sacrificing some of our commitments to people who are important to us. Or perhaps we know that we are just not working to the best of our ability. Whatever the situation, any incongruence will mean that we are limiting or even blocking ourselves from achieving what we are really capable of. Sometimes this incongruence occurs because we choose to delete what we intuitively know is not right and hope that things will sort themselves out over time. And although this might sometimes happen, it is more likely that things will deteriorate. The longer we ignore the issues, the more of a challenge they become to resolve.

One of the simplest and yet sometimes most powerful ways of using the logical levels of change model is to coach using questions to chunk up and chunk down the levels to recognize in what ways you are (or are not) making a decision that is congruent. The questions with which to do this are shown in the following diagram.

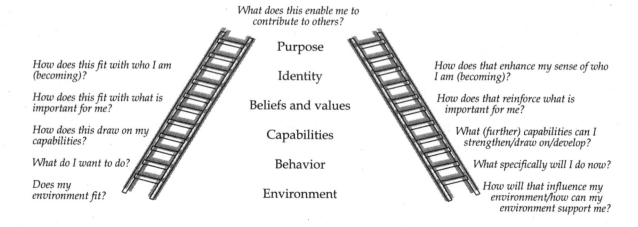

How does this fit with who I am (becoming)?

How does this fit with what is important for me?

How does this draw on my capabilities?

What do I want to do?

Does my environment fit?

Purpose

Identity

Beliefs and values

Capabilities

Behavior

Environment

What does this enable me to contribute to others?

How does that enhance my sense of who I am (becoming)?

How does that reinforce what is important for me?

What (further) capabilities can I strengthen/draw on/develop?

What specifically will I do now?

How will that influence my environment/how can my environment support me?

PRESUPPOSE EXCELLENCE

One of the biggest influences we have as a coach is our belief in the person with whom we are working. If we cannot imagine the person we are coaching achieving the kinds of outcomes they express, or if we cannot imagine them realizing any kind of higher potential, then we should not be coaching them. If, on the other hand, we can imagine this person being the person they want to be or being someone realizing a greater potential, then that is what we communicate to them.

If I think of you as stupid I will engage with the "stupid" part of you. If I think of you as stubborn, that is what I am going to encourage and experience in my dealings with you. If, however, I can see the confident part of you, my interactions with you invite that part of you to emerge. If I can see, hear, and feel you letting go of any limiting patterns and being fully and congruently who you are, then that is the "you" that can increasingly emerge.

I see the confident part of you – not the part of you with which I engage

Suppose that you have a colleague, a member of your family, or an associate with whom you feel frustrated. Maybe you feel that they could be achieving more than they currently are. It often helps to pay attention to the situations that are the most personal and then extend your thinking out to the others. It may be that this person has not excelled in what they have done to date—but coaching is not about facts, it is about processes and beliefs.

Maybe you can recall someone who, irrespective of the facts of the situation, demonstrated a belief in you at a key point in your life to the degree that it inspired you to achieve something beyond anything you had done previously. Perhaps it was a teacher who took that special interest in what they believed you were capable of. Maybe it was a boss who showed a trust in you that you had not experienced before. Or maybe it was your parents who stuck by their belief in you no matter what happened. This is the foundation of great coaching.

We influence others by the beliefs we hold in them, irrespective of the facts or the circumstances. Coaching is an emotional process. Think of your children, your family, your colleagues, and your associates. Is there any one of them in whom you show this outstanding belief? And is there any one of them about whom you hold doubt? Your belief can strengthen their belief. Your doubt potentially deepens their doubt. It is your responsibility as a coach to believe in the people you are coaching, whether they are members of your family or people with whom you work.

Your belief can strengthen their belief

How do you strengthen belief in others? Belief comes from our ability to imagine either ourselves or other people achieving outcomes. If we can see, hear, and emotionally experience them realizing their dreams, that translates itself into a belief and we communicate this to them whatever we do and say. You might do this imagining when you are out of their company or while you are interacting with them. If you are doing it during an interaction, step back and imagine this person realizing a potential beyond what they are demonstrating right now.

She sees beauty in everyone

One of my colleagues is exceptional in her ability to advise people on issues relating to their image. She sees beauty in everyone she meets.

WHO IS COACHING WHOM?

When someone comes to me for a coaching session for the first time and tells me their issue, one of my first reactions is to ask myself, "Do I want to deal with this issue in my life right now?" Coaching is a mutual process. I can only offer the structure of what I have managed for myself or what I am managing for myself in my life at this time.

In essence, when we interact with another person we are one system. We are not "doing coaching" to others, we are part of a coaching system. What we offer is what we receive and what we receive and accept for ourselves is what we can give.

With the people we are coaching we bring out and engage with those parts of ourselves that we need to resolve or that we have we resolved and for which we can now be an example. *We teach what we need the most.* I may not behave in exactly the same way as the people I am coaching, but I will have a parallel structure or capability in my experience. For example:

What I experience in the other person

They are dismissive in the way they speak to colleagues.

They avoid making a commitment to change.

They are aggressively focused on what they want and insensitive to the needs of others in the way they behave in a meeting.

What I am doing myself

I am dismissive in the way I speak to a member of my family.

I avoid commitment to one of my stated outcomes.

I am single-mindedly aggressive in my focus on my work goals and oblivious to the effect on my friends and family.

However, while I am resolving issues for myself I begin to recognize and consequently reinforce these kinds of issues in others. For example:

Issues you might deal with for yourself

Your willingness to let go of something of material importance to you.

Your ability to tell someone close to you how much you care/love them.

A decision to reinvent yourself and move on to new approaches or new business.

Your ability to let go of trying to control others (family members or work colleagues) and let them find their own solutions.

Issues you might support in others

Their ability to let go of behaviors, people, or material possessions that are familiar and comfortable yet limiting.

Their ability to forgive and let go of past judgments and be intimate.

Their ability to let go of the must haves or the should haves to have what they really want despite the cost.

Their ability to truly delegate and give people the space to find their own motivation.

WARWICKSHIRE COLLEGE LIBRARY

SHORTCUT TO COACHING

Some of the most powerful coaching is the simplest. At its roots NLP is a state of interest and curiosity. Applying these two principles, here is a shortcut to coaching.

1 Invite someone to tell you an issue for which they would like new choices or increased understanding.
2 Get into a state of curiosity and acceptance.
3 Get yourself into a similar posture and way of moving as the other person. This is approximate—you don't have to mimic. Think of yourself as being connected to them.
4 Listen intently to what they are telling you. Mentally note the words they are using and the gestures they are making.
5 Ask them open questions (see precision questions in Chapter 6) using only the words they give you. Don't in any way try to give suggestions or make changes to what they are saying, just be curious to the degree that you understand fully what they are saying, only exploring those aspects of the situation that they are giving you.
6 Summarize back to them from time to time, using their language. Keep to their vocabulary and use their nonverbal style of communicating when you do this summary.
7 While they are talking, identify how you have the structure of this issue within yourself too and how you either have or are dealing with it in your life.
8 Imagine the other person achieving what they really want. See, hear, and feel it until you believe that they are capable of a greater potential than they have demonstrated to date, either with respect to this issue or in their lives as a whole. Think this as you speak to them (keep this vision to yourself).
9 Recognize that the person is bringing this issue to you so that you can learn too.
10 Summarize what you have heard and what you believe the other person is feeling.
11 Ask them if there is anything else they would like from you.

SUMMARY

NLP high performance coaching is founded on the study of our subjective experience. By discovering how we structure our memories, our imagination, and our thoughts, we can find out how we are making our work and our lives exactly what they are. Compare eliciting the code of a computer program to understand how we are getting the output that we are getting. And if we are not getting what we want we can look for the "bugs" in the program and "debug" it.

THOUGHT PROVOKERS

1 Ask a colleague or friend if they will take part in an exercise with you. Tell them you are going to talk with them about their goals. Ask them to tell you about their progress toward their goals. For the first few minutes (no more than that) think about how unlikely it is that they will achieve their goals. Think of the difficulties and the impossibility of what they are saying. You do not have to say what you are thinking, but do engage in some interaction with them as they are speaking.

    After a few minutes, change your thinking so that you are imagining them achieving all they are saying and more. Picture what they are doing and hear how they sound in this future desired state. Notice how you feel toward them as you do this and engage with them as they continue to tell you about these goals. Do this for a few minutes or more.

    At the end of this time, ask your colleague how they felt during the conversation. Did they notice or experience any differences in how you were toward them or even how they felt about themselves? Did you notice any changes in their responses to you as you changed your inner thinking? What were they?

2 Think of someone you find it difficult to work with. Ask yourself about the image of this person that you have had prior to and during each interaction that you have experienced as difficult. Now think of someone you find easy and a pleasure to deal with. What is in your mind before and during your interactions with them?

3 Think of an outcome that you want to achieve in your life or your work right now. What is your desired state? What is your present state? What quality do you need to find in yourself to begin to bridge the gap between the two? How might you re-experience that quality so that you can bring it to bear on the outcome that you want to achieve today?

4 Think of someone in your work, your personal life, and your community with whom you don't get on as well as you might. What is it about each of them that you feel is the cause of the difficulty? How is the aspect of each that you have identified true about you?

5 Think of someone in your work, your personal life, and your community with whom you do get on well. What is it about each of them that you admire? How is that aspect of each true about you?

REFERENCES

Ian McDermott & Wendy Jago (2001) *The NLP Coach*, Piatkus.

John Whitmore (2002) *Coaching for Performance: GROWing People, Performance, and Purpose*, Nicholas Brealey Publishing.

Robert Dilts already knew this strategy when a young boy who had been categorised as learning disabled was brought to him to see if Robert could help him progress with his learning. The boy was about 11 years old and was certainly not recognised as being able to spell. Many adult good spellers will see the word that they want to spell on something like an overhead projection screen. It is unlikely that this boy had ever seen such a thing. Robert asked him what his favourite film was and he replied "Star Wars". He then asked the boy who was his favourite character in the film and he said it was the Wookie. For those of you who have never seen Star Wars *then the Wookie is a large bear like creature.*

Robert asked the boy if he would be willing to play a game and he agreed. He asked the boy if he could see the Wookie now and the boy looked up momentarily and said he could. Robert asked him if he could make the Wookie put his arms out horizontally by his sides (he demonstrated this) and the boy (looking up again) said yes. "Now," said Robert, "I want you to hang some letters underneath the Wookie's arm—put a P, now an H and then an E underneath his arm side by side." He paused between each one. "Have you done that?" The boy nodded. "Can you make the Wookie open his mouth?" Again the boy nodded. "I want you to see the Wookie open his mouth and you will see some letters come out. The first letter is N. Can you do that?" Once again a nod. "Now see the Wookie open his mouth again and this time the letter that comes out is an O. And again and this time the letter is M and finally as the Wookie opens his mouth again an M comes out. And now an E. Have you done that?"

"Yes," said the boy, although Robert already knew the answer.

"Finally I want you to hang some more letters under the Wookie's other arm. First an N now an O and now an N." When the boy indicated that he had done all of that Robert said to him, "Now tell me what letters are hanging under the Wookie's right arm" (he indicated which arm he meant).

The boy said without hesitation "P, H, E."

"And now the Wookie is opening his mouth and the letters are coming out again — what are they?"

"N, O, M, E" the boy replied.

"And now tell me the letters hanging under the Wookie's left arm."

"N, O, N," said the boy, who had just spelt (without hesitation) PHENOMENON

Glossary

Anchoring The process of making associations that work through conscious choice so that you can re-access your own or trigger others' chosen state when appropriate.

Association The state of being inside one's skin, seeing the world from your own eyes, hearing the world from your own ears, and feeling the emotions of the situation whether current, remembered, or imagined.

Beliefs Emotionally held opinions treated as facts and the basis of our everyday decisions, skills, and behaviors.

Congruence Having all parts of oneself working in harmony, without conflict.

Criteria The values and standards used as the basis for decisions.

Dissociation The state of observing yourself as if you were an outsider. Seeing and hearing yourself from the outside, i.e., you can see you in your entirety, not the way you see yourself from within your own body. The effect of dissociation is to disconnect with emotion.

Eye accessing cues Movements of a person's eyes that indicate visual, auditory, or feelings thinking.

Filters Levels of thinking that determine where we put our attention, how we make our perception what it is, and what defines how we respond to situations and people.

Linguistic The study of language and, in the context of NLP, the patterns in language that communicate our thinking strategies.

Logical levels of change A form of personal and organizational hierarchy that affects change and how effectively we bring about change for ourselves or for others, consisting of environment, behavior, capabilities, values, beliefs, identity, and spirituality or systems.

Metaphor A parallel means of describing or observing. Metaphors can be parables, stories, analogies, pictures, and actions.

Modeling The process of unpacking our own and others' conscious and especially unconscious strategies in order to duplicate the results.

Neuro The way we use our brain.

Neuro linguistic programming Defined as the study of the structure of subjective experience. The name was developed by John Grinder and Richard Bandler in 1975. It is a process of modeling and increasingly the term is used to encompass the techniques and skills uncovered as a result of this process.

Outcome (well formed) A goal that is characteristic of someone who consistently achieves what they want in ways that are a win for others as well as themselves. Different from traditional methods of goal setting in that it involves the use of all senses, including emotion.

Pacing Respecting the values, needs, and style of another person in a way that leads to rapport. Going along with aspects of what is important to another and yourself.

Perceptual positions The mental strategy used by skillful negotiators, involving moving mentally between being in one's own shoes, the shoes of the other person, and an outside detached position. There is an old Indian saying, "You must first walk two moons in a man's moccasins before you can understand him."

Programming Not the computer kind, but similar in that it is to do with the sequences of thinking and behavior patterns that constitute our strategies for achieving the results we do.

Rapport Our ability to relate to ourselves and others in ways that create a climate of respect, trust, and cooperation.

Reframing The ability to make meanings of events in ways that work for you and create desirable emotional states.

State The mental, physical, and emotional condition of a person.

Strategies A set of thinking and behavioral steps to achieve a result.

TOTE Test→operate→test→exit, the feedback loop used to guide behavior.

Well-formed outcomes *See* Outcomes.

Taking Your Learning Further

Sue Knight provides inhouse training and open programs leading to recognized certification in NLP. For examples of inhouse training programs take a look at www.sueknight.co.uk.

Open programs leading to certification in NLP follow these stages:

❑ Stage 1—Introduction to NLP, a practical and comprehensive introduction to the foundations of NLP.
❑ Stage 2—Business Practitioner training, leading to certification in NLP. This program covers the material that is included in this book.
❑ Stage 3—Master Practitioner training, advanced program leading to certification concentrating on the skills of modeling and centered around delegates' modeling projects.
❑ Stage 4—Trainer training, not only for trainers but for anyone who wishes to learn how to communicate and train or coach others in the principles of NLP. Successful completion of this program gives you the authority to issue NLP certifications to others on acceptance by the Association for NLP.

Sue Knight can be contacted at:

PO Box 1008   Telephone: +44 (0) 1628 604438
Slough   Email: sue@sueknight.co.uk
Berkshire SL1 8DB   Web page: www.sueknight.co.uk
UK

Sue Knight works both in the UK and internationally. She collaborates with consultancies and training centers throughout the world who work to similar values. These are listed below with contact numbers for each. If any company would like to discuss future collaboration and inclusion in this list, please contact Sue Knight on sue@sueknight.co.uk.

AUSTRALIA

Universal Events, Australia's largest NLP training company, was established by Karen Corban in 1993 to provide people with the world's leading NLP training and resources. Our mission is to provide information to support individuals and companies to fast track their success and achieve their greatest potential.

We are committed to learning and sharing knowledge with people to help enhance their lives. The values that we aspire to are integrity, passion, growth, service, support, love, continuous learning, commitment, excellence, and fun.

We believe that NLP changes people's lives in the shortest amount of time and offers people the opportunity for fast and lasting change. We hold the belief that anything is possible and that it is easy to transform and live the life of your dreams.

Universal Events
Level 10, 118 Alfred Street,
Milsons Point NSW 2061
Australia

Telephone: +61 2 9460 1530
Fax: +61 2 9460 1539
Email: info@universalevents.com.au
Website: www.universalevents.com.au

CANADA

Success Strategies/Stratégies de réussite is an international training and consulting company specializing in communication and influencing. We help solve impossible communication problems. Success Strategies' president, Shelle Rose Charvet, is author of the international bestseller *Words That Change Minds: Mastering the Language of Influence*. This book describes the below-conscious motivation triggers that drive people's behaviour, based on the applied NLP model called the Language and Behaviour Profile.

1264 Lemonville Road
Burlington, ON
Canada
L7R 3X5

Telephone: +1 (905) 639 6468
Fax: +1 (905) 639 4220
Email: info@successstrategies.com
Website: www.successstrategies.com

DENMARK AND SCANDINAVIA

Strandgaard-Gruppen Consultants supply both short and long leadership development programs as well as open programs in coaching and NLP, such as NLP Business Practitioner with Sue Knight.

Vagn Strandgaard and Lotte Møller Sørensen are the co-founders of Strandgaard Consulting A/S, an international business consultancy that provides tailor-made education and training in the principles of the learning organization, coaching, and NLP. We have specialized in executive project management and strategy implementation. We are among the pioneers of NLP in Danish business life, but NLP has always been a fundamental part of this organization's culture and in its work with clients.

Therefore we have for the past six years had close cooperation with Sue Knight and held a number of inhouse and open NLP Business Process programs. Lotte Møller Sørensen has also translated NLP *at Work*, the first NLP book on the Danish market that talked directly to businesses and managers who want to be leaders.

INDIA

U and Infinity, founded by S. Ashok in April 2001, is one of the premier training institutes in India, spearheading the spread of NLP in the country. The main objective of this institution is to support people in their journey from "U to Infinity," and to serve as a resource center, for those who crave to unleash the infinite power from within.

Our mission is to improve the quality of life of people by aiding them to rediscover themselves.

Our vision is to make a significant and constructive difference in the lives of at least 1,000,000 people, before April 2006.

We hold introductory lectures and Business Practitioner training, supported and contributed to by Sue Knight. We also run short lectures every week on selected NLP topics. These are open to the public. We also cater to students and the staff of leading educational institutions and colleges on an invitation basis. Business consultancy to corporates based on NLP and TQM concepts for building sustainable change is our specialty area, where we attempt some new models for excellence, on a research basis for selective companies.

U and Infinity
853, 13th Main Road
Anna Nagar
Chennai 600040, India

Telephone: (+91) 44 628 7049 and (+91) 44 620 7592
Cellphone: +91 98410 52573
Website: www.uandinfinity.com
Email: office@uandinfinity.com

USA

NLP University was founded by Todd Epstein and Robert Dilts and is now run by Robert Dilts, Judith Delozier, and Teresa Epstein.

We at NLPU like to offer a comprehensive education in NLP, including a sense of the history and development of the discipline, as well as the most recent developments.

NLP University is dedicated to presenting the best possible NLP seminars to the international NLP community and we are proud of our legacy as the home of NLP and a catalyst where people gather to research and develop the future of NLP. We are committed to bringing the best trainers in the world to NLP University, each year, to teach the latest and most comprehensive range of NLP seminars available. NLPU is the place where the latest developments, generative applications, and creative activity in the field of NLP are most focused. Above all, NLPU is a place to live the NLP presuppositions with a group of peers—In other words, to create a real-life reference experience for an NLP community.

Telephone: +1 831 336 3457
Fax: +1 831 336 5854
Website: www.nlpu.com
Email: teresanlp@aol.com

NLP COMPREHENSIVE

We are here to help individuals and businesses make the fullest use of their talents and resources. We teach the thought processes and communication strategies of exceptional performers through workshops, books, and tapes.

PO Box 927
Evergreen
CO 80437
USA

Telephone: +1 303 987 2224
Fax: +1 303 987 2228
Website: 222.nlpco.com
Email: learn@nlpco.com